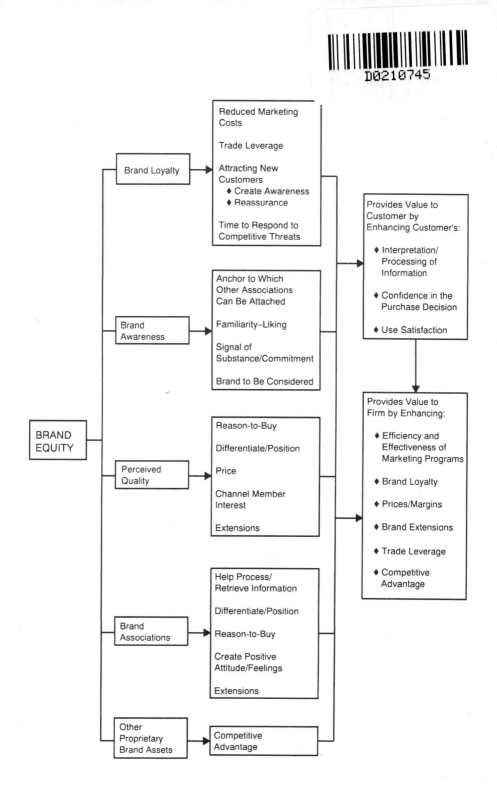

Managing Brand Equity

Managing Brand Equity

•

Capitalizing on the Value of a Brand Name

David A. Aaker

THE FREE PRESS
A Division of Macmillan, Inc.
NEW YORK

Maxwell Macmillan Canada
TORONTO

Maxwell Macmillan International
NEW YORK—OXFORD—SINGAPORE—SYDNEY

The Free Press
A Division of Macmillan, Inc.
866 Third Avenue, New York, N.Y. 10022

Maxwell Macmillan Canada, Inc.
1200 Eglinton Avenue East
Suite 200
Don Mills, Ontario M3C 3N1

Macmillan, Inc. is part of the Maxwell Communication Group of Companies.

Printed in the United States of America

printing number

1   2   3   4   5   6   7   8   9   10

Library of Congress Cataloging-in-Publication Data

Aaker, David A.
　　Managing brand equity: capitalizing on the value of a brand name /
　　David A. Aaker.
　　　　p.　　cm.
　　Includes bibliographical references and index.
　　ISBN 0-02-900101-3
　　1. Brand name products—Valuation—United States—Management.
2. Intangible property—Valuation—United States—Management.
I. Title.
HD69.B7A22　　　1991
658.8'27—dc20　　　　　　　　　　　　　　　　　　91–10380
　　　　　　　　　　　　　　　　　　　　　　　　　　　　CIP

Contents

Preface and
Acknowledgments

THE POWER OF BRANDS

Larry Light, a prominent advertising research professional, was asked by the editor of the *Journal of Advertising Research* for his perspective on marketing three decades into the future. Light's analysis was instructive:

> The marketing battle will be a battle of brands, a competition for brand dominance. Businesses and investors will recognize brands as the company's most valuable assets. This is a critical concept. It is a vision about how to develop, strengthen, defend, and manage a business. . . . It will be more important to own markets than to own factories. The only way to own markets is to own market-dominant brands.

> The power of brand names is not restricted to consumer markets. In fact, brand equity may be more important in industrial goods markets than in consumer marketing. Brand-name awareness often is pivotal in being considered by an industrial buyer. Further, after analysis, many industrial purchase alternatives tend to be toss-ups. The decisive factor then can turn upon what a brand means to a buyer.

THE INTEREST IN BRANDING

Brand equity is one of the hottest topics in management today. The Marketing Science Institute recently did a survey of its membership, which includes 50 or so of the top marketing companies in the country, to learn their opinion as to what were the pressing questions in need of research. The runaway winner was brand equity. Academic research interest has also mushroomed: A recent research proposal competition sponsored by the Marketing Science Institute received 28 proposals.

The growing interest is reflected in the proliferating conferences, articles, and press attention on branding. Another indicator is the experimentation with different organizational forms in order to better enhance and protect brand equity. Some, like Colgate–Palmolive and Canada Dry, have created a management of brand equity position to be a guardian of the value of brands.

There are several driving forces behind the interest in branding. First, firms have shown a willingness to pay substantial premiums for brand names because alternative development of new brand names either is not feasible or is too costly. This phenomenon raises several questions, such as: How much is brand equity worth? On what is it based? Why should so much be paid?

Second, marketing professionals sense that an increased emphasis upon price, often involving the excessive use of price promotions, is resulting in the deterioration of industries into commodity-like business areas. They believe that more resources should be diverted into brand-building activities, to develop points of differentiation. The recognized need is to develop sustainable competitive advantages based upon non-price competition. The problem is that brand-building efforts, unlike price promotions, have little visible impact upon sales in the short run. How then are such activities justified in a world with extreme pressures for delivering short-term performance?

Third, managers realize a need to fully exploit their assets in order to maximize the performance of their business. A key asset is usually the brand name. How can it be exploited? Can it be extended to new products, or exposed to new markets? Is there an opportunity to get more out of it by strengthening it or by altering its components? Conversely, how might it be damaged, and how can that be avoided?

THE APPROACH OF THE BOOK

This book has several objectives. One objective is to define and illustrate brand equity, providing a structure that will help managers see more clearly how brand equity does provide value. Another is to document research findings and illustrative examples which demonstrate that value has emerged (or has been lost) from marketing decisions or environmental events that have enhanced (or damaged) the brand. A third objective is to discuss how brand equity should be managed: How should it be created, maintained, and protected? How should it be exploited? A fourth objective is to raise questions and suggest issues that should be addressed by thoughtful managers who are trying to think strategically.

I have written this book for managers having either direct or indirect responsibility for brands and their equity. Such managers will represent firms that are either large or small, consumer or industrial, service- or product-focused. They will be concerned with the need to develop and protect the equity in their core brands. In addition, they will (or should) be addressing such questions as the following: What is the role of the company name in the branding equation? Should we develop a subbrand name? Should the brand name be extended to other products? I hope also, however, that it will be used in schools of management where faculty and students are attempting to improve our ability to, in general, manage strategically and, in particular, manage brand equity.

The first chapter discusses the Ivory brand, provides an historical background, and both defines brand equity and suggests a variety of approaches to place a value on it. Four dimensions of brand equity are the focus of the next six chapters, which collectively define the dimensions, specify how each creates value for the customer and the firm, and discuss their measurement and management.

Chapter 2 considers the importance of the brand loyalty. Chapter 3 covers the creation, measurement, and role of brand awareness. Chapter 4 discusses perceived quality, how it can be managed, and the evidence as to its role in business performance. Chapter 5 introduces the concept of associations and positioning. Methods to measure associations are covered in Chapter 6. Selecting, creating, and maintaining associations is the subject of Chapter 7. Clearly, the management of associations, covering three chapters, is both important and complex.

The brand is identified by the name, and often by a symbol *and* a slogan as well. Chapter 8 discusses these indicators and their selection. Brand extensions (the good, the bad, and the ugly) is the topic of Chapter 9. Chapter 10 presents methods to revitalize a tired brand—to breathe new life into both it and its context. It also discusses the end game: how to allow a brand a graceful decline and, if needed, death. Chapter 11 provides a discussion about global branding, presents a summary model of brand equity, and concludes with a set of observations from each chapter that collectively summarize the major points presented in the book.

An historical analysis of a brand that has experienced a dramatic event, or has been especially good or bad at building brand equity, begins each chapter. There is much to be learned from history: Each of these analyses provides a vivid illustration of how a wide variety of actions can affect a brand. In several cases a dollar value is placed upon a set of actions affecting a brand, even though it is impossible to know for sure what caused what. Too, there is a host of case studies throughout, to illustrate the concepts and methods and to make them more tangible and understandable.

In addition to the historical flavor—what has happened to individual brands—more systematic studies are sought out and reported. The past 15 years have seen the development of studies about such brand constructs as market share, awareness, brand extensions, perceived quality, and others that provide significant evidence about their role. Some of these studies have been based upon large-scale data bases. Others come from controlled experiments. They all help provide substance to an area that has too long relied upon opinion.

Each chapter closes with a set of questions to consider. The goal is to provide a vehicle with which to translate the ideas in the chapter into a diagnostic and action agenda. Some questions will stimulate new ways of looking at your brand and its environment, and others will suggest a need to find out more information.

ACKNOWLEDGMENTS

Many people helped in the writing of this book. Let me offer my special thanks here to the following: Bob Wallace, my editor at The Free Press, for his enthusiasm for the project and Kevin Keller, my research colleague on the first two branding research efforts in which I was involved, for his stimulating ideas. From among those who read large portions of the manuscript and gave helpful comments: Stuart Agres of Lowe & Partners; Alec Biel of Ogilvy; Patrick Crane of Kodak; Stephen King of WPP Group; Vijay Mahajan of Texas; Larry Percy of Lintas; and Al Riley of Campbell Soup. Among my colleagues who read chapters or gave helpful suggestions: Jennifer Aaker of Lowe & Partners; Russell Berg of H-P; Pete Bucklin and Rashi Glazier of Berkeley; Robert Jones of Ruhr/Paragon; Kent Mitchel of MSI; August Swanenberg of Nielsen; Al Shocker of Minnesota; Doug Stayman of Cornell; and Bill Wells of DDB Needham. Lisa Cuff of The Free Press and Serena Joe of Berkeley were extremely helpful. Then there was MSI, who sponsored three branding conferences, provided inspiration and support. And a series of research assistants and students who helped enormously—including Susan Anderson, Ziv Carmon, Anastasia Jackson, Andy Keane, Said Saffari, and Iegor Siniavski.

Finally, I would like to thank my family, who put up with yet another writing project.

David A. Aaker
Berkeley

Managing Brand Equity

1
·

What Is Brand Equity?

A product is something that is made in a factory; a brand is something that is bought by a customer. A product can be copied by a competitor; a brand is unique. A product can be quickly outdated; a successful brand is timeless.

Stephen King
WPP Group, London

THE IVORY STORY

O ne Sunday in 1879 Harley Procter, one of the founders of the candle and soap firm Procter & Gamble (P&G), heard a sermon based on the Forty-fifth Psalm, "All thy garments smell of myrrh, and aloes, and cassia, out of ivory palaces."[1] The word "ivory" stuck in his mind—and became the name of the firm's white soap.

In December, 1881, P&G ran their first Ivory ad in a religious weekly, stating that the soap "floated" and that it was "99 44/100% pure," a dual claim which has become one of the most famous ad slogans ever. That ad is shown in Figure 1–1. Figure 1–2 shows a 1920 Ivory ad illustrating the consistency of the positioning over time. Note the imagery created by the forest, the barefoot girl, and the clear water.

The purity claim was supported by a chemist, who had tested Ivory and found that only 56/100% contained impurities. The flotation property, first created by a production mistake which fed air into the soap mixture, was discovered by customers—who attempted to reorder the "floating" soap.

FIGURE 1–1 The First Ivory Ad Appearing in 1881

VITALIZED PHOS-PHITES

Aid wonderfully in the mental and bodily growth of Infants and Children. Under its use the teeth come easier, the bones grow better, the skin plumper and smoother; the brain acquires more readily, and rests and sleeps more sweetly. An ill-fed brain learns no lessons and is excusable if peevish. It gives a happier childhood. For sale by druggists, or mail, $1.00.

F. CROSBY CO., 6th Avenue, N. Y.

STAMPS—50 different, 10c.; 100 rare, 25c.; 200 obsolete, $1.25; 500 from all parts of the globe, $5.00; 50 Foreign Revenue, 50c.; 50 U. S. Revenue, 50c.; Complete Set of 11 War, 60c. Stamp and Album circular free.

E. F. GAMBS,
621 South 5th Street,
ST. LOUIS, MO.

HARPER'S
YOUNG PEOPLE SERIES.

MILDRED'S BARGAIN AND OTHER STORIES. By Lucy C. Lillie, Author of "Prudence." Illustrated. 16mo, Cloth, $1 00.

THE FOUR MACNICOLS. By William Black, Author of "A Princess of Thule." Illustrated. 16mo, Cloth, $1 00.

WHO WAS PAUL GRAYSON? By John Habberton, Author of "Helen's Babies." Illustrated. 16mo, Cloth, $1 00.

TOBY TYLER; or, TEN WEEKS WITH A CIRCUS. By James Otis. Illustrated. 16mo, Cloth, $1 00.

MR. STUBBS'S BROTHER. A Sequel to "Toby Tyler." By James Otis. Illustrated. 16mo, Cloth, $1 00.

THE MORAL PIRATES. By W. L. Alden. Illustrated. 16mo, Cloth, $1 00.

THE CRUISE OF THE "GHOST." By W. L. Alden. Illustrated. 16mo, Cloth, $1 00.

THE TALKING LEAVES. An Indian Story. By W. O. Stoddard. Illustrated. 16mo, Cloth, $1 00.

Published by HARPER & BROTHERS, New York.

☞ Sent by mail, postage prepaid, to any part of the United States, on receipt of the price.

THE "IVORY" is a Laundry Soap, with all the fine qualities of a choice Toilet Soap, and is 99 44-100 per cent. pure.

Ladies will find this Soap especially adapted for washing laces, infants' clothing, silk hose, cleaning gloves, and all articles of fine texture and delicate color, and for the varied uses about the house that daily arise, requiring the use of soap that is above the ordinary in quality.

For the Bath, Toilet or Nursery, it is preferred to most of the Soaps sold for toilet use, being purer and much more pleasant and effective, and possessing all the desirable properties of the finest unadulterated White Castile Soap. The Ivory Soap will "float."

The cakes are so shaped that they may be used entire for general purposes, or divided with a stout thread (as illustrated into two perfectly formed cakes, of convenient size for toilet use.

The price, compared to the quality and the size of the cakes, makes it the cheapest Soap for everybody and every want. **Try it.**
SOLD EVERYWHERE.

FOR THE LITTLE GIRLS
NEW STYLE
DOLLS!

Eight inches tall, with beautiful life-like features. Banged hair and dark eyes, or curls and blue eyes.

10 cents each, or two for 15 cents, which *includes dresses* with each doll. 1 doz. dolls and 12 different dresses for 75 cents. Mailed free. Special Offer to the readers of this Paper. Every person sending 15 cents will receive 2 dolls with dresses and 50 page Illus. Book free. A lady in Tipton, Iowa, writes that she sold 25 the first afternoon. Postage stamps taken.

HOPE MANUFACTURING CO., Providence, R. I.

WATCHES.

Stem Winders, Stem Setters, Reliable, Warranted. Prices from $10 to $60. Circulars with full descrip-

Print Your Own Cards, &c. Press $3

Large sizes for circulars, &c., $8 to $90. For pleasure, money-making, young or old. Everything easy, printed instructions. Send 2 stamps for Catalogue of Presses, Type, Cards, &c., to the factory.

KELSEY & CO., Meriden, Conn.

$66 a week in your own town. Terms and $5 outfit free. Address H. Hallett & Co., Portland, Maine.

BOYS who are Hunting and Fishing, and want to make money and have fun, send name and two 3c. stamps, and we will send you an article that will please you. Centre Mfg. Co., East Providence Centre, R. I.

FIGURE 1–2 A 1920 Ivory Ad

Ivory was a remarkable product in a time in which most soaps were yellow or brown, irritated skin, and damaged clothes. The fact that it floated had practical value to those used to being frustrated by trying to find their soap in the bath water. It was thus well positioned—a soap that was pure, was mild, and floated. From the outset, the fact that it was mild enough for babies was stressed, and babies were often featured in the advertising. The claims of purity and mildness were supported by the white color, the name Ivory, the twin slogans, and the association with babies. The soap's brand name, along with its distinctive wrapping, gave customers confidence that they were getting the mild, gentle soap they wanted. The "aggressive" 1882 national advertising budget of $11,000 provided a start toward high brand awareness, and customer confidence that the manufacturer was backing the product and would stand behind it.

Ivory, now over 110 years old, is a prime example of the value of creating and sustaining brand equity. Brand equity will be carefully defined and detailed later in this chapter. Briefly, it is a set of assets such as name awareness, loyal customers, perceived quality, and associations (e.g. being "pure" and "it floats") that are linked to the brand (its name and symbol) and add (or subtract) value to the product or service being offered.

Curiously, in 1885 a yellow soap named Sunlight, when introduced to dreary, sun-starved England, became the start of Unilever, now one of the largest firms in the world. Unlike Ivory, however, Sunlight gave way to other brands, such as Lifebuoy, Lux, and Rinso.

Nearly thirty years later, in 1911, P&G introduced Crisco, the first all-vegetable shortening, using an ad showing a woman in her kitchen admiring a freshly baked rhubarb pie. The ad was the precursor of the "slice of life" type of advertising (linking brands to people's life contexts) that was to be a P&G staple over the years. By 1933 the firm had added Chipso, a washing-machine soap; Dreft, a synthetic detergent; Ivory Flakes; Ivory Snow; and Camay, a competitor to Ivory.

P&G demonstrated its commitment to Ivory's brand equity during the depression. In the face of tremendous economic hardships, P&G resisted pressures to reduce advertising. In fact, in part by sponsoring "The O'Neills," a radio "soap opera," Ivory doubled its sales between 1933 and 1939.

The loyalty and market presence that Ivory had built was challenged in 1941 by an Ivory clone called Swan from Lever Brothers. It was billed as "The first really new floating soap since the Gay Nineties." P&G reacted with aggressive advertising to protect Ivory. Without any clear product difference, Lever could not dislodge Ivory, and ultimately withdrew from the market.

In May of 1931 a memo by Neil McElroy, then working on P&G's Camay account and frustrated by being in the shadow of Ivory, put forth the idea of developing a brand management team. He argued that there were not enough people caring about Camay. The marketing effort (and the effort to create and maintain equity) was diffused and uncoordinated, and lacked a budget commitment. The solution, creating a brand management team responsible for the marketing program and its coordination with sales and manufacturing, was a key event in the history of branding.

During the late 1940s and 1950s the firm added Spic & Span cleaner, Tide detergent, Prell shampoo, Lilt home permanent, Joy dishwashing detergent, Blue Cheer, Crest toothpaste, Dash low-sudsing detergent, Comet cleanser with bleach, Duz soap, Secret cream deodorant, Jif peanut spread, Duncan Hines, Charmin, and Ivory Liquid. The sixties and seventies saw the addition of Pampers disposable diapers, Folger's coffee, Scope mouthwash, Bounty paper towels, Pringles potato chips, Bounce fabric softener, Rely tampons, and Luv disposable diapers.

In the late 1980s, P&G had 83 advertised brands and annual sales of nearly $20 billion. In the U.S. it had the No. 1 brand in 19 of the 39 categories in which it competed, and one of the top three brands in all but five. In these 39 categories, P&G commanded an average market share close to 25%.

Most firms will focus efforts upon one brand, protecting its position by pursuing a given positioning strategy. New segments are usually therefore uncovered by competitors who are attempting to gain a position in the market. One striking aspect of P&G has been its willingness to develop competing brands in order to serve new segments, even if the new brands pressure (or even threaten) existing brands. The mature, fragmented laundry detergent category is an excellent example of how a set of brands can combine to reach a variety of segments and result in a dominant position: P&G holds a 50%-plus share of the market.

P&G's ten brands use different associations to target different market segments. Thus:

Ivory Snow—"Ninety-nine and forty-four one-hundredths percent pure," the "Mild, gentle soap for diapers and baby clothes"

Tide—For extra-tough family laundry jobs—"Tide's in, dirt's out"

Cheer—Works in cold, warm, or hot water—"All-temperature Cheer"

Gain—Originally an "enzyme" detergent but now a detergent with a fragrance—"Bursting with freshness"

Bold 3—Includes fabric softener—"Cleans, softens, and controls static"

Dash—Concentrated power, less suds to avoid clogging washing machines

Dreft—With "Borax, nature's natural sweetener" for baby's clothes

Oxydol—Contains bleach—for "Sparkling whites—with color-safe bleach"

Era—Concentrated liquid detergent—with proteins to clean stains

Solo—Heavy-duty, with a fabric softener

In few other companies is the power of branding so apparent. Without question the key to the success of P&G is its commitment to the development of brand equity, the brand management system that supports it, and the ongoing investment in marketing that sustains it.

There are a few publicly available numbers that allow a crude estimate of the profits that the Ivory brand name has provided to P&G over the past century. We know that just over $300 million was spent on U.S. measured media during the 10-year period from 1977 to 1987. It is estimated that during this period measured media was about 75% of total advertising at P&G. If similar ratios hold for Ivory products, the total Ivory advertising expenditures would be around $400 million.

Assuming an ad-to-sales ratio of 7% (the ratio for P&G as a firm ranged from 6% to 8% during this period), worldwide sales of Ivory products would have been $5.7 billion. Assuming an exponential sales-growth curve since 1887, the total sales of Ivory products since Ivory was first introduced would be around $25 billion. Assuming an average profitability of 10% (the average profitability for laundry and cleaning products from 1987 to 1989 was 10%), a reasonable estimate of total Ivory profits would be $2 to $3 billion.

Interestingly and not coincidentally, P&G is known on Wall Street as a firm which takes a long-term view of its brand profitability. Although this can be frustrating and risky in the short term for an investor, P&G is patient with brands even when they absorb losses over a long time period. Their persistence with Pringles chips, Duncan Hines ready-to-eat soft cookies, and Citrus Hill orange juice in the face of substantial losses are examples. The long-term perspective of P&G may in part be due to the fact that it is 20% owned by its employees.

In this book we shall explore brand equity. As the P&G example illustrates, the development of brand equity can create associations that can drive market positions, persist over long time periods, and be capable of resisting aggressive competitors. However, it can also involve an initial and ongoing investment which can be substantial and will not necessarily result in short-term profits. Payoffs, when they come, can involve decades. Thus, management of brand equity is difficult, requiring patience and vision.

In the following pages we will define brand equity and suggest that it is based on a set of dimensions each of which potentially needs to be managed. Several perspectives on how to place a value on a brand will then be detailed. First, however, several basic questions must be addressed. For example: What exactly is a brand? Have brand equities been eroding? How do price promotions affect brands? What is behind the pressures for short-run financial results? Can a focus on brand equity provide a counterpoint to the tyranny of short-term financials?

THE ROLE OF BRANDS

A brand is a distinguishing name and/or symbol (such as a logo, trademark, or package design) intended to identify the goods or services of either one seller or a group of sellers, and to differentiate those goods or services from those of competitors. A brand thus signals to the customer the source of the product, and protects both the customer and the producer from competitors who would attempt to provide products that appear to be identical.

There is evidence that even in ancient history names were put on such goods as bricks in order to identify their maker.[2] And it is known that trade guilds in medieval Europe used trademarks to assure the customer and provide legal protection to the producer. In the early sixteenth century, whiskey distillers shipped their products in wooden barrels with the name of the producer burned into the barrel. The name showed the consumer who the maker was and prevented the substitution of cheaper products. In 1835 a brand of Scotch called "Old Smuggler" was introduced in order to capitalize on the quality reputation developed by bootleggers who used a special distilling process.

Although brands have long had a role in commerce, it was not until the twentieth century that branding and brand associations became so central to competitors. In fact, a distinguishing characteristic of modern marketing has been its focus upon the creation of differentiated brands. Market research has been used to help identify and develop bases of brand differentiation. Unique brand associations have been established using product attributes, names, packages, distribution strategies, and advertising. The idea has been to move beyond commodities to branded products—to reduce the primacy of price upon the purchase decision, and accentuate the bases of differentiation.

The power of brands, and the difficulty and expense of establishing them, is indicated by what firms are willing to pay for them. For example, Kraft was purchased for nearly $13 billion, more than 600% over its book value, and the collection of brands under the RJR Nabisco umbrella brought over $25 billion. These values are far beyond the worth of any balance sheet item representing bricks and mortar.

An even clearer example of the value of a brand name is licensing. For example, Sunkist in 1988 received $10.3 million in royalties by licensing its name for use on hundreds of products such as Sunkist Fruit Gems (Ben Myerson candy), Sunkist orange soda (Cadbury Schweppes), Sunkist juice drinks (Lipton), Sunkist Vitamin C (Ciba–Geigy), and Sunkist fruit snacks (Lipton).[3] Lipton used the name Sunkist Fun Fruits to overcome an established Fruit Corner line of fruit snacks from General Mills. The Fruit Corner tag line, "Real fruit and fun rolled up in one," was overshadowed by Sunkist Fun Fruits, a name that said it all.

The value of an established brand is in part due to the reality that it is more difficult to build brands today than it was only a few decades ago. First, the cost of advertising and distribution is much higher: One-minute commercials and sometimes even half-minute commercials are now considered too expensive to be practical, for example. Second, the number of brands is proliferating: Approximately 3,000 brands are introduced each year into supermarkets. There were at this writing 750 nameplates of cars, over 150 brands of lipstick, and 93 cat-food brands. All this meant, and continues to mean, increased competition for the customer's mind as well as for access to the distribution channel. It also means that a brand often is relegated to a niche market, and so will lack the sales to support expensive marketing programs.

BRAND-BUILDING NEGLECT

Despite the often obvious value of a brand, there are signs that the brand-building process is eroding, loyalty levels are falling, and price is becoming more salient. The accompanying insert suggests a series of indicators of a lack of attention to brands which most firms will find familiar.

Indicators of an Underemphasis on Brand-Building

- Managers cannot identify with confidence the brand associations and the strength of those associations. Further, there is little knowledge about how those associations differ across segments and through time.
- Knowledge of levels of brand awareness is lacking. There is no feel for whether a recognition problem exists among any segment. Knowledge is lacking as to top-of-mind recall that the brand is getting, and how that has been changing.
- There is no systematic, reliable, sensitive, and valid measure of customer satisfaction and loyalty—nor any diagnostic model that guides an ongoing understanding of why such measures may be changing.
- There are no indicators of the brand tied to long-term success of the business that are used to evaluate the brand's marketing effort.
- There is no person in the firm who is really charged with protecting the brand equity. Those nominally in charge of the brand, perhaps termed brand managers or product marketing managers, are in fact evaluated on the basis of short-term measures.
- The measures of performance associated with a brand and its managers are quarterly and yearly. There are no longer-term objectives that are meaningful. Further, the managers involved do not realistically expect to stay long enough to think strategically, nor does ultimate brand performance follow them.
- There is no mechanism to measure and evaluate the impact of elements of the marketing program upon the brand. Sales promotions, for example, are selected without determining their associations and considering their impact upon the brand.
- There is no long-term strategy for the brand. The following questions about the brand environment five or ten years into the future are unanswered, and may have not been addressed: What associations should the brand have? In what product classes should the brand be competing? What mental image should the brand stimulate in the future?

There is evidence that loyalty levels for supermarket products have declined.[4] Nielsen charted the market share for 50 selected major supermarket brands and found that it fell 7% from 1975 to 1987. The research firm NPD revealed that in a study of 20 supermarket product categories the average number of brands purchased in a six-month period increased by 9% from 1975 to 1983.

The ad agency BBDO found a surprising perception of brand parity among consumers throughout the world in 13 consumer product categories.[5] They asked consumers whether they felt that the brands they had to choose from in a given product category were more or less the same. The percent who indicated brand parity ranged from 52% for cigarettes to 76% for credit cards. It was noticeably higher for such products as paper towels and dry soup, which emphasize performance benefits, than for products like cigarettes, coffee, and beer, for which imagery has been the norm.

One survey of department-store shoppers involving 11 product categories such as underwear, shoes, housewares, furniture, and appliances documented the erosion of price.[6] Only 39% of a national probability sample of 400 randomly dialed adults indicated that they paid full price, while 41% waited for a sale and 16% more bought discounted merchandise not on sale. Interestingly, the study found a high negative correlation between media advertising in a product category and category sales at full price. Advertising, of course, creates strong brands which can hold share in the face of discounting.

THE USE OF SALES PROMOTION

It is tempting to "milk" brand equity by cutting back on brand-building activities, such as advertising, which have little impact upon short-term performance. Further, declines in brand equity are not obvious. In contrast, sales promotions, whether they involve soda pop or automobiles, *are* effective—they affect sales in an immediate and measurable way. During a week in which a promotion is run, dramatic sales increases are observed for many product classes: 443% for fruit drinks, 194% for frozen dinners, and 122% for laundry detergents.[7]

Promotions provide a way to keep a third- or fourth-ranking brand on the shelf. They are also attractive to the Pepsis of the world that want to beat Coke and, not so incidentally, squeeze out the 7-Up's of the world.

There has been a dramatic increase in sales promotion during the past two decades or so, both customer-directed (such as couponing and rebates) and trade-directed (such as wholesale case discounts). Just over a decade ago there was a 40/60 relationship between expenditures in promotions and advertising. The ratio is now 60/40 and still changing. Coupon distributions grew at an annual rate of 11.8% through the 1980s.[8] Even in categories such as automobiles, price promotions have been the norm.

Unlike brand-building activities, most sales promotions are easily copied. In fact, competitors must retaliate or suffer unacceptable losses. When a promotion/price-cutting cycle begins it is most difficult to stop because both the customer and the trade become used to it and begin planning their purchases around the promotion cycle. The inevitable result is a great increase in the role of price. There is pressure to reduce the quality, features, and services offered. At the extreme, the product class starts to resemble a commodity, since brand associations have less importance. At that point, promotions look even better with respect to short-term impact, but their value declines. One recent study of more than 1,000 promotions concluded that only 16% paid off when costs and forward-buying were factored in.[9]

The enhanced role of promotions is in part driven by measurement. With the advent of the scanner-based databases in food and drug stores, the short-term measures of some marketing actions are better than ever. They show that price promotions affect sales. However, they are not well suited to measure long-term results, in part because such results are difficult to detect in a noisy marketplace, and also because experiments covering multiple years are very expensive to conduct. Because there are no easy, defensible ways to measure the long-term effects of marketing actions, short-term measures have added influence. The situation is a bit like that of the drunk who looks for car keys under a street light because the light is better than where the keys were actually lost.

The visibility of the short-term success of price promotions and other potentially brand-debilitating activities is fed by the short-term orientation of many marketing organizations. Brand managers and other key people often are rotated regularly so that they can expect to stay in any one position for only two to five years. This then becomes their time horizon. Worse, during this time they are evaluated on the basis of short-term measures such as market share movements and short-term profitability. This is in part because such measures are available and reliable while indicators of long-term success are elusive, and, too, because the organization itself is concerned with short-term performance.

PRESSURES FOR SHORT-TERM RESULTS

Branding decisions take place in organizations experiencing extreme pressures to deliver short-term performance, particularly in the U.S. A myriad of diverse spokespeople, including the chairman of Sony, a political scientist from Harvard, and the authors of the MIT Commission on Productivity, have forcefully concluded that U.S. managers have an excessive preoccupation with short-term profits at the expense of long-range strategy.

A prime reason why American managers might have a short-term focus is the prominence and acceptance of the maximization of stockholder value as the prime objective of U.S. firms. The problem is that shareholders are inordinately influenced by quarterly earnings. Their crude model is that future returns will be related to current performance. The resulting need for managers to demonstrate good quarterly earnings percolates into organizational objectives and brand-management evaluation. As a result, there is intense pressure throughout the firm to deliver good short-term financials.

A basic problem is that shareholders usually are incapable of understanding the strategic vision of a firm, in part because they are not privy to strategic decision-making, and also because they cannot interpret the uncertain strategic environment or the complexities of the organization. Further, there is an absence of credible alternative indicators of long-term performance.

After decades of effort, we have been markedly unsuccessful at modeling the long-term value of advertising in the absence of multiple-year field experiments. Measure of new-product effort is similarly difficult to quantify. Firms can keep track of new product research expenditures, the number of new products, the percent of business associated with products introduced within five years, and so on, but it is difficult to generate measures that are convincing surrogates for long-term performance. The long-term value of activities which will enhance or erode brand equity are similarly difficult to convincingly demonstrate. Without alternatives, short-term financials fill a vacuum and come to dominate performance measurement.

Managing with a long-term perspective is difficult in the face of the shareholder value emphasis, and other pressures, facing U.S. managers. What is to be done? Simply put, we need to find measures of long-term performance to supplement or replace short-term financials, measures that will be convincing enough to satisfy shareholders.

The Brand-Building Potential of Advertising

A rare effort to document the brand-building effect of advertising was made by the research firm IRI.[10] An analysis of hundreds of heavy-up advertising experiments (where heavy advertising is compared to moderate or normal advertising) was conducted. On average over half of such heavy-up tests show no significant change in sales at all during the test period. IRI examined 15 of these experiments that did achieve significant sales gains during a test year. Sales averaged 22% over the base period. Sales in years 2 and 3, after the heavy advertising was withdrawn, were still above the base period, 17% and 6% respectively. Thus, the impact of advertising may be grossly underestimated if only a one year perspective is employed. Of course, advertising and promotion results are more often expected in months, or even weeks.

THE ROLE OF ASSETS AND SKILLS

One approach to introducing a strategic orientation is to change the primary focus from managing short-term financials to the development and maintenance of assets and skills.[11] An asset is something a firm possesses, such as a brand name or retail location, which is superior to that of the competition. A skill is something a firm does better than its competitors do, such as advertising or efficient manufacturing.

Assets and skills provide the basis of a competitive advantage that is sustainable. What a business *does* (the way it competes and where it chooses to do so) usually is easily imitated. It is more difficult to respond to what a business *is*, since that involves acquiring or neutralizing specialized assets or skills. Anyone can decide to distribute cereal or detergent through supermarkets, but few have the clout to do it as effectively as, say, General Mills. The right assets and skills can provide the barriers to competitor thrusts that allow the competitive advantage to persist over time and thus lead to long-term profits. The challenges are to identify key assets and skills on which the firm should base its competitive advantage, to build upon and maintain them, and then to use them effectively.

The concept of an asset as a generator of a profit stream is familiar, especially when that asset is capitalized and appears on the balance sheet. A government bond is the prototypical example. A factory which houses plant, equipment, and people is another example. But of course a factory, unlike a government bond, requires active management and must be maintained.

The most important assets of a firm, however (such as the people in the organization and the brand names), are intangible in that they are not capitalized and thus do not appear on the balance sheet. Depreciation is not assessed, on "intangible assets," and thus maintenance must come directly out of cash flow and short-term profits. Everyone understands that even in bad times a factory must be maintained, in part because of the depreciation term in the income statement and also because maintenance needs are visible. An intangible asset, by contrast, is more vulnerable, and its "maintenance" is more easily neglected.

MANAGING THE BRAND NAME

One such intangible asset is the equity represented by a brand name. For many businesses the brand name and what it represents are its most important asset—the basis of competitive advantage and of future earnings streams. Yet, the brand name is seldom managed in a coordinated, coherent manner with a view that it must be maintained and strengthened.

Instead of focusing upon an asset such as a brand, too often American "fast-track" managers get caught up in day-to-day performance measures which are easily available. What caused the share drop in the Northeast? Would a promotion fight off a new product challenge? How can we combat a new entry? Can we put a name on another division's product and thus provide an interim solution? How can growth be sustained? Can a brand name be used to gain entry into a new product market?

A focus on short-run problems facing the brand can result in an operation that performs well, sometimes over a long time-period. However, the danger is that this performance is achieved by exploiting the brand and allowing it to deteriorate. The brand might be extended so far that its core associations are weakened. Its associations might be tarnished by expanding its market to include less-prestigious outlets and customers. Price promotions might be used to provide a perceived bargain for customers. The brand should be thought of as an asset, such as a timber reserve. Short-term profits can be substantial if the reserve is depleted without regard to the future but the asset can be destroyed in the process.

It is not enough to avoid damaging a brand—it needs to be nurtured and maintained. A more subtle danger facing a brand is from a firm with a strong cost/efficiency culture. The focus is on improving the efficiency of operations including purchasing, product design, manufacturing, promotions, and logistics. A problem, however, is that in such a culture the brand may not be nurtured, and thus may slowly deteriorate. Further, efficiency pressures lead to difficult compromises between cost goals on the one hand and customer satisfaction on the other.

The value of brand-building activities on future performance is not easy to demonstrate. The challenge is to understand better the links between brand assets and future performance, so that brand-building activities can be justified. What are the assets that underlie brand equity? How do they relate to future performance? Which assets need to be developed, strengthened, or maintained? What exactly is the nature of the payoff/risk of such activities? What is the value of an improvement in perceived quality or brand awareness, for example? If answers to such questions would emerge, there would be more support for brand-building and more resistance to short-term expediency.

All brand-building activities require justification. However, the need is particularly acute in advertising because of the large expenditures involved that are often vulnerable to short-term pressures. Peter A. Georgescu, president of Young & Rubicam, captured the pressure on advertising by noting a need to learn how to measure, forecast, and manage the communication elements that go into the making of strong brands.[12] He warned: "We have to find ways to measure and justify the megamillions our clients have to spend to build strong brands—or else." The "or else" referred to brands becoming "faceless, lifeless" commodities.

The first step in identifying the value of brand equity is to understand what it is—what really contributes to the value of a brand. Thus, we now turn to the definitional issue. Subsequently, we shall look at several methods of placing a value upon a brand which will provide additional insight regarding the brand concept. And, finally, some issues facing those who create or manage brands will be introduced.

WHAT IS BRAND EQUITY?

Brand equity is a set of brand assets and liabilities linked to a brand, its name and symbol, that add to or subtract from the value provided by a product or service to a firm and/or to that firm's customers. For assets or liabilities to underlie brand equity they must be linked to the name and/or symbol of the brand. If the brand's name or symbol should change, some or all of the assets or liabilities could be affected and even lost, although some might be shifted to a new name and symbol. The assets and liabilities on which brand equity is based will differ from context to context. However, they can be usefully grouped into five categories:

1. Brand loyalty
2. Name awareness
3. Perceived quality
4. Brand associations in addition to perceived quality
5. Other proprietary brand assets—patents, trademarks, channel relationships, etc.

The concept of brand equity is summarized in Figure 1–3. The five categories of assets that underlie brand equity are shown as being the basis of brand equity. The figure also shows that brand equity creates value for both the customer and the firm.

PROVIDING VALUE TO THE CUSTOMER

Brand-equity assets generally add or subtract value for customers. They can help them interpret, process, and store huge quantities of information about products and brands. They also can affect customers' confidence in the purchase decision (due to either past-use experience or familiarity with the brand and its characteristics). Potentially more important is the fact that both perceived quality and brand associations can enhance customers' satisfaction with the use experience. Knowing that a piece of jewelry came from Tiffany can affect the experience of wearing it: The user can actually feel different.

PROVIDING VALUE TO THE FIRM

As part of its role in adding value for the customer, brand equity has the potential to add value for the firm by generating marginal cash flow in at least half a dozen ways. First, it can enhance programs to attract new customers or recapture old ones. A promotion, for example, which provides an incentive to try a new flavor or new use will be more effective

FIGURE 1–3 Brand Equity

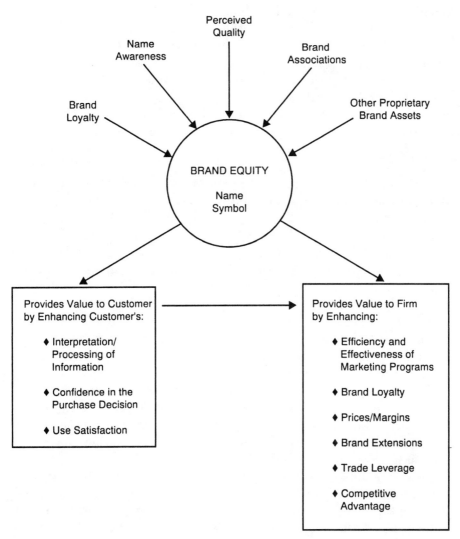

if the brand is familiar, and if there is no need to combat a consumer skeptical of brand quality.

Second, the last four brand equity dimensions can enhance brand loyalty. The perceived quality, the associations, and the well-known name can provide reasons to buy and can affect use satisfaction. Even when they are not pivotal to brand choice, they can reassure, reducing the incentive to try others. Enhanced brand loyalty is especially important in buying time to respond when competitors innovate and obtain product advantages. Note that brand loyalty is both one of the dimensions of brand equity and is affected by brand equity. The potential influence on loyalty from the other dimensions is significant enough that it is explicitly listed as one of the ways that brand equity provides value to the firm.

It should be noted that there exist similar interrelationships among the other brand equity dimensions. For example, perceived quality could be influenced by awareness (a visible name is likely to be well made), by associations (a visible spokesperson would only endorse a quality product), and by loyalty (a loyal customer would not like a poor product). In some circumstances it might be useful to explicitly include other brand equity dimensions as outputs of brand equity as well as inputs, even though they do not appear in Figure 1–3.

Third, brand equity will usually allow higher margins by permitting both premium pricing and reduced reliance upon promotions. In many contexts the elements of brand equity serve to support premium pricing. Further, a brand with a disadvantage in brand equity will have to invest more in promotional activity, sometimes just to maintain its position in the distribution channel.

Fourth, brand equity can provide a platform for growth via brand extensions. Ivory, as we have seen, has been extended into several cleaning products, creating business areas that would have been much more expensive to enter without the Ivory name.

Fifth, brand equity can provide leverage in the distribution channel. Like customers, the trade has less uncertainty dealing with a proven brand name that has already achieved recognition and associations. A strong brand will have an edge in gaining both shelf facings and cooperation in implementing marketing programs.

Finally, brand-equity assets provide a competitive advantage that often presents a real barrier to competitors. An association—e.g., Tide is the detergent for tough family laundry jobs—may preempt an attribute that is important for a given segment. For example, another brand would find it difficult to compete with Tide for the "tough cleaning job" segment.

A strong perceived quality position, such as that of Acura, is a competitive advantage not easily overcome—convincing customers that another brand has achieved quality superior to the Acura (even if true) will be hard. Achieving parity in name awareness can be extremely expensive for a brand with an awareness liability.

We now turn to the five categories of assets that underlie brand equity. As each is discussed, it will become clear that brand-equity assets require investment to create, and will dissipate over time unless maintained.

Brand Loyalty

For any business it is expensive to gain new customers and relatively inexpensive to keep existing ones, especially when the existing customers are satisfied with—or even like—the brand. In fact, in many markets there is substantial inertia among customers even if there are very low switching costs and low customer commitment to the existing brand. Thus, an installed customer base has the customer acquisition investment largely in its past. Further, at least some existing customers provide brand exposure and reassurance to new customers.

The loyalty of the customer base reduces the vulnerability to competitive action. Competitors may be discouraged from spending resources to attract satisfied customers. Further, higher loyalty means greater trade leverage, since customers expect the brand to be always available.

Awareness of the Brand Name and Symbols

People will often buy a familiar brand because they are comfortable with the familiar. Or there may be an assumption that a brand that is familiar is probably reliable, in business to stay, and of reasonable quality. A recognized brand will thus often be selected over an unknown brand. The awareness factor is particularly important in contexts in which the brand must first enter the consideration set—it must be one of the brands that are evaluated. An unknown brand usually has little chance.

Perceived Quality

A brand will have associated with it a perception of overall quality not necessarily based on a knowledge of detailed specifications. The quality perception may take on somewhat different forms for different types of industries. Perceived quality means something different for Hewlett Packard or IBM than for Solomon Brothers or Tide or Heinz. However, it will always be a measureable, important brand characteristic.

Perceived quality will directly influence purchase decisions and brand loyalty, especially when a buyer is not motivated or able to conduct a detailed analysis. It can also support a premium price which, in turn, can create gross margin that can be reinvested in brand equity. Further, perceived quality can be the basis for a brand extension. If a brand is well-regarded in one context, the assumption will be that it will have high quality in a related context.

A SET OF ASSOCIATIONS

The underlying value of a brand name often is based upon specific associations linked to it. Associations such as Ronald McDonald can create a positive attitude or feeling that can become linked to a brand such as McDonald's. The link of Karl Malden to American Express provides credibility, and (to some) may stimulate confidence in the service. The association of a "use context" such as aspirin and heart-attack prevention can provide a reason-to-buy which can attract customers. A life-style or personality association may change the use experience: The Jaguar associations may make the experience of owning and driving one "dif-

---

Branding an Ingredient: Nutrasweet

Perdue chickens and Chiquita bananas illustrate that a commodity product can be successfully branded. Each has developed a formidable awareness level and quality reputation for a product that was thought not long ago to be a pure commodity.

The Nutrasweet Company, a unit of Monsanto, faced an even more difficult task: to brand a patented ingredient, the sugar substitute aspartame.[13] The brand had to be strong enough to survive the expiration of the patent in the early 1990s.

Their strategy was to create a consumer-level brand name (drawing upon the words "nutrition" and "sweet") and symbol (the familiar swirl) and establish it so firmly that consumers will prefer products with Nutrasweet over the same products from a low-cost competitor. Although Nutrasweet has advertised extensively, the cornerstone of the brand-creation effort has been their insistence that each of the some 3,000 products that use Nutrasweet display the brand name and symbol. The brand has been extremely successful in the market: In 1989, only six years after its introduction, it had profits of $180 million on sales of over $850 million.

Some fascinating questions emerge: How strong will the Nutrasweet brand be in the face of cheap substitutes? What will Nutrasweet do to help retain consumer loyalty? Can the firm repeat its success with its newest commodity, the fat substitute Simplesse? Will a similar strategy work again?

ferent." A strong association may be the basis of a brand extension: Hershey's chocolate milk provides the drink with a competitive advantage based upon Hershey's associations.

If a brand is well positioned upon a key attribute in the product class (such as service backup or technological superiority), competitors will find it hard to attack. If they attempt a frontal assault by claiming superiority via that dimension, there will be a credibility issue. It would be difficult for a competing department store to make credible a claim that it has surpassed Nordstrom on service. They may be forced to find another, perhaps inferior, basis for competition. Thus, an association can be a barrier to competitors.

OTHER PROPRIETARY BRAND ASSETS

The last three brand-equity categories we have just discussed represent customer perceptions and reactions to the brand; the first was the loyalty of the customer base. The fifth category represents such other proprietary brand assets as patents, trademarks, and channel relationships.

Brand assets will be most valuable if they inhibit or prevent competitors from eroding a customer base and loyalty. These assets can take several forms. For example, a trademark will protect brand equity from competitors who might want to confuse customers by using a similar name, symbol, or package. A patent, if strong and relevant to customer choice, can prevent direct competition. A distribution channel can be controlled by a brand because of a history of brand performance.

Assets, to be relevant, must be tied to the brand. If distribution is a basis for brand equity, it needs to be based on a brand rather than on a firm (such as P&G or Frito–Lay). The firm could not simply access the shelf space by replacing one brand with another. If the value of a patent could easily be transferred to another brand name, its contribution to brand equity would be low. Similarly, if a set of store locations could be exploited using another brand name, they would not contribute to brand equity.

WHAT IS THE VALUE OF A BRAND?

Developing approaches to placing a value on a brand is important for several reasons. First, as a practical matter, since brands are bought and sold, a value must be assessed by both buyers and sellers. Which approach makes the most sense? Second, investments in brands in order to enhance brand equity need to be justified, as there always are competing uses of funds. A bottom-line justification is that the investment will enhance the value of the brand. Thus, some "feel" for how a brand should be valued may help managers address such decisions. Third, the valuation question provides additional insight into the brand-equity concept.

What is the value of a brand name? Consider IBM, Boeing, Betty Crocker, Ford, Weight Watchers, Bud, and Wells Fargo. What would happen to those firms if they lost a brand name but retained the other assets associated with the business? What would it cost in terms of expenditures to avoid damage to their business if the name were lost? Would any expenditure be capable of avoiding an erosion, perhaps permanent, to the business?

Black & Decker bought the GE small-appliance business for over $300 million, but only had the use of the GE name for three years. After going through the effort to change the name, their conclusion was that they might have been better off simply to enter the business without buying the GE line. The cost to switch equity from GE to Black & Decker was as high as developing a new line and establishing a new name. Clearly, the GE name was an important part of the business.

At least five general approaches to assessing the value of brand equity have been proposed. One is based on the price premium that the name can support. The second is the impact of the name on customer preference. The third looks at the replacement value of the brand. The fourth is based on the stock price. The fifth focuses on the earning power of a brand. We shall now consider these in the listed order.

PRICE PREMIUMS
GENERATED BY THE BRAND NAME

Brand equity assets such as name awareness, perceived quality, associations, and loyalty all have the potential to provide a brand with a price premium. The resulting extra revenue can be used (for example) to enhance profits, or to reinvest in building more equity.

One approach to the measurement of a price premium attached to a brand is simply to observe the price levels in the market. What are the differences, and how are they associated with different brands? For example, what are the price levels of comparable automobiles? How much are the different brands depreciating each year? How responsive is the brand to a firm's own price changes, or to price changes of competitors?

Price premiums can also be measured through customer research. Customers can be asked what they would pay for various features and characteristics of a product (one characteristic would be the brand name). Termed a dollarmetric scale, this survey device provides a direct measure of the value of the brand name.

Using a variant of the dollarmetric measure, American Motors tested a car (then called the Renault Premier) by showing an "unbadged" (unnamed) model of it to customers and asking them what they would pay for it.[14] The same question was then asked with the car identified by various names. The price was around $10,000 with no name, and about $3,000 more with the Renault Premier name on it. When Chrysler bought American Motors the car became the Chrysler Eagle Premier, and it was sold for a price close to the level suggested by the study.

Additional insight is acquired by obtaining buyer-preference or purchase-likelihood measures for different price levels. In such a study, the resistance of a buyer preference to price decreases of competition, and the responsiveness to a brand's own decrease in price, can be determined. A high-equity brand will lose little share to a competitor's lower price, and will gain share when its own relative price is decreased (up to a point).

Trade-off (conjoint) analysis is still another approach. Here, respondents are asked to make trade-off judgments about brand attributes. For example, suppose that the attributes of a computer included on-site service (supplied vs. not supplied), price ($3,200 vs. $3,700) and name (Compaq vs. Circle). A respondent would prefer on-site service, a low price, and an established brand name. To determine the relative value of each, the respondent would be asked to choose between:

Compaq at $3,700 vs. Circle at $3,200

Service at $3,700 vs. No Service at $3,200

Compaq with No Service vs. Circle with Service

The output of trade-off analysis would be a dollar value associated with each attribute alternative. The dollar value of the brand name would thus be created in the context of making judgments relative to other relevant attributes of the product class.

Given that a price premium can be obtained, the value of the brand name in a given year would be that price differential multiplied by the unit sales volume. Discounting these cash flows over a reasonable time horizon would provide one approach to valuing the brand.

BRAND NAME AND CUSTOMER PREFERENCE

Considering the price premium earned by a brand may not be the best way to quantify brand equity especially for product classes like cigarettes and air travel where prices are fairly similar. An alternative is to consider the impact of the brand name upon the customer evaluation of the brand as measured by preference, attitude, or intent to purchase. What does the brand name do to the evaluation?

One study showed that the approval rating for Kellogg's Corn Flakes went from 47% to 59% when the consumers were told the identity of the brand name.[15] And when Armstrong tested a line of tiles against comparable products, the Armstrong name resulted in the preference going from 50–50 to 90–10. The issue often is how much the brand name provides to market share and brand loyalty.

The value of the brand would then be the marginal value of the extra sales (or market share) that the brand name supports. Suppose, for example, it was believed that sales would be 30% less if the brand name was discarded, or sales would decline 30% over a five-year period if the advertising support for the name was eliminated. The profits on the lost marginal sales would represent the value of the brand.

The size of any price premium and the preference rating of a brand can both be measured and tracked over time using survey research. They can become one basis of tracking brand equity. However, this approach is static, in that it looks at the *current* power of the brand—a view which does not necessarily take into account the *future* impact of changes (such as improvements in quality).

REPLACEMENT COST

Another perspective is the cost of establishing a comparable name and business. Kidder Peabody estimates that it would cost from $75 million to $100 million to launch a new consumer product, and that the chances of success would be around 15%. If it was felt that it would cost $100 million to develop and introduce a product and that the chance for success was 25%, on average four products costing a total of $400 million would need to be developed to ensure one winner. A firm should thus be willing to pay $400 million for an established brand with prospects comparable to those being developed.

BRAND VALUE BASED
UPON STOCK PRICE MOVEMENTS

Another approach, suggested by finance theory and implemented by University of Chicago professors Carol J. Simon and Mary W. Sullivan, is to use stock price as a basis to evaluate the value of the brand equities of a firm. [16] The argument is that the stock market will adjust the price of a firm to reflect future prospects of its brands.

The approach starts with the market value of the firm, which is a function of the stock price and the number of shares. The replacement costs of the tangible assets (such as plant and equipment, inventories and cash) are subtracted. The balance, intangible assets, is apportioned into three components: the value of brand equity, the value of nonbrand factors (such as R&D and patents), and the value of industry factors (such as regulation and concentration). Brand equity is assumed to be a function of the age of a brand and its order of entry into the market (an older brand has more equity), the cumulative advertising (advertising creates equity), and the current share of industry advertising (current advertising share is related to positioning advantages).

To estimate the model, the stock-market valuation of 638 firms (less the value of their tangible assets) was related to the indicators of the three types of intangible assets. The resulting estimates allowed an estimate of the brand equities for each firm. The model operates at the level of a publically traded firm and thus will be most valid and useful for a firm with a dominant brand. However, it does have the attraction of being based upon the stock price, which reflects future rather than past earnings, and generates some interesting results.

Table 1–1 shows the average brand equity as a percent of firm tangible asset value by industry, based upon 1985 data for 638 firms. As expected, there is little in the way of brand-equity in industries such as metals and primary building products, whereas firms in the apparel and tobacco industries have substantial brand equities. Applying the model to specific firms suggests that Dreyers Ice Cream (which uses the Edy's name in Eastern markets) and Smucker's have high levels of brand equity relative to their tangible assets and Pillsbury has a lower, but still very substantial, level.

An analysis of the soft drink industry using this model dramatically demonstrates how marketing actions can affect brand equity. The introduction of Diet Coke in July of 1982 caused brand equity for Coke to increase by 65% while that of Pepsi was unchanged. In contrast, the

TABLE 1–1 Brand Equity as a Percent of Firm
Tangible Assets

Industry	Brand Equity
Apparel	61
Tobacco	46
Food products	37
Chemicals	34
Electric machinery	22
Transportation equipment	20
Primary metals	1
Stone, glass, and clay	0
Food Product Firms	Brand Equity
Dreyers	151
Smucker	126
Brown–Forman	82
Kellogg's	61
Sara Lee	57
General Mills	52
Pillsbury	30

introduction of the ill-fated New Coke in April of 1985 caused the Pepsi
brand equity to increase by 45% (even though soft drinks are only 40%
of sales at the Pepsi firm) while the brand equity at Coke declined by
10%.

BRAND VALUE BASED
UPON FUTURE EARNINGS

The best measure of brand equity would be the discounted present
value of future earnings attributable to brand-equity assets. The problem
is how to provide such an estimate.

One approach is to use the long-range plan of the brand. Simply
discount the profit stream that is projected. Such a plan should take into
account brand strengths and their impact upon the competitive environment. One firm that uses the brand's plan to provide a value for
brand equity adjusts the manufacturing costs to reflect the industry
average rather than the actual costs. The logic is that any above (or below)
average efficiency should be credited to manufacturing and not to brand
equity.[17]

Another approach that can be used even when a brand profit plan is unavailable or unsuitable is to estimate current earnings and apply an earnings multiplier. The earnings estimate could be current earnings with any extraordinary charges backed out. If the current earnings are not representative because they reflect a down or up cycle, then some average of the past few years might be more appropriate. If the earnings are negative or low due to correctable problems, then an estimate based upon industry norms of profit as a percent of sales might be useful.

The earnings multiplier provides a way to estimate and place a value upon future earnings. To obtain a suitable earnings multiplier range, the historical price earnings (P/E) multipliers of firms in the involved industry or in similar industries should be examined. For example, a multiplier range for a brand might be 7 to 12 or 16 to 25 depending upon the industry.

The use of an industry-based P/E ratio provides a judgment that stock-market investors have placed upon the industry prospects—its growth potential, the future competitive intensity from existing and potential competitors, and the threat of substitute products. The question remains, which P/E multiplier within the identified range should be used for the brand?

To determine the actual multiplier value within that range, an estimate of the competitive advantage of the brand is needed. Will the brand earnings strengthen over time and generally be above the industry average, or will they weaken and be below average? The estimate should be based upon a weighted average of an appraisal of the brand on each of the five dimensions of brand equity.

APPRAISING BRAND ASSETS

An appraisal of the brand upon the five dimensions involves addressing and obtaining answers to questions such as the following:

Brand Loyalty. What are the brand-loyalty levels by segment? Are customers satisfied? What do "exit interviews" suggest? Why are customers leaving? What is causing dissatisfaction? What do customers say are their problems with buying or using the brand? What are the market-share and sales trends?

Awareness. How valuable an asset is brand awareness in this market? What brand awareness level exists as compared to that of competitors?

What are the trends? Is the brand being considered? Is brand awareness the problem? What could be done to improve brand awareness?

Perceived Quality. What drives perceived quality? What is important to the customer? What signals quality? Is perceived quality valued—or is the market moving toward a commodity business? Are prices and margins eroding? If so, can the movement be slowed or reversed? How do competitors stack up with respect to preceived quality? Are there any changes? In blind-use tests, what is our brand name worth? Has it changed over time?

Brand Associations. What mental image, if any, does the brand stimulate? Is that image a competitive advantage? Is there a slogan or symbol that is a differentiating asset? How are the brand and its competitors positioned? Evaluate each position with respect to its value/relevance to customers and how protected/vulnerable it is to competitors: Which

---

Should the Value of a Brand Be Reported to Shareholders?

A case can be made that the brand value should be placed on the balance sheet or at least reported to shareholders as part of a firm's financial report. In fact, several British firms have added brand equity to the balance sheet. For example, in 1988 Ranks Hovis McDougall decided to put a balance sheet value of $1.2 billion on its 60 brands. First, such an intangible asset can easily exceed in value that of tangible assets which are scrupulously reported and affect shareholder's valuation of firms. Second, reported brand equity can focus attention upon intangible assets and thus make it easier to justify brand building activities that are likely to pay off in the long term. Without such information, shareholders must rely upon short-term financials.

The major difficulty involves a question of whether any valuation of brand equity can be both objective and verifiable. Unless brand valuation can be defended, it will not be helpful and can result in legal liability. It is no coincidence that in England, where brand value has been placed upon the balance sheet, there is a less litigious environment.

position is the most valuable and protected? What does the brand mean? What are its strongest associations?

Other Brand Assets. Are sustainable competitive advantages attached to the brand name that are not reflected in the other four equity dimensions? Is there a patent or trademark that is important? Are there channel relationships that provide barriers to competitors?

ESTIMATING A MULTIPLIER

In addition to an appraisal of brand strength, it is important to know the importance/relevance of that strength in the market, the firm's ability to exploit it, and the commitment to protecting it.

The various dimensions of brand equity are not equally important in all markets. The need is to determine their relative value. Which dimensions represent, or could represent, a sustainable competitive advantage that matters? Do awareness levels explain the relative success of competitors? Or is there awareness parity among the relevant competitors? Perceived quality may be critical in a cleaning product or high-technology device, but in a mature market where it is difficult to convince customers that brands differ, it might be of less consequence.

Another issue is whether a brand asset such as a strong customer base is being, or will be, exploited. A brand asset will have little value if it is not used. Brand loyalty will not generate value by itself. Programs are needed to increase satisfaction and switching costs—to make sure that the customer base is protected so that the costs of regaining customers will not have to be incurred. A perceived quality advantage should result in either a price premium or a perceived value advantage. Programs will be needed to make sure that the market does not become a commodity area that weakens the value of a perceived quality advantage.

Finally, the brand asset needs to be protected. The exploitation of perceived quality, for example, may be short-lived if programs are not in place to maintain the perceived quality level.

Thus, a relatively high multiplier will be appropriate when there is strength in the more important asset categories, and when that strength is both exploited and protected. The multiplier will be lower when strength in the key asset areas is lacking, or when strengths are not being either protected or exploited.

Two Qualifications

The evaluation of brand equity needs to deal with two problems: the evaluation of other firm assets, and the value of brand extensions.

First, some part of the discounted present value of a business is due to such tangible assets as working capital, inventory, buildings, and equipment. What portion should be so attributed? One argument is that such assets are book assets that are being depreciated, and their depreciation charge times an earnings multiplier will reflect their asset value. Another tact would be to focus upon cash flow instead of earnings, and provide an estimate of such assets using book value or market value. This estimate would then be subtracted from the estimate of discounted future earnings.

A second problem is to estimate the earnings streams from brand extensions (the use of the brand name to enter new product classes— for example, Kellogg's bread products, or Hershey's ice cream). Usually, the value of potential brand extensions will have to be estimated separately.

The extension value will depend upon the attractiveness of market area of any proposed extension, its growth and competitive intensity, and the strength of the extension. The extension strength will be a function of the relevance of the brand association and perceived quality, the extent to which it could translate into a sustainable competitive advantage, and the extent to which the brand will fit the extension. Chapter 9 will elaborate.

ISSUES IN MANAGING BRAND EQUITY

The introduction of the brand-equity concept raises a host of practical issues about the management of a brand. An overview of some of these issues will set the stage for the following chapters.

1. *The bases of brand equity:* On what should the brand equity be based? What associations should form the basis of the positioning? How important is awareness? Among which segments? Can barriers be created to make it more difficult for competitors to dislodge loyal customers?

2. *Creating brand equity:* How is brand equity created? What are the driving determinants? What is the role in any given context of the name, the channel, the advertising, the spokesperson, and the package, and how do they interrelate? As a practical matter, decisions on such elements need to be made as brand equity is created or changed.

3. *Managing brand equity:* How should a brand be managed over time? What actions will meaningfully affect the elements of equity—in particular the associations and perceived loyalty? What is the "decay rate" if supporting activities (such as advertising) are withdrawn? Often a reduction of advertising results in no detectable drop in sales. Is there damage to the equity if a reduction is prolonged? How can the impact of a promotion or another marketing program be determined?

4. *Forcasting the erosion of equity:* How can erosion of brand equity, and other future problems, be forecast? The danger is that by the time that damage to the brand is recognized, it is too late. The cost of correcting a problem can be extremely high relative to the cost of maintaining equity. The forecasting issue is especially crucial in durables like automobiles, where the time needed to replace a product can be as long as five years. If a decline can be detected two years before the brand's damage becomes obvious, then the remedy can be more timely. A disaster such as the Tylenol tampering case has the advantage that the threat to brand equity, and the need to take action, are both obvious. More commonly, a brand is eroded so slowly that it is difficult to generate a sense of urgency.

5. *The extension decision:* To what products should the brand be extended? How far can the brand be extended before brand equity is affected? Of particular concern is the vertical brand extension: Can an upscale version of the brand be marketed? If so, will there be spillover impact upon the brand name? Do the Earnest and Julio Gallo varietals help the basic Gallo line? What about the temptation to exploit the brand by putting the name on a downscale product? How can the extent of damage to brand equity be predicted? Will the new associations of an extension be helpful or harmful?

6. *Creating new names:* The investment in a new brand name (an alternative to a brand extension) will generate a name with a new set of associations which can provide a platform for another growth stream. What are the trade-offs between these alternatives? Under what circumstances should the one be preferred over the other? How many brand names can a business support?

7. *Complex families of names and subnames:* How should different levels of brand-name families be managed? What mix of advertising should Black & Decker place behind the Black & Decker name, the Space Saver name that indicates a product subgroup, or the Black & Decker Dustbuster? Should the recruiting effort of the U.S. government be centered around the individual military branches, or should the U.S.

defense team be the focus? Delicate considerations of the vertical re-lationships among brands and "subbrands" have to be made.

8. *Brand-equity measurement:* A basic question which underlies all these issues is how to measure brand equity and the assets on which it is based. If it can be conceptualized in a given context precisely enough to measure and monitor it, the other problems become manageable. Clearly, there are several approaches to brand equity and its measure-ment. The need is to determine which is the most appropriate and to select a measurement method.

9. *Evaluating brand equity and its component assets:* A pressing re-lated issue is how to value a brand. Given that there is a market for brands, it is of enormous practical value to actually provide methods to estimate that value. Of even more importance is to place a value upon the underlying assets (such as awareness and perceived quality). The key to justifying investment in building such assets is to be able to estimate the value of such activities. Although some progress has been made, this area remains a signficant challenge for marketing professionals.

THE PLAN OF THE BOOK

This book has several objectives. One is to define and illustrate brand equity, providing a structure which will help managers see more clearly how brand equity provides value. Another is to document research find-ings and illustrative examples that demonstrate that value has emerged (or has been lost) from marketing decisions or environmental events that have enhanced (or damaged) the brand. A third objective is to discuss how brand equity should be managed. How should it be created, main-tained, and protected? How should it be exploited? A fourth objective is to raise questions and suggest issues that should be addressed by thoughtful managers who are trying to think strategically.

The next chapter will discuss the brand loyalty of the customer base and its link to brand equity. Chapters 3 and 4 cover brand awareness and perceived quality. Chapter 5 introduces the concept of associations and positioning. Methods to measure associations are covered in Chapter 6. Selecting, creating, and maintaining associations is the subject of Chapter 7. Clearly the management of associations, covering three chapters, is both important and complex.

The brand is identified by the name, and often by a symbol and a slogan as well. Chapter 8 discusses these indicators and their selection.

Brand extensions—the good, the bad, and the ugly—is the topic of Chapter 9. Chapter 10 presents methods to revitalize a tired brand, to breathe new life into it and its context; and the end game—how to allow a brand a graceful decline and, if needed, death. Chapter 11 contains some thoughts about global brands, a recap of some major themes of the book, and the presentation of an overall "model" of brand equity.

2

·

Brand Loyalty

You have to have a brand become a friend.

Fred Posner
N W Ayer

Reputation, reputation, reputation! O! I have lost my reputation.
I have lost the immortal part of myself and what remains is bestial.

William Shakespeare

THE MICROPRO STORY

In 1979, MicroPro introduced a word-processing program called WordStar to run on CP/M, the standard operating system of the day for personal computers.[1] The first reliable, full-featured word-processing program, WordStar came to dominate the market for serious word-processing users. With a clever use of pairs of keystrokes, a touch typist could do a wide variety of word-processing tasks extremely quickly.

MicroPro's sales exploded:

1.5 million in 1980
4.4 million in 1981
22.3 million in 1982
43.8 million in 1983
66.9 million in 1984

In 1981, IBM entered the personal computer business, thereby legitimatizing both the product and its supporting word-processing programs for business use. The IBM computer and its operating system, MS–DOS, became the new *de facto* industry standard. The following year, MicroPro adapted WordStar to MS–DOS. However, in doing so they did not really utilize the 10 function keys that were a main attribute of the new computer, choosing instead to retain the use of their multi-keystroke command structure. A true touch typist had little interest in the new function keys, but then the emerging business user often was not a skilled touch typist anyway, and *was* attracted to the power of the function keys.

The entry of IBM brought dozens of competitors, the most serious of which turned out to be WordPerfect, introduced in 1982, and Microsoft Word, which appeared in 1983. Both offered several advances, including the full use of function keys. MicroPro responded with WordStar Release 3.3, which largely closed the gap. However, it was to be the last release for four years in a field which saw continuous refinement of programs in response to competitive software innovations and hardware improvement.

MICROPRO'S FINANCIAL PERFORMANCE

In 1983, MicroPro literally dominated the market, and (more importantly) by early 1984 had an installed base of over 800,000 WordStar users. Because there are large switching costs in word processing, and because new buyers rely heavily upon colleagues and friends who are "knowledgeable," the value of the installed base is substantial. However, in the context of a rapidly growing industry, MicroPro's sales fell to $42.6 million in 1985 and then remained flat through 1990. Much more importantly, market share fell precipitously to 12.7% by 1987, and by late 1989 to under 5%. After earning over $4 million in 1983 and nearly $6 million in 1984, earnings virtually disappeared during the next three years (averaging well under $1 million per year) and substantial losses followed (averaging over $4 million a year from 1988 to 1990). The stock price fell from over $10 in July of 1984 to under $1 in April of 1990, providing a company value of under $10 million.

During the same time frame WordPerfect, the upstart firm, went from zero share in 1982 to over 30% at end of 1987, and during 1989 soared to over 70%. Although their stock is not traded, it holds a value of from $1 billion (assuming profitability and price-earnings ratio at the industry average) to over $2 billion (with the more likely assumption their profitability and price-earnings ratio are comparable to that of Microsoft).

Of course, literally hundreds of other word-processing firms did not survive, largely because they could not get off the ground; they could not get enough distribution and sales to be viable. However, they also never had the installed base that WordStar enjoyed.

WHY DID WORDSTAR LOSE IT?

WordStar lost position in large part because it turned its back upon its installed base. First, it failed to adequately provide support for existing customers. Second, the major follow-on product was not backward-compatible with the original WordStar, and in fact competed with it.

As late as 1987, MicroPro was deservedly known as being indifferent to customers, who would call with problems and not be able to get through. The firm had the industry nickname "MicroPro-please-hold." Further, the calls were at the customers' expense. Worse, when customers did get through, they often were referred to their dealer—even though the dealer might be either unwilling or unable to help. Understandably, the customer frustration level was high.

By contrast, WordPerfect developed an unlimited-access, toll-free, phone-in advisory service which became an important point of distinction in part because of the MicroPro legacy. One writer noted that the WordPerfect systems provided a no-questions-asked, all-questions-answered technical help with a style and class that others lacked, and sarcastically concluded: "Paying customers like the idea of a software vendor that answers the phone when they call."[2] Figure 2-1 shows a WordPerfect ad that focuses upon their customer support system.

In November of 1984, MicroPro started to ship WordStar 2000, which was eagerly awaited by WordStar users who wanted to upgrade the program they loved. Although WordStar 2000 was competitive with respect to other features, it remained slow—and used more memory than WordStar. Worse, it was not backward-compatible with the prior version: It involved learning a new set of instructions. Further, WordStar touch typists now were forced to use the function keys set apart from the keyboard.

In fact, WordStar 2000 proved to be the product that launched WordPerfect, in that it virtually endorsed the kind of function-key processing that WordPerfect (and Microsoft Word) had touted. More importantly, WordStar users now knew that to have the most advanced features, they would have to learn a new program. It was no easier to switch to WordStar 2000 than to Wordperfect or Microsoft Word.

FIGURE 2–1 Supporting the Customer

Courtesy of WordPerfect Corporation.

EFFORTS TO GAIN BACK LOYALTY

In early 1986 a second release of WordStar 2000 corrected many of its problems and made it a more competitive product, but it still was not backward-compatible with WordStar—nor was the November 1987 Release 3 of WordStar 2000.

Meanwhile (late in 1986), MicroPro had bought Newstar Software, which had developed a "modern WordStar" program, for $3.1 million. The program was introduced in February of 1987 as WordStar Professional Release 4. At long last Wordstar users had an update—but it was years late. It was followed in August of 1988 by WordStar Professional Release 5, which got favorable reviews in the trade press, and by Release 5.5 in 1989.

There were, however, a pair of serious problems with the two product lines Wordstar Professional and Wordstar 2000. First, they competed with each other: Both basically were after the same market, with similar features. Second, the double offering was confusing to customers—and even to MicroPro's salespeople and retail representatives. Which one should a customer select? There was no obvious answer.

The confusion between the two was not helped by the advertising. In 1987, WordStar Professional had a "Word Stars on WordStar" campaign, featuring testimonials from such famous users as Tom Wolfe. However, the campaign broke *just after* WordStar 2000 Release 3 was introduced!

In 1989, MicroPro made a belated effort to turn it all around. WordStar 2000 was de-emphasized in favor of WordStar Professional—the program that was backward-compatible with the installed base of 1.9 million WordStar users. The WordStar Professional was positioned as a productivity tool for touch typists who could exploit the unique control-key commands. A responsive telephone customer back-up system was installed, and "WordStar News," a customer newsletter which provided additional support, first appeared. WordStar graphics were sharpened up. A "Lost Stars Come Home" upgrade, targeted at prior WordStar users, was presented. And (hardly the least important) a direct sales force, bypassing the national distributors who might have helped them stay removed from their customers, was developed. It appears that WordStar will survive, but as a bit player in a market they once commanded.

OBSERVATIONS

We have seen that an enormous asset that WordStar had in 1984 was its dominant installed base, in an industry in which there are high switching costs and customer world-of-mouth is pivotal. And that WordStar, by inadequately supporting its product and going to the WordStar 2000, turned its back on this asset—the result being an incredible opportunity that competitors (the makers of WordPerfect and Microsoft Word) exploited.

It is not impossible to create a new model that obsoletes the old one, particularly if an established name can be used. In the mid–1960s, IBM came out with the System 360, a completely new line that entirely replaced the old one. However, there were two sharp distinctions between IBM then, and WordStar back in 1984. First, unlike the WordStar 2000, the IBM 360 was a superior state-of-the-art product. Second, IBM had a loyal customer base which had confidence that IBM would back up the product. In contrast WordStar, instead of a reservoir of good will, had a substantial customer group unhappy with MicroPro's attitude.

BRAND LOYALTY

The brand loyalty of the customer base is often the core of a brand's equity. If customers are indifferent to the brand and, in fact, buy with respect to features, price, and convenience with little concern to the brand name, there is likely little equity. If, on the other hand, they continue to purchase the brand even in the face of competitors with superior features, price, and convenience, substantial value exists in the brand and perhaps in its symbol and slogans.

Brand loyalty, long a central construct in marketing, is a measure of the attachment that a customer has to a brand. It reflects how likely a customer will be to switch to another brand, especially when that brand makes a change, either in price or in product features. As brand loyalty increases, the vulnerability of the customer base to competitive action is reduced. It is one indicator of brand equity which is demonstrably linked to future profits, since brand loyalty directly translates into future sales.

LEVELS OF BRAND LOYALTY

There are several levels of loyalty as Figure 2–2 suggests. Each level represents a different marketing challenge and a different type of asset to manage and exploit. All may not be represented in a specific product class or market.

The bottom loyalty level is the nonloyal buyer who is completely

FIGURE 2-2 The Loyalty Pyramid

indifferent to the brand—each brand is perceived to be adequate and the brand name plays little role in the purchase decision. Whatever is on sale or convenient is preferred. This buyer might be termed a switcher or price buyer.

The second level includes buyers who are satisfied with the product or at least not dissatisfied. Basically, there is no dimension of dissatisfaction that is sufficient to stimulate a change especially if that change involves effort. These buyers might be termed habitual buyers. Such segments can be vulnerable to competitors that can create a visible benefit to switching. However, they can be difficult to reach since there is no reason for them to be on the lookout for alternatives.

The third level consists of those who are also satisfied and, in addition, have switching costs—costs in time, money, or performance risk associated with switching. Perhaps they have invested in learning a system associated with a brand, as in the MicroPro case. Or perhaps there is a risk that another brand may not function as well in a particular use context. To attract these buyers, competitors need to overcome the switching costs by offering an inducement to switch or by offering a benefit large enough to compensate. This group might be called switching-cost loyal.

On the fourth level we find those that truly like the brand. Their preference may be based upon an association such as a symbol, a set of use experiences, or a high perceived quality. However, liking is often a general feeling that cannot be closely traced to anything specific; it has a life of its own. People are not always able to identify why they like something (or someone), especially if the relationship has been a long one. Sometimes just the fact that there has been a long-term relationship can create a powerful affect even in the absence of a friendly symbol or other identifiable contributor to liking. Segments at this fourth level might be termed friends of the brand because there is an emotional/ feeling attachment.

The top level are committed customers. They have a pride of discovering and/or being users of a brand. The brand is very important to them either functionally or as an expression of who they are. Their confidence is such that they will recommend the brand to others. The value of the committed customer is not so much the business he or she generates but, rather, the impact upon others and upon the market itself.

The ultimate committed customer is the Harley Davidson rider who wears the Harley symbol as a tattoo, the Macintosh user who attends shows and will spend considerable effort to insure that an acquaintance does not buy IBM and forego the pleasure of the user-friendly Macintosh, or the Beetle owner of the 1960s who flaunted the funkiness of the car. A brand that has a substantial group of extremely involved and committed customers might be termed a charismatic brand. Not all brands should aspire to be charismatic, of course, but when a Macintosh, NEXT, Beetle, or Harley does achieve that aura, there can be a big payoff.

These five levels are stylized; they do not always appear in the pure form and others could be conceptualized. For example, there will be customers who will appear to have some combination of these levels— i.e., buyers who like the brand and have switching costs. Others may have profiles somewhat different from those represented—i.e., those who are dissatisfied but have sufficient switching costs to continue buying the brand in spite of being dissatisfied. These five levels do, however, provide a feeling for the variety of forms that loyalty can take and how it impacts upon brand equity.

BRAND LOYALTY AS ONE BASIS OF BRAND EQUITY

A set of habitual buyers has considerable value because they represent a revenue stream that can go forward for a long time. The attrition rate for those with stronger levels of loyalty will be lower, causing their value to be higher. If a relationship between loyalty and the frequency of buying a brand can be estimated, the value of a change in brand loyalty can be estimated. A conceptual approach to providing such an estimate is discussed at the close of the chapter.

Brand loyalty is qualitatively different from the other major dimensions of brand equity in that it is tied more closely to the use experience.

Brand loyalty cannot exist without prior purchase and use experience. In contrast, awareness, associations, and perceived quality are characteristics of many brands that a person has never used.

Brand loyalty is a basis of brand equity that is created by many factors, chief among them being the use experience. However, loyalty is influenced in part by the other major dimensions of brand equity, awareness, associations, and perceived quality. In some cases, loyalty could arise largely from a brand's perceived quality or attribute associations. However, it is not always explained by these three factors. In many instances it occurs quite independent of them and, in others, the nature of the relationship is unclear. It is very possible to like and be loyal to something with low perceived quality (e.g., McDonald's) or dislike something with

---

Perrier's Bubble Burst

Perrier developed a special niche during the 1980s.[3] With its distinctive bottle, naturally sparkling water, and remarkable cache, Perrier enjoyed intense loyalty especially in the restaurant market. In 1989, it held nearly 50% of the market for bottled water in the face of intensive marketing efforts by a host of new entrées. For many, Perrier was bottled water.

In February of 1990, Perrier recalled its product worldwide after it was found to be contaminated by traces of benzene, a suspected carcinogen. Off the shelves for over five months, the effect was devastating—its share by late 1990 had dropped to under 20% even with aggressive price promotions.

The Perrier image was tainted by the realization that its "natural water" ("Earth's First Soft Drink") may not be so premium, the use of price promotions to attempt to regain distribution and customers, and the fact that it was no longer stocked in the finest restaurants and bars.

However, the biggest factor was that the habit of ordering Perrier had been broken. A large part of the Perrier success was the loyalty of its installed base. Many customers simply always ordered Perrier—never just bottled water (Perrier was like Kleenex—it represented the product to many). When the supply was interrupted, by necessity customers had to sample other brands. They found that they were as good or better than Perrier. Because Perrier had little real product advantages, such a break in supply disrupted its customer base. The bubble had burst. Perrier may never bounce back.

---

high perceived quality (e.g., a Japanese car). Thus, brand loyalty provides an important basis of equity that is sufficiently distinct from the other dimensions.

In fact, all the brand equity dimensions have causal interrelationships. Perceived quality, for example, will in part be based upon associations and even awareness (a visible brand might be considered more able to provide quality). An association with a symbol, for example, might affect awareness. Thus, there is no claim that the four major dimensions of brand equity are independent.

A key premise is that the loyalty is to the brand—that it is not possible to transfer it to another name and symbol without spending substantial amounts of money and forgoing significant sales and profits. If the loyalty is to a product rather than the brand, equity would not exist. Buying a commodity like oil or wheat rarely involves loyalty to the product itself, although the surrounding service may be attached to a brand and it could engender considerable loyalty.

A customer base can too easily be taken for granted when the interest is in short-term sales rather than in building and maintaining equity. The focus is often upon faceless sales statistics to be analyzed and controlled rather than on the people and organizations who are the customers. As a result, brand loyalty often is treated with benign neglect, and is neither nurtured nor exploited. Considering brand loyalty is a key, core bases of brand equity should help a firm treat customers as the brand assets that they are.

MEASURING BRAND LOYALTY

To more clearly understand brand loyalty and its management, it is useful to consider approaches to its measurement. A consideration of several measurement tacks will provide additional insights into its scope and nuances as well as provide a practical tool in using the construct and linking it to profitability. One approach is to consider actual behavior. Other approaches are based upon the loyalty constructs of switching costs, satisfaction, liking, and commitment.

BEHAVIOR MEASURES

A direct way to determine loyalty, especially habitual behavior, is to consider actual purchase patterns. Among the measures that can be used are:

Repurchase rates: What percent of Oldsmobile owners purchase an Oldsmobile on their next car purchase?

Percent of purchases: Of the last five purchases made by a customer, what percent went to each brand purchased?

Number of brands purchased: What percent of coffee buyers bought only a single brand? Two brands? Three brands?

The loyalty of customers can vary widely among some product classes, depending upon the number of competing brands and the nature of the product. The percentage of users buying only one brand is over 80% for products like salt, cooking spray, waxed paper, and pet shampoos, and under 40% for gasoline, tires, canned vegetables, and garbage bags.[4]

Behavior data, although objective, has limitations. It may be inconvenient or expensive to obtain, and provides only limited diagnostics about the future. Further, using behavior data, it can be difficult to discriminate between or among those who actually switched brands and the purchases of multiple brands by different members of a family (or by different units in an organization). Thus, an apparent switch from IBM to Compaq could be simply because the one group in an organization is loyal to IBM, and another to Compaq.

SWITCHING COSTS

An analysis of switching costs can provide insight into the extent to which switching costs provide a basis for brand loyalty. If it is very expensive or risky for a firm or a consumer to change suppliers, then the attribution rate from the customer base will be lower.

The most obvious type of switching cost is an investment in a product or system. When a firm buys a computer system, the hardware investment is only part of the investment involved. They have to also invest in software, and in training people. Thus, when an industry standard such as IBM DOS becomes entrenched, it is hard to be dislodged by, for example, Apple or NEXT. The firm would have to reinvest in software and training, a process which would cost in time and productivity as well as money.

Another type of switching cost is the risk of change. If the current system works, even if there are problems, there is always the risk that a new system will be worse. A consumer who has a relationship with a particular hospital and doctor may be reluctant, even when unhappy, to try unknowns. There is a reluctance to fix something that is not demonstrably broken. Operationally, customers might be queried to see what risks are associated with change. A lack of awareness of certain risks in changing from AT&T to MCI, for example, might suggest the need for a communication effort.

A business should value the switching costs that it enjoys. WordStar, of course, did not follow that maxim. Further, it should work to increase the dependence of the customer upon its product or service.

MEASURING SATISFACTION

A key diagnostic to every level of brand loyalty is the measurement of satisfaction and, perhaps more important, dissatisfaction. What problems are customers having? What are the sources of irritation? Why are some customers switching? What are the precipitating reasons? A key premise of the second and third levels of loyalty is that the dissatisfaction is absent or low enough to avoid precipitating a decision to switch.

It is important that any measure of satisfaction be current, representative, and sensitive. Asking users of a service to return cards on which they can check whether the service (such as courtesy on the phone) is usually satisfactory is neither representative nor sensitive. By such measures, the firms in the insurance industry (with 95% + approval) looked good just prior to the passing of Proposition 103 which mandated a 20% reduction in insurance rates in California. Clearly, there was an enormous level of resentment and frustration among customers which was not reflected in the surveyed measures of satisfaction that were used.

LIKING OF THE BRAND

The fourth loyalty level involves liking. Do the customers "like" the firm? Are there feelings of respect or friendship toward the firm or brand? Is there a feeling of warmth toward the brand? A positive affect can result in resistance to competitive entries. It can be much harder to compete against a general feeling of liking rather than a specific feature.

General overall liking can be scaled in a variety of ways, such as:

- Liking
- Respect
- Friendship
- Trust

The concept is that there is a general liking or affect which is distinct from specific attributes that underlie it. People simply *like* a brand, and this liking cannot be explained completely by their perceptions and beliefs about the brand's attributes. It is rather reflected by general statements of liking, such as those listed above. The concept of reliability may, in some cases, represent a specific attribute. However, it also is often highly correlated with general affect.

Another measure of liking is reflected in the additional price that customers would be willing to pay to obtain their brand and the price advantage that competitors would have to generate before they could attract a loyal buyer. Several approaches to estimating the price premium that the brand name can support were discussed in Chapter 1. The simplest, the dollarmetric, asks how much a customer would pay to get his or her preferred brand.

COMMITMENT

The strongest brands, the ones with extremely high equity, will have a large number of committed customers. When a substantial commitment level exists, it can be relatively easy to detect because it usually manifests itself in many ways. One key indicator is the amount of interaction and communication that is involved with the product. Is it something that the customer likes to talk about with others? Does he or she not only recommend the product but tell others why they should buy it? Another is the extent to which the brand is important to a person in terms of his or her activities and personality. Is it particularly useful or enjoyable to use?

THE STRATEGIC VALUE OF BRAND LOYALTY

The brand loyalty of existing customers represents a strategic asset that, if properly managed and exploited, has the potential to provide value in several ways as Figure 2–3 suggests.

REDUCED MARKETING COSTS

A set of customers with brand loyalty reduces the marketing costs of doing business. It is simply much less costly to retain customers than to get new ones. Because potential new customers usually lack motivation

FIGURE 2–3 The Value of Brand Loyalty

to change from their current brands, they will be expensive to contact, in part because they are not making an effort to locate brand alternatives. Even when they are exposed to alternatives, they will often need a substantial reason to risk buying and using another brand. A common mistake—attempting to grow by attracting new customers while neglecting existing ones—will be discussed at the close of this chapter.

Existing customers, by contrast, usually are relatively easy to hold if they are not dissatisfied. The familiar is comfortable and reassuring. It is usually far less costly to keep existing customers happy, to reduce the reasons to change, than to find new ones. Of course, the higher the loyalty, the easier it is to keep customers happy. Yet, customers will leave, especially if their problems and concerns are not addressed. The challenge is to reduce this flow.

Loyalty of existing customers represents a substantial entry barrier to competitors. Entering a market in which existing customers are loyal or even satisfied with an established brand, and must be enticed to switch, can require excessive resources. The profit potential for the entrant is thus reduced. For the barrier to be effective, potential competitors must know about it; they cannot be allowed to entertain the delusion that customers are vulnerable. Thus, signals of strong customer loyalty which can be sent to competitors, such as advertisements about documented customer loyalty or product quality, can be useful.

TRADE LEVERAGE

Brand loyalty provides trade leverage. Strong loyalty toward brands like Nabisco Premium Saltines, Cheerios, or Tide will ensure preferred shelf space because stores know that customers will have such brands on their shopping list. At the extreme, brand loyalty may dominate store choice decisions. Unless a supermarket, for example, carries brands like Weight Watchers frozen dinners, Paul Newman's salad dressing, Asahi Super Dry beer, or Grey Poupon mustard, some customers will switch stores. Trade leverage is particularly important when introducing new sizes, new varieties, variations, or brand extensions.

ATTRACTING NEW CUSTOMERS

A customer base with segments that are satisfied and others that like the brand can provide assurance to a prospective customer, especially when the purchase is somewhat risky. A purchase will thus not represent an adventuresome thrust away from the crowd. The old phrase that "You won't get fired for buying IBM" is largely based upon this logic. Especially in product areas that are new or otherwise risky, the acceptance of the brand by a group of existing customers can be an effective message, a way to exploit the installed base. Using existing customers to sell new customers rarely happens automatically; it usually takes an explicit program.

A relatively large satisfied customer base provides an image of the brand as an accepted, successful product which will be around and will be able to afford service backup and product improvements. In many businesses where follow-on service and product support are important, such as computers and automobiles, two of the main concerns often are whether the firm is healthy and committed enough to be around when it is needed, and whether its products are accepted. For example, Dell computer, a mail-order computer firm, in 1989 advertised an installed base of 100,000 customers (including over 50% of the Fortune 500 companies) to reassure prospective customers wary of buying a mail-order computer.

Brand awareness can also be generated from the customer base. Existing customers and dealers will enhance recognition merely by being there. Friends and colleagues of users will become aware of the product just by seeing it. Further, this type of exposure—actually seeing it "in action" or even on a retailer's shelf—will be much more vivid and have more impact than only seeing an ad several times (unless the ad is highly unusual and effective). Seeing a product being used by a friend will generate the kind of memory links to the use context and the user that any advertisement would have great difficulty in doing. Brand recall thus would be stronger. In selecting target markets, one consideration should be their potential to create visibility and awareness for the brand.

TIME TO RESPOND TO COMPETITIVE THREATS

Brand loyalty provides a firm with time to respond to competitive moves—some breathing room. If a competitor develops a superior product, a loyal following will allow the firm time needed for the product improvements to be matched or neutralized. For example, some newly developed high-tech markets have some customers who are attracted by the most advanced product of the moment; there is little brand loyalty in this group. In contrast, loyal, satisfied customers will not be looking for new products, and thus may not learn of an advancement. Further, they will have little incentive to change even if exposed to the new product. With a high level of brand loyalty, a firm can allow itself the luxury of pursuing a less risky follower strategy.

MAINTAINING AND ENHANCING LOYALTY

In many situations it is difficult to get rid of customers—to get them to move to a competitor. You literally have to work at it. For perhaps two decades General Motors had, by many objective measures, inferior cars. Logically its share of the U.S. market should have fallen to nearly zero—yet it remained in the 33% range: One of every three cars sold domestically still was a GM product. The fact is that customers do not like to change; you almost have to beat some of them off with a baseball bat. Incredibly, some firms (such as MicroPro) have done just about that.

Changing brands requires effort, especially if the decision involves substantial investment or risk. Further, positive attitudes toward an incumbent brand are likely to develop which will not only justify but enhance prior decisions. People do not like to admit that they were wrong—it is much easier to rationalize prior decisions. In truth an enormous inertia exists in consumer choice. The familiar is comfortable and reassuring.

Consider the efforts of Coca-Cola to popularize "new" Coke. The large and loyal group of "real" Coke users rebelled. They (even those who could not tell the difference between "new" Coke, "old" Coke, and Pepsi in blind-taste tests) wanted their product back! And they ultimately carried the day: The withdrawn original Coke formula reappeared— although this time it was forced to bear the dubiously distinctive name Coke Classic.

The bottom line is that it should be easy to keep customers merely by following some basic rules, as Figure 2–4 suggests.

FIGURE 2–4 Creating and Maintaining Brand Loyalty

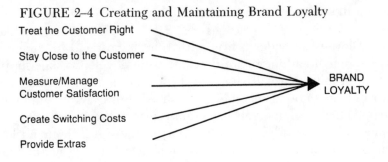

TREAT THE CUSTOMER RIGHT

Tom Peters talks about the "secret" to the success of Maytag—they deliver a washing machine that works—it washes clothes. Hardly an unbelievable concept. The point is that a product or service that works— that functions as expected—provides a basis for loyalty, a reason not to switch. Again, customers need reasons to change. The key to keeping them often is simply to avoid driving them away.

To get rid of customers, a business often actually has to be rude, uncaring, unresponsive, and/or disrespectful. It should not be difficult to avoid such behavior, yet customers experience it all the time. The goal, of course, is to have the interaction be positive—to treat the customer as any person would like to be treated: with respect.

Among the keys to ensuring a positive customer experience are training and culture. In Japan, where a negative customer interaction is rare, the training is intense and detailed, and the customer culture usually is very strong. A bank teller will spend weeks learning and practicing exactly how to respond to various customer contacts. Further, the bank's culture would not tolerate negative customer interaction.

STAY CLOSE TO THE CUSTOMER

The companies that have strong customer cultures find ways to stay close to the customer. Even the top executives at IBM, for example, have account contact and responsibility. Disneyland executives work in the Park in an "on stage" capacity for two weeks each year. Worthington Steel sends its production people to meet customers who are using the product, so they realize that real people with real concerns are depending upon the quality. Focus groups can be used to see and hear real customers voice concerns. Just the act of encouraging customer contact can help send signals to both the organization and the customers that the customer is valued.

MEASURE/MANAGE CUSTOMER SATISFACTION

Regular surveys of customer satisfaction/dissatisfaction are particularly useful in understanding how customers feel and in adjusting products and services. These surveys need to be timely, sensitive, and comprehensive, so that the firm can learn why overall satisfaction is changing. If no change is detected from period to period, perhaps the surveys either are being conducted too frequently, or are too insensitive.

For customer satisfaction measures to have impact they need to be integrated into day-to-day management. Marriott Hotels, for example, uses weekly measures of guest satisfaction to identify current problems and stimulate responsive programs. For example, the manager of the front desk will be concerned with the measures associated with waiting time, with checking in, and with checking out. The satisfaction instrument will prompt detailed discussions of problems and possible responses.

One way to ensure that satisfaction surveys are used is to make them part of the compensation system. Domino's Pizza, for example, conducts weekly phone surveys of customers measuring dimensions such as response time, lumpiness of dough, freshness of pepperoni, and attitude of delivery people. Indicators are developed for each outlet. A bonus pool is distributed monthly based upon these measures. Such a system will elevate the satisfaction measures so that operations will be affected.

CREATE SWITCHING COSTS

One way to create switching costs is to create a solution for a customer problem that may involve redefining the business. Drug wholesaling once was characterized by a host of distributors, each with a sales force negotiating price. Then McKesson installed computer terminals for their drug retailers, and basically provided them with inventory control and automated ordering services. By doing this they created enormous switching costs for the retailer, and transformed the entire drug wholesaling business.

Another approach is to reward loyalty directly. The airlines' frequent-flyer clubs have become a way to reward and keep customers. The concept has been extended to other products. A program termed "The Great Payback" provides customers of such brands as Post cereals, Weight

Watchers entrees, and Clorox with points that they can use to obtain merchandise in a Sears store. Another system, termed the GiftLink Shoppers Reward, provides buyers of products of Kraft, Campbell soup, Ocean Spray, and P&G with merchandise from Samsonite, Sony, and others.

PROVIDE EXTRAS

It is often relatively easy to change customer behavior from tolerance to enthusiasm just by providing a few extra unexpected services. A mint on a pillow, an explanation of a procedure, or a sample from a bakery can really make a good impression. A simple apology can have the potential to turn even a disastrous situation into a tolerable one. Yet how many times has an appropriate apology not been forthcoming in a customer contact?

Nordstrom's department store is legendary for providing extra services not afforded by its competition. A pianist, a full-service concierge, and a shoeshine stand complete with telephone are among the extras. Even more impressive are the salespeople who help customers throughout the store, often write letters to customers, and go to extraordinary lengths to accommodate customers' needs. A business doesn't have to try to be another Nordstrom's, but it can't go wrong by following its example in certain respects.

SELLING OLD CUSTOMERS
INSTEAD OF NEW ONES

Perhaps the most common mistake that firms make is to attempt to grow mainly by attracting new customers. Often, aggressive marketing programs are involved. The problem is that new customers are almost always difficult to attract. They simply may have little reason to consider moving from another brand. Further, they may be expensive to contact—after all, they are not generally making an effort to read ads for alternatives, or to contact salespeople.

In contrast, there usually is an enormous payoff in retaining existing customers, in part because retention programs are relatively inexpensive. If the migration of existing customers to competitors can be reduced, growth will *naturally* occur. New customers, even without much effort to attract them, will appear, some influenced by existing customers. A customer base is like a leaky bucket: Increasing the input may be more wasteful than patching the leaks.

What is needed here is a reduction of dissatisfied customers' motivation to leave, and an increase in the switching costs of those who are satisfied. The first step is to analyze irritations and problems causing people to switch brands by contacting lost customers. They often represent the best source of information about the dynamics of the customer base. Why did they leave? Exactly what was the motivation, and what can be done to remove it? A systematic program of exit interviews can aid in the detection of problems. Too often a bank manager, for example, will know exactly how many new accounts were opened last month, and perhaps why those new customers selected his or her bank, but little or nothing about why existing customers became dissatisfied and left.

An aggressive customer-retention program will move beyond removing sources of discontent, to building switching costs by rewarding customers. Waldenbooks, for example, developed a "preferred reader" program to reward customers and create switching costs. A preferred reader has a card which allows the member to:

- Access a toll-free line, to order books by phone.
- Save 10% on all purchases.

The Subaru Drive Program

The Subaru DRIVE program provides each Subaru owner with a series of personal messages from the dealer through a four-year period after purchasing the car, including:

- A welcome letter
- A series of coupons redeemable for Subaru service
- A quarterly 16-page newsletter covering new products, driving tips, and special offers
- Maintenance reminders
- A vehicle identification card to aid in service
- Request for opinions via questionnaires

The program keeps the owner in touch with Subaru, provides a feeling of being a valued customer, and generates service business for the dealer.

- Earn a $5 coupon for each $100 spent.
- Get instant check approval.

The program provides a strong incentive for a Waldenbook customer to increase his or her loyalty toward Waldenbooks.

A CUSTOMER-RETENTION ANALYSIS

How should a customer-retention program be justified? Will it pay off in terms of future profit streams? The answers to these and related problematical questions are to be found in systematically analyzing customer retention.

One approach to the needed analysis is to estimate the relationship between customer-retention levels and profitability.[5] Given current levels of annual retention as the base, how much would marginal annual profit change if annual retention were increased or decreased by one, five, or ten percentage points? Figure 2–5 illustrates. Over some range the dominant cost consideration would be the variable cost involved. With only the variable cost affected, there will be high leverage associated with affecting retention.

The annual profit achieved by a change in retention needs to be converted into a net present value. Basically, the annual profit is projected into the future, then discounted by both the firm's cost of capital and

FIGURE 2–5 Customer-Retention Analysis

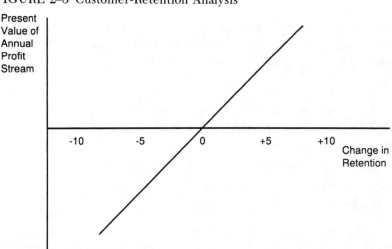

the retention rate. Thus, given a cost of capital of 15% and a retention rate of 90%, an annual profit of $100 *this* year would be expected to deliver *next* year $100 × .85 (the cost of capital) × .90 (the retention rate), or $76.50.

One analysis showed that a 5% reduction in customer defections resulted in dramatic increases in the profit stream for the average customer. The profit increase depended upon the type of business.[6] For auto-service firms, where loyalty tends to be low, a 30% profit increase was estimated. It was 35% for software. For industries with higher levels of loyalty like credit cards and bank deposits, it was over 75%.

The hardest part of the analysis is to link a retention program to a change in retention rates. What impact will any given program have upon retention? At times judgment and experience, perhaps supported by market research, can provide guidance, but usually some kind of market experiment is needed. To judge its impact, try the program out on a subset of customers.

One associated problem is that, in most contexts, the decision to change brands is so rare that retention becomes an insensitive measure, and it becomes necessary to use measures such as satisfaction, dissatisfaction, and the likelihood of a decision to change brands. The link between these measures and retention then needs to be established, perhaps using past data of changes in retention—either over time or over different customer units.

QUESTIONS TO CONSIDER

1. Who are your customers? Is the customer base being exploited to help sell other customers by providing referrals, reassurance, or awareness?

2. What are the brand-loyalty levels by segment? Would alternative methods to measure loyalty be helpful? Why are some low and some high? Is there a program of "exit interviews" for those who are no longer users of the brand?

3. What are the levels of satisfaction? Of dissatisfaction? What is causing dissatisfaction? How is this changing over time?

4. Should you audit the existing programs to improve loyalty? Hire a "consumer consultant" to determine how the consumer could use the product or service better? Are there customer needs which remain unmet? What sort of programs should be considered to improve loyalty levels. What is the relationship between retention and profitability?

3
·
Brand Awareness

A good name is better than riches.

Cervantes
Don Quixote

*Ever since Morton's put a little girl in a yellow slicker and declared
"When it rains, it pours" no advertising person worth his or her
salt has had any excuse to think of a product as having parity with
anything.*

Malcolm MacDougal
Jordan Case McGrath

THE DATSUN-BECOMES-NISSAN STORY

In 1918 a Japanese automobile firm soon to become Nissan produced
a two-seat automobile they called Datson—"the son of Dat." In part
an acronym, this name reflected the initials of the car's three main
financial backers: Den, Aoyama, and Takeuchi.[1] The name was later
changed to Datsun, in part to avoid confusion with a similar word which
in Japanese meant "to lose money."

When the firm returned to making cars after World War II, they chose
to market them in Japan under the name Nissan. However, in 1961 the
U.S. car market was entered under the old Datsun name—perhaps in
part to minimize the Japanese relationship. By 1981 the name Datsun
was used not only in the U.S. but in many other countries, even though

the firm was marketing its cars, trucks, and other products under the name Nissan in Japan. In fact, the awareness level of Nissan in the U.S. was only 2% as compared to 85% for the Datsun name.

The decision to change the name from Datsun to Nissan in the U.S. was announced in the fall of 1981. The rationale was that the name change would help the pursuit of a global strategy. A single name worldwide would increase the possibility that advertising campaigns, brochures, and promotional materials could be used across countries and simplify product design and manufacturing. Further, potential buyers would be exposed to the name and product when traveling to other countries.

Industry observers, however, speculated that the most important motivation was that a name change would help Nissan market stocks and bonds in the U.S. They also presumed substantial ego involvement, since the absence of the Nissan name in the U.S. surely rankled Nissan executives who had seen Toyota and Honda become household words.

During the years 1982–1984 the change was implemented. The products were changed gradually. On the 1982 models the Nissan name appeared on the car's front grille while the rear carried the Datsun name on the left and the Nissan name on the right. Other Datsun models simply had a "by Nissan" tag line. A lot of cars were thus sold with both names on them. In 1983 some models were switched over completely. For example, with the 1983 model the Datsun 510 was replaced by the Nissan Stanza. It wasn't until the 1984 line that the entire transition was complete.

Advertising was of course the cornerstone of the name-change effort. The successful "Datsun: We Are Driven" campaign (exemplified by Figure 3–1), which was initiated in 1977 and had a $60 million budget in 1981, was dropped. In its place appeared a "Come Alive, Come and Drive: Major Motion from Nissan" and "Major Motion: The Name Is Nissan" set of campaigns supported by a budget which grew from $120 million in 1983 to $180 million in 1987. Around $240 million was estimated spent on advertising implementing the "The Name Is Nissan" campaign (illustrated by Figure 3–2). The enlarged advertising budget was undoubtedly in part due to the added mission: to register the new name. It seems very likely that "The Name is Nissan" campaign with its name registration mission was considerably less effective than the successful Datsun campaign it replaced.

The most incredible aspect of this story is the resilience of the Datsun name. In the spring of 1988, a national survey found that the recognition and esteem of the Datsun name was essentially the same as that of the Nissan name, despite the virtual absence of the Datsun name from the

FIGURE 3–1 "Datsun: We Are Driven"

Permission to reprint this advertisement granted by Nissan Motor Corporation in U.S.A.

FIGURE 3–2 "The Name Is Nissan"

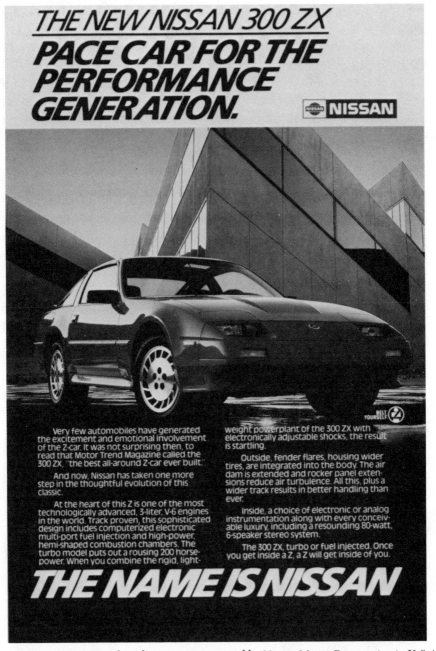

Permission to reprint this advertisement granted by Nissan Motor Corporation in U.S.A.

commercial scene for five years, and the money effort placed behind the Nissan name.[2]

The greatest potential cost of the name change was the bottom-line effect upon sales. Nissan saw its share drop from 5.9% in 1982 to 5.5% in 1983, and to 4.5% in 1984—a loss of 1.4 share points as compared to the 0.9 share points that Toyota lost during the same period. However, during that time period there also were import restrictions, some quality problems with the Nissan line, and growth in the Honda line. Thus it is impossible to determine precisely to what extent the share drop was caused by the confusion of the name change—yet that surely was a contributory factor of some notable degree.

The cost to change the name could easily have exceeded half a billion dollars, and probably was much more. First, it is known that the operational costs, including changing signs at the 1,100 dealerships, cost around $30 million. Second, one may assume that $200 million was spent on advertising between 1982 and 1984 because of the name change, and that another $50 million was wasted because the "Datsun, We Are Driven" campaign was prematurely stopped. Finally, assume even that .3% market share was lost for a three-year period because of buyer confusion. That loss alone would represent many hundreds of millions of dollars in marginal profit. And the cost would go much higher if the reasonable assumption were made that the name change has had effects that have lingered into the nineties.

THE GE-BECOMES-BLACK & DECKER STORY

In contrast, Black & Decker, which in 1985 acquired GE's small-appliance business, decided on an abrupt name change even though they had the freedom to use the GE name for several years. They immediately changed the name on the products, and supported the effort with an investment of $100 million of advertising—mainly to establish awareness of the new name. As a result of the advertising, awareness of Black & Decker as a maker of small kitchen appliances increased from 15% to 57% during the first 18 months. Yet Black & Decker concluded that the name-awareness campaign took much longer than they thought it would, and also was much more difficult and expensive than planned.

Again, just as in the Nissan story, the most remarkable aspect of the Black & Decker story is the persistence of the GE name. A random sample of 1,000 households was polled for a discount-store trade magazine in late 1988, more than three years after the Black & Decker name change.[3] Among other questions, each respondent was asked which brand they would buy in a variety of product categories. For housewares the percent of shoppers who selected each brand were tabulated (as shown in Table 3–1)

A reasonable person might have forecast that the GE name would recede after over three years of having no presence in the housewares category. Incredibly, however, the GE name was preferred over four times more often than that of Black & Decker.

WHAT IS BRAND AWARENESS?

Brand awareness is the ability of a potential buyer to recognize or recall that a brand is a member of a certain product category. A link between product class and brand is involved. Publicity about the Metropolitan Museum does not necessarily help the awareness of Metropolitan Life. Similarly, the use of a large balloon with the word Levi's on it may make the Levi name more salient, but it will not necessarily help improve name awareness. However, if the balloon is shaped to resemble a pair of Levi's 301 jeans, the link to the product is provided, and the balloon's effectiveness at creating awareness is enhanced.

Brand awareness involves a continuum ranging from an uncertain feeling that the brand is recognized, to a belief that it is the only one in the product class. As Figure 3–3 suggests, this continuum can be

TABLE 3–1 Consumer Brand Preferences in Housewares

Brands	Percent Would Prefer
Rubbermaid	14.6
General Electric	12.8
Corning	9.9
Cannon	5.7
Corelle	5.1
Ecko	4.0
Visions	3.5
Sunbeam	3.3
Black & Decker	3.0
Libbey	2.8

SOURCE: Reprinted by permission from *Discount Store News*, October 24, 1988 Issue. Copyright Lebhar-Friedman, Inc., 425 Park Avenue, New York, NY 10022.

FIGURE 3–3 The Awareness Pyramid

represented by three very different levels of brand awareness.[4] The role of brand awareness in brand equity will depend upon both the context and upon which level of awareness is achieved.

The lowest level, brand recognition, is based upon an aided recall test. Respondents, perhaps in a telephone survey, are given a set of brand names from a given product class and asked to identify those that they had heard of before. Thus, although there needs to be a link between the brand and the product class, it need not be strong. Brand recognition is a minimal level of brand awareness. It is particularly important when a buyer chooses a brand at the point of purchase.

The next level is brand recall. Brand recall is based upon asking a person to name the brand in a product class; it is termed "unaided recall" because, unlike as in the recognition task, the respondent is not aided by having the names provided. Unaided recall is a substantially more difficult task than recognition, and is associated with a stronger brand position. A person can recall many more items on an aided recall basis than when unaided.

The first-named brand in an unaided recall task has achieved top-of-mind awareness, a special position. In a very real sense, it is ahead of the other brands in a person's mind. (Of course, there may be another brand close behind.)

A still stronger recall position, not represented in Figure 3–3, would be that of a dominant brand, a brand that is the only brand recalled for a high percentage of the respondents.[5] Consider Arm & Hammer baking soda (which has 85% of the market and a symbol with a 95% recognition level), Band-Aid adhesive bandages, Jell-O gelatin, Crayola crayons, Morton Salt, Lionel trains, Philadelphia cream cheese, V-8 vegetable juice, and A-1 steak sauce. In each case, how many other brands can you name? Having a dominant brand provides a strong competitive advantage. In many purchase situations it means that no other brand will even be considered.

HOW AWARENESS WORKS
TO HELP THE BRAND

Brand awareness creates value in at least four ways as Figure 3–4 suggests.

ANCHOR TO WHICH OTHER
ASSOCIATIONS CAN BE ATTACHED

Brand recognition is the basic first step in the communication task. It usually is wasteful to attempt to communicate brand attributes until a name is established with which to associate the attributes. A name is like a special file folder in the mind which can be filled with name-related facts and feelings. Without such a file readily accessible in memory, the facts and feelings become misfiled, and cannot be readily accessed when needed.

Figure 3–5 illustrates using an anchor metaphor. The associations, such as Golden Arches, clean/efficient, Ronald McDonald, kids, fun, and Big Mac, are linked to the McDonald's name via chains (representing links in memory). Note that the chain can be thick and sturdy or rather weak. Note also that the structure can be strengthened by links between the associations—there is a chain connecting Ronald McDonald and kids.

FIGURE 3–4 The Value of Brand Awareness

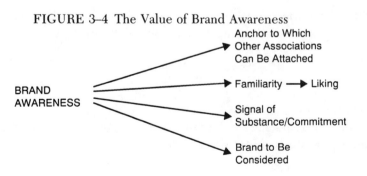

FIGURE 3–5　The McDonald's Associations

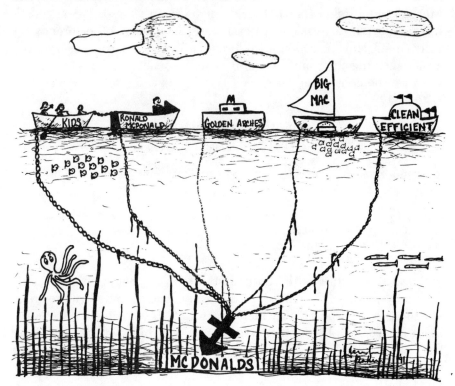

Courtesy of Jennifer Aaker.

A new product or service is, of course, particularly concerned with gaining recognition. Virtually all models attempting to forecast new-product success have brand recognition as a key initial construct; only rarely can a purchase decision occur without recognition. Further, learning about features and benefits of the new product is difficult without achieving recognition. With recognition established, the task is simply to attach a new association, such as a product attribute.

FAMILIARITY/LIKING

Recognition provides the brand with a sense of familiarity—and people like the familiar. Especially for low-involvement products like soap, chewing gum, paper towels, sugar, disposable pens, or facial tissues, familiarity can sometimes drive the buying decision. In the absence of motivation to engage in attribute evaluation, familiarity may be enough.

Studies have shown a positive relationship between the number of exposures and liking, whether the stimuli are abstract pictures, names, music, or whatever. One study, for example, showed Turkish-like words either three or six times. Even though different words were used so that there could be no inherent appeal of a word, those words that were recognized were liked more than those that were not recognized.

Interestingly, these recognition studies have found that exposure repetition can affect liking even when the recognition level apparently is unaffected.[6] One explanation is that the recognition (or familiarity) effect can exist below the threshold of recognition measurement.

Consider the case of such old brand names as Ipana and Black Jack, which have been reissued and have done well. The recognition value of the brand undoubtedly contributed.

SUBSTANCE/COMMITMENT

Name awareness can be a signal of presence, commitment, and substance, attributes which can be very important even to industrial buyers of big-ticket items, and consumer buyers of durables. The logic is that if a name is recognized, there must be a reason—such as:

- The firm has advertised extensively.
- The firm has been in the business for a long time.
- The firm is widely distributed.
- The brand is successful—others use it.

These suppositions are not necessarily based upon knowledge of specific facts about the brand. Even if a person has not been exposed to advertising and knows little about the firm, brand awareness could still lead to the assumptions that the firm is substantial and backs the brand with advertising. If a brand is completely unknown before it was put forth as a choice alternative, there is a suspicion that it is not substantial with a committed firm behind it.

Sometimes, even in the case of large and involved purchase decisions, brand familiarity and perceptions of substance associated with brand awareness can make all the difference. When there is no clear winner after extensive analyses as to (let us say) which computer or which advertising agency to select, the strength of brand awareness can be pivotal.

BRANDS TO CONSIDER

The first step in the buying process often is to select a group of brands to consider—a consideration set. In selecting an advertising agency, a car to test-drive, or a computer system to evaluate, for example, three or four alternatives might be considered. The buyer probably will not

---

Brand Recall and Buying Decisions

Toronto's Professor Prakash Nedungadi, in a clever experiment, demonstrated how brand recall influences purchase decisions.[7] In a product category (e.g., fast foods) two subcategories (e.g., national chains and local stores) were created. Within each subcategory, a major brand (e.g., McDonald's, Joe's Deli) and a minor brand (e.g., Wendy's, Subway) were identified on the basis of usage and liking surveys. Subjects first answered a series of 12 yes/no questions about four brands (e.g., Irish Spring is a laundry detergent). Each subject had three of the questions involve one of the four test brands (the brand name was "primed") unless they were in a control group. Subjects were then asked what brand they would select for a specific lunch and what others they would consider. Later, they were asked to indicate their intentions of visiting a list of different restaurants. The findings (which were replicated using burger condiments and alcohol mixers) were intriguing:

When one of the major brands was primed (McDonald's or Joe's Deli) the percent selecting that brand went up dramatically EVEN THOUGH the relative liking of that brand (as measured by the intentions question) DID NOT change. Brand recall (as measured by the consideration set question) was enhanced and affected choice WITHOUT affecting liking.

For the local store subcategory, a similar dramatic increase in choice for the major brand (Joe's Deli) occurred when the minor brand in the subcategory (Subway) was primed. Brand recall for Joe's Deli was indirectly enhanced—introducing Subway made the subject think of local stores which reminded them of Joe's Deli. This finding shows that recall is complex and that a strong position in a subcategory can create recall by calling attention to the subcategory as well as by creating notice for the brand.

be exposed to many brand names during the process, except by happenstance. Thus, brand recall can be crucial to getting into this group. Who makes computers? The first firms that come to mind will have an advantage. A firm which lacks recall may not even hear about the opportunity.

The role of brand recall (or, better yet, top-of-mind recall) can also be crucial for frequently purchased products like coffee, detergent, and headache remedies, for which brand decisions usually are made prior to going to the store. Further, in some categories (such as cereal) there are so many recognized alternatives that the shopper is overwhelmed. Thus, even though Nut & Honey is prominently displayed, it may be critical that it be a "recalled" brand, or even "top-of-mind recalled," to get the purchase.

Certain studies have shown a relationship between recall and consideration sets: Generally, if a brand does not achieve recall it will not be included in the consideration set. However, people usually will *also* recall brands that they *dislike* strongly. Several other studies have demonstrated the relationship between top-of-mind recall and attitudes/purchase behavior. One such study, of six brands in three product classes (fast food, soda, and banking), showed large differences in preference and purchase likelihood, depending on whether the brand was the first, second, or third mentioned in an unaided recall task.[8]

THE COFFEE STUDY

A study of the coffee market clearly showed the impact of awareness.[9] For 19 successful bimonth periods, market-share and advertising expenditure data were obtained and linked to the results of 19 coincident telephone surveys that measured unaided recall and attitudes toward the brands. The results are summarized in Figure 3–6. Advertising impacted on market share only indirectly through its impact upon awareness and attitude. Further, there was as much influence from a change in

FIGURE 3–6 Impact of Awareness upon Sales in the Coffee Market

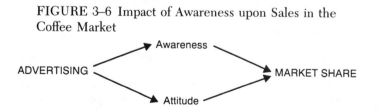

awareness as there was via a change in attitude, suggesting that awareness can be an important factor independent of changes in attitude. The implication is that awareness, influenced by reminder advertising, affects purchase decisions.

LANDOR'S IMAGEPOWER

Landor Associates has developed a measure of the power of a brand name; the measurement is based upon a survey of 1,000 American consumers.[10] Two dimensions are averaged. The one, termed "the share-of-mind score," is a measure of brand recognition. The other, termed "esteem," is a measure of favorable opinon that people have for companies and brands they know. The ratings are averaged to form an overall "ImagePower" score. Table 3–2 shows the ratings for several of the 667 brands tested (in 1988).

Of interest is how dominant Coca-Cola is in the survey. The gap between Coca-Cola and the second name, Campbell's, is as large as the

TABLE 3–2 The Most Powerful Brands in the U.S.

ImagePower Rank Order	Company/Brand	Esteem Index	Share of Mind Index
1	Coca-Cola	68	78
2	Campbell's	67	60
3	Pepsi-Cola	61	67
4	AT&T	64	63
5	McDonald's	50	77
6	American Express	60	65
7	Kellogg's	58	64
8	IBM	65	58
9	Levi's	63	58
10	Sears	59	62
⋮			
30	Rolls–Royce	63	46
⋮			
169	Nissan	43	66
⋮			
177	Datsun	41	67
⋮			
667	Asahi	28	27

SOURCE: Mim Ryan, "Assessment: The First Step in Image Management," *Tokyo Business Today*, September 1988, pp. 36–38. (The numbers shown are approximate indices.)

gap between Campbell's and the number 50 brand, Dole (not shown). The high recognition score as reflected in the Landor work was undoubtedly the basis of the remarkably successful launch of brand extensions, some with very little marketing support. In the mid–1980s, the Coke name was attached to nine different soft drinks, including Diet Cherry Coke, a brand which received no advertising support at all.

One finding from the Landor study is that there is a high correlation between awareness and esteem. Of course, this correlation is in part caused because people are aware of and like brands they use. However, it may also in part reflect the fact that familiar brands do tend to be liked. There are exceptions, of course. Some brands such as Greyhound, Playboy, and Warner Bros. have their relatively high recognition but not-so-high esteem. Others, like Rolls–Royce, Hilton, Harley–Davidson, Windex, and Rolex, are in the opposite situation, having the intriguing opportunity to capitalize upon their esteem by building awareness.

Using the same technique in Japan and Europe, Landor has utilized its potential to identify the relative success that firms have had in creating world brands. In fact, with data for all three areas combined, Coca-Cola is the number one brand, followed by IBM, Sony, Porsche, and McDonald's.

THE LIMITATIONS OF AWARENESS

Awareness, although a key brand asset, cannot by itself create sales, especially for a new product. An unusual and controversial advertising campaign introducing the Infiniti (by Nissan) illustrates.[11] Using ads which showed scenes involving birds, fields, and lakes (but not the car), the campaign created a recognition level of 90%, and some unique associations. However, sales were disappointing during the early months of the product, and critics were claiming that the absence of a "reason-to-buy" in the ads was a contributing factor. One comic suggested that the advertising was working fine: Sales of rocks and trees were up 300%!

THE POWER OF OLD BRAND NAMES

Certainly there is a decay factor over time, especially when top-of-mind recognition is involved. However, a remarkable phenomenon is that when a brand becomes really well established, with high recognition created as a result of many exposures and usage experiences, recognition tends to stay high over a long time-period even if advertising support is dropped.

In the mid–1980s, for example, an awareness study was conducted on blenders. When test subjects were asked to recall all the brand names of blenders they could, GE scored as number two, even though they had not made blenders for 20 years. Also, Unilever's Lux Beauty Bar, a brand which has not been advertised for more than 15 years, still generates sales of $25 million, half of which may be gross profit.[12]

One study of brand-name familiarity asked 100 housewives in four cities to name as many brands as they could. They were paid for each name.[13] On average they came up with 28, and 15% named more than 40. Half of the brands were food names. The age of the brands named was most remarkable: As Table 3–3 shows, over 85% were over 25 years old, and 36% were over 75 years old!

Another remarkable study, this one by The Boston Consulting Group, compared the leading brands of 1925 with those of 1985 in 22 product categories.[14] In 19 categories the leader was the same. In the other three, the prior leader was still a factor. Table 3–4 summarizes the results. Of course, there are categories (such as frozen dinners, and granola bars) that did not exist in 1925, and so the marketplace is more dynamic than the table suggests. However, the power of the old brand names still is incredible. In part, this is certainly based upon their recognition levels— which in turn are based upon exposures that probably were in the thousands for some.

What are the implications? One is that the establishment of a strong name anchored by high recognition creates an enormous asset. Further, the asset gets stronger over the years as the number of exposures and

TABLE 3–3 Ages of Best-Known Brand Names

Age of Brand	Percentage of 4,923 Brands Mentioned
Over 100 years	10
75 to 99 years	26
50 to 74 years	28
25 to 49 years	4
15 to 24 years	4
Under 14 years	3

SOURCE: Adapted from Leo Bogart and Charles Lehman, "What Makes a Brand Name Familiar?" *Journal of Marketing Research*, February 1973, pp. 17–22.

TABLE 3–4 The Leading Brands: 1925 and 1985

Product	Leading Brand 1925	Current Position 1985
Bacon	Swift	Leader
Batteries	Eveready	Leader
Biscuits	Nabisco	Leader
Breakfast cereal	Kellogg	Leader
Cameras	Kodak	Leader
Canned fruit	Del Monte	Leader
Chewing gum	Wrigley	Leader
Chocolates	Hershey	No. 2
Flour	Gold Medal	Leader
Mint candies	Life Savers	Leader
Paint	Sherwin–Williams	Leader
Pipe tobacco	Prince Albert	Leader
Razors	Gillette	Leader
Sewing machines	Singer	Leader
Shirts	Manhattan	No. 5
Shortening	Crisco	Leader
Soap	Ivory	Leader
Soft drinks	Coca-Cola	Leader
Soup	Campbell	Leader
Tea	Lipton	Leader
Tires	Goodyear	Leader
Toothpaste	Colgate	No. 2

SOURCE: Thomas S. Wurster, "The Leading Brands: 1925–1985," *Perspectives*, The Boston Consulting Group, 1987.

experiences grows. As a result, a challenging brand—even with an enormous advertising budget and superior product or service—finds it difficult to fight its way into the memory of the customer.

There is widespread belief, especially among lay people, that with enough advertising and a good enough product, a new brand will win, even in a mature-product class. It is just not that easy: Consider all the unsuccessful challenges to those brands that led the 22 product categories in the 60-year period of the study. In some mature-product classes the only way to become the leading brand is to have been born that way.

To challenge in a mature product class, it is usually best to revitalize an existing, established brand in the product class than to attempt a new entry. If a new entry is attempted, one route is to extend a brand name established in a related product class. The revitalization and extension options will be discussed in later chapters.

HOW TO ACHIEVE AWARENESS

Achieving awareness, both recognition and recall, involves two tasks; gaining brand name identity and linking it to the product class. For a new brand, both tasks are required. However, in other contexts one is already accomplished, and the assignment becomes different. For example, a brand name such as Pizzaplace implies the product class and the need is only to establish the brand name. When Roto-Rooter, an established name, went into plumbing, the need was to link the established name to a product class.

How should awareness be achieved, maintained, or improved? The best approach will depend upon the context, but there are several helpful guidelines that are based upon formal studies from both psychology and advertising and upon observing brands that have done well in creating and maintaining awareness levels.

BE DIFFERENT, MEMORABLE

An awareness message should provide a reason to be noticed and it should be memorable. There are many tacks that work but one key is simply to be different, unusual. Consider, for example, the talking Parkay margarine box. It provides a humorous approach to linking the Parkay name to margarine and is very different from the communication of other brands.

Too many product classes have brands with very similar communication approaches, making it difficult to break out of the clutter. For example, most ads for perfume, sports cars, menthol cigarettes, and soft drinks have a sameness that inhibits the task of achieving recognition. One advertiser switched the sound track from a Coca-Cola television commercial with one for 7-UP—and the effect was barely noticeable.

Of course, it is necessary to create a link between the brand and the product class. Putting a car on the top of an isolated mountain, for example, may be memorable but the audience may have trouble recalling which car was placed on the mountain top.

INVOLVE A SLOGAN OR JINGLE

A slogan or jingle can make a big difference. The slogans "It Floats" or "You Deserve a Break Today" can help recall. When a product class such as soap is the stimulus, it might be easier to come up with "It

Floats" and then Ivory, rather than to name Ivory directly. The link to the slogan might be stronger because it involves a product characteristic that can be visualized. Thus, it can pay to create and establish a slogan with strong links to brand and the product class.

A jingle can be a powerful awareness-creating device. One new-product model that was designed to predict awareness levels, achieved 13 weeks after launch, was tested on 58 new product introductions.[15] One finding was that a catchy jingle was extremely important in explaining why some new products gained higher levels of recall than others. One of the high recall brands used the jingle "Oh O, Spaghettios."

SYMBOL EXPOSURE

If a symbol is available or can be developed, such as Colonel Sanders, the Transamerica pyramid, or the Travelers umbrella, which can be closely linked to a brand, it can play a major role in creating and maintaining awareness. A symbol involves a visual image which is much easier to learn and to recall than a word or phrase. Further, there are often creative ways to gain symbol exposure besides using advertising—for example, Betty Crocker baking contests, exhibitions of Budweiser's Clydesdale horse team, and apples in various forms at computer shows.

Consider the Goodyear blimp, one of which is shown in Figure 3–7, which has been used by Goodyear for public relations since 1925. The current fleet of three airships have contributed substantially to the name recognition of Goodyear. They provide exposure to a 116-foot-long logo consisting of the Goodyear name plus its winged foot, supplemented by a lighted sign consisting of 7,560 programmed lights. The major exposure occurs from the 80-plus TV performances each year in many telecast outdoor events, such as the Super Bowl and the World Series. One journalist wrote, "An event isn't an event unless you've got the Goodyear blimp." The symbol is so strong that competitor Goodrich once ran a series of ads showing a blue sky with white clouds, to emphasize the point that *they* are the company *without* the blimp.

PUBLICITY

Advertising is well-suited to generating awareness because it allows the message and audience to be tailored to the job at hand and because it is generally an efficient way to gain exposures. However, publicity

FIGURE 3–7 A Goodyear Blimp

Courtesy of The Goodyear Tire & Rubber Company.

should usually play a role and can sometimes carry the ball. It can be not only much less expensive than media advertising but also effective. People are more often interested in learning about a news story than in reading advertising. The Goodyear blimp, for example, gets several thousand press clippings each year. The problem is to generate events or issues associated with the brand that are newsworthy.

The ideal situation occurs when the product is inherently interesting, such as a new-car concept—the two seat Mazda Miata sports car—or a new computer chip. However, if the product is not newsworthy, an event, symbol, or other device needs to be created. For example, Ben and Jerry's "cowmobile," a mobile ice cream shop that dispensed free Ben and Jerry's ice cream as it crossed the country, was newsworthy at least in the small towns it visited.

EVENT SPONSORSHIP

The primary role of most event sponsorship is to create or maintain awareness. Thus the Volvo tennis circuit, the Virginia Slims women's tour, and the Transamerica tennis tournament all generate exposure from spectators, who view them either live or on television, and from others who read about them either before or after their occurrence. Beer brands long ago discovered the value of promotions, and Budweiser, Miller, Coors, and other brands have become prominently associated with hundreds of events.

CONSIDER BRAND EXTENSIONS

One way to gain brand recall, to make the brand name more salient, is to put the name on other products. Coca-Cola, Heinz, Weight Watchers, and Sunkist all get name exposure when their names are attached to additional products which are advertised, displayed, and used.

At an extreme, many prominent Japanese firms such as SONY, Honda, Mazda, Mitsubishi, and Yamaha use their names on all their products. In fact, the name SONY was deliberately selected so that it could be widely used and thus benefit from multiple promotion efforts. The ubiquitous Mitsubishi name and three diamond symbol appear on more than 25,000 products including automobiles, financial products, and mushrooms.

Of course, there is always a trade-off. Although brand recall is often enhanced by the broad use of a brand name, different names provide the opportunity to develop different associations for each name. Chapter 9 will elaborate on the issues involved in brand extensions.

USING CUES

An awareness campaign often can be aided by cues of either the product class, the brand, or both. One brand cue that is particularly useful is the package, since the package is the actual stimulus with which the shopper is confronted. The Morton Salt or Lean Cuisine package will cue a product. A person like Andre Agassi, e.g., can cue a product class such as tennis rackets. Sometimes cues can be used to remind people of the link developed in the advertising.[16] The Life cereal Mikey ads, in which a cute boy named Mikey enjoys Life cereal to the disbelief of his brother, are leveraged by a small picture of Mikey printed on the package in order to cue the ads.

RECALL REQUIRES REPETITION

Developing recall is more difficult than developing recognition. The brand name needs to be made more salient, and the link from the brand to the product class needs to be stronger. While recognition, even based on only a few exposures, persists, recall decays through time. It is a bit like the fact that we recognize the face but cannot recall the name. Recall is difficult, requiring either an in-depth learning experience or many repetitions. Top-of-mind recall is, of course, even more demanding. For a brand like Budweiser to maintain high levels of top-of-mind recall, relatively high levels of repetition may be needed indefinitely.

THE RECALL BONUS

Maintaining a strong top-of-mind awareness through constant exposure can create not only brand awareness, but also brand salience that can inhibit the recall of other brands. A series of studies have found that when people were given a brand name, or set of brand names, and asked to generate names of competitive products, their effort was inhibited—they came up with fewer names. In one such experiment, respondents who were asked to evaluate a Dristan TV ad could think of fewer names of cold remedies than those not exposed to the Dristan ad.[17] The salient brand, Dristan, got in the way of the memory retrieval task.

QUESTIONS TO CONSIDER

1. What is the role of recognition and recall for your brand? Exactly how does each affect purchase decisions?

2. What is your level of recognition and recall by segment? Is there any problem with achieving recognition among new customers? Is the brand name salient enough to the key segments—is recall being maintained?

3. Evaluate your communication program designed to generate recognition or recall and its various components. What is working? What

areas merit an extensive review? What about packaging? Are the programs consistent with the brand associations?

4. What promotions and other communication devices designed to generate recognition or recall have worked well for competitors? Are all avenues of public relations being exploited?

4

·

Perceived Quality

Quality is the only patent protection we've got.

James Robinson
CEO, American Express

It pays to give most products an image of quality—a First Class ticket.

David Ogilvy

Quality is free.

Phil Crosby

THE SCHLITZ STORY

The Joseph Schlitz Brewing Company started in 1850 as a small brewhouse supplying a Milwaukee restaurant. It received a growth impetus when the 1871 Chicago fire destroyed many of that city's breweries.[1] In 1872 the slogan "The beer that made Milwaukee famous" was born. By the turn of the century, Schlitz was the third-largest beer, trailing only Pabst and Anheuser-Busch. The firm remained healthy during the first 50 years of the twentieth century, surviving Prohibition during the 1920s by producing malt and yeast syrups. In 1947 it became the leading beer in the U.S. Although it lost its lead to Budweiser in 1957, it remained a strong No. 2 brand through the early 1970s.

[78]

FIGURE 4–1 A Schlitz Gusto Ad

Courtesy of The Stroh Brewery Company.

The 1960s saw the Leo Burnett Company create the well-regarded "Real gusto in a great light beer" and "when you're out of Schlitz, you're out of beer" ad themes. Figure 4–1 shows one of the "gusto" ads of the 1960s. Also in the 1960s, Schlitz successfully introduced both Schlitz Malt Liquor and the trademarked "pop top" can. In the early 1970s a lifestyle approach featured "men of the sea," providing a heavy-beer drinker as hero while retaining the gusto theme. The slogan was "You only go around once in life—so grab all the gusto you can."

SCHLITZ TUMBLES

As late as 1976 the Joseph Schlitz Brewing Company, producing the popularly priced Old Milwaukee plus a newly introduced Schlitz Light in addition to the flagship Schlitz brand, still held 16.1% of the market, as compared to 19.5% for Anheuser–Busch and 12.2% for Miller. However, in 1977 the Schlitz firm lost the No. 2 position to Miller, and thereafter its fortunes tumbled. The Schlitz firm's market share went from 15.8 in 1976 to 13.9 in 1977, and from there to 11.8 in 1978. The profits fell steadily, from $48 million in 1974 to a negative $50 million in 1979.

Figure 4–2 shows the sales decline of the Schlitz brand (excluding malt light beers). It dropped from 17.8 million barrels per year in 1974 to 16.6 million in 1976 (when it benefited from a major strike at Anheuser-Busch) to 7.5 million in 1980, and under 1 million in 1986—when it had all but disappeared. In the mid-eighties its role was that of a price brand—it had dropped from the premium category.

The Joseph Schlitz Brewing Company was publicly traded until it was bought by Stroh in 1982. Thus, there is a record of how much the firm has been worth over time. We assume that the percent of that value which should be assigned to the Schlitz name is equal to the percent of the Joseph Schlitz Brewing Company sales associated with the products carrying the Schlitz brand. Table 4–1 summarizes. By this logic, the value of the brand name (the brand equity) fell from over $1 billion in 1974 to $75 million only six years later. Over 93% of the brand equity was lost.

MANAGING QUALITY AT SCHLITZ

Why? What happened? The story starts with the first signs of disaster, which appeared in 1974.

In Schlitz's Milwaukee plant in 1974 the "accelerated batch fermentation" (ABF) process was finally put into production after a 10-year development. The revolutionary, yeast-centered brewing process, which changed the fermentation process from 12 days to four, both reduced cost and improved the uniformity of the product. Although there apparently was a reduction in shelf life, the taste was otherwise unaffected. However, on the street the word was that Schlitz was making "green beer." One employee noted that in the brewing business, people think it is good to use the same process your ancestors used to make beer in

FIGURE 4–2 Schlitz Sales
(Millions of Barrels)

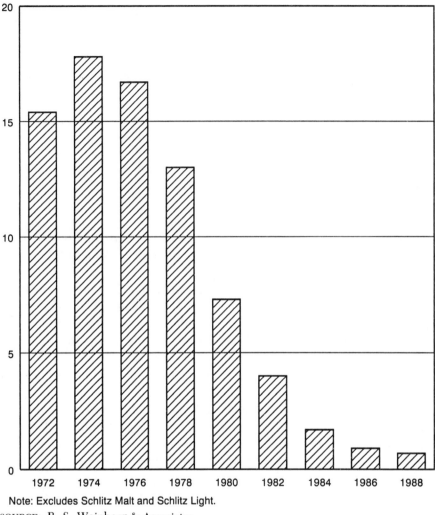

Note: Excludes Schlitz Malt and Schlitz Light.
SOURCE: R. S. Weinberg & Associates.

1700, but would question your sanity if you say you use the same transportation your ancestors used in 1700.

The new production process was not the only attempt by Schlitz to gain a sustainable competitive cost advantage. For some time they had reduced costs by substituting corn syrup for barley malt. Although internally the belief (or hope) was that the average beer drinker could not tell the difference between the taste of the new, cheaper beer and the original version, in fact the new beer did have a lighter taste.

TABLE 4-1 The Brand Equity of Schlitz

Year	Total Market Value Year High (in $ millions)	Total Market Value—Less Debt Year High (in $ millions)	Percentage of Revenues from Schlitz	Schlitz Brand Market Value (in $ millions)
1974	1,670	1,374	71	1,082
1975	875	596	68	447
1976	698	426	65	307
1977	530	300	62	207
1978	487	311	60	207
1979	388	231	56	145
1980	287	150	45	75
1981	495	345	36	138
1982	465	318	28	98

The fact that Schlitz was attempting to save money by going to less-expensive ingredients and processes was difficult to keep quiet and defend, especially since Anheuser–Busch had made the explicit decision to retain the more expensive ingredients. In early 1975, Anheuser–Busch president, August Busch said: "Our competition has changed their ingredients and processes in a quest for higher profits and a greater return on investment. But when it comes to quality you can only fool the consumer for a short time. Consequently, we chose to let our earnings decline rather than lessen our quality. After all, we are in the business for the long term."

The image problem was compounded when Schlitz used its cost savings in part to aggressively discount and use promotions to build sales. This effort was consistent with a strategy of achieving cost advantage through lower production costs, and volume-based economies of scale. The belief was that cost would be a decisive market factor. However, the discounts and promotions were inconsistent with the premium beer category that Schlitz had always occupied.

In 1975 a serious quality-image problem emerged, fanned by whispering campaigns of competitors. The advertising attempted to respond by emphasizing a quality theme. The "gusto" line was dropped for "There's just one word for beer: Schlitz! And you know it!" and "When it's right, you know it." However, this campaign, like ones to come, could not correct the deteriorating situation.

In 1976 the worst happened. On January 1, Schlitz changed the foam stabilizer used to give the beer shelf life. The motivation was to avoid having to add an ingredient to the label in order to comply with a new labeling law. The new stabilizer would be filtered out during the brewing process, and thus would not become a part of the final product. However, the new stabilizer reacted with some other components to form tiny flakes in the product. The result was described as either flaky or cloud beer—but for months the problem was ignored. In early summer one attempted fix (removing the stabilizer) caused the beer to go flat when it sat for a time on a shelf. In the fall of 1976, some 10 million bottles and cans of Schlitz were "secretly" recalled and destroyed. Subsequently, the secret got out, and Schlitz became something of a joke.

Attempting to Recover

In 1977, in yet another attempt to counter the image problem, an advertising campaign was run showing burly men growling at individuals who tried to get them to switch brands. The slogan was "You want to take away my Schlitz? My gusto?" The aggressive ads became known in the industry as the "Drink Schlitz or I'll kill you" campaign. There was a rather widespread belief within the advertising industry that the short-lived campaign was a disaster. Schlitz never really recovered.

In 1978 Schlitz hired the brewmaster from Anheuser–Busch, who changed the production process and ingredients so that the beer was again the same premium product it had been in the 1960s. He became the spokesperson for an advertising campaign with the tag line "Beer makes it good, Schlitz makes it great." In 1979 the slogan "Go for it!" was used, to be followed by a return to the "Gusto" theme. But sales still declined.

In 1980, in desperation, Schlitz even spent $4 million on five live taste tests, in which they had 100 drinkers of a competing brand (either Budweiser, Miller, or Michelob) involved in a blind taste test on live television. One such test, which took place at the 1981 Super Bowl, featured a prominent football referee—to generate as much excitement as possible. As their best result, Schlitz got 50% of the Michelob drinkers to say they preferred the unmarked Schlitz beer. However, *nothing* would convince customers that Schlitz was back, even though the physical product had, since 1978, used the old formula and process.

Assessing the Blame

Of course, a lot happened in the beer industry during the 1970s that affected Schlitz. Phillip Morris acquired Miller in 1970 and repositioned

"The champagne of bottled beer" to the blue-collar working man who enjoys "Miller time," using dramatically increased advertising budgets. They also introduced 7-ounce cans, and improved the product quality by instituting a policy of removing beer that had been on shelves for 120 days. Further, in 1975 they launched Miller Lite and targeted "real" beer drinkers who wanted a "less filling" beer. One of the most successful new products ever introduced, its sales passed Schlitz in 1979 and in 1983 became the No. 2 brand behind Bud.

In the late 1970s, Anheuser–Busch reacted to Miller by substantially increasing advertising expenditures and aggressively sponsoring sports events (they sponsored over 400 in 1982, as opposed to 20 in 1976). They also expanded capacity and introduced Natural Light and Michelob Light. As a result, the beer-industry environment was a lot less attractive to competitors during the late 1970s and 1980s than it had been.

The efforts of Miller and Anheuser–Busch came primarily at the expense of regional brands and Schlitz. Including light brands, the sales patterns for Schlitz looked very different from those of comparable brands, Pabst and Coors. While Schlitz fell from 13 million barrels in 1978 to 1.8 million in 1984, Pabst also fell (from 12.7 to 6.8) but Coors actually grew (from 12.1 to 12.6). The stock market value of Coors fell from $809 million in 1975, when it went public, to 46% of this level in 1980. In contrast, in 1980, Schlitz had fallen to 17% of its 1975 value, which was less than half of its 1974 value.

Schlitz had problems in addition to the quality fiasco. A management void was created when a CEO died in 1977. This loss was compounded by some legal problems in 1978 which led to the loss of four top marketing people. However, it seems clear that the collapse of the Schlitz brand equity was caused largely by the loss of the perceived quality of the product.

A retired Schlitz ad manager during the glory days summarized it well: "Schlitz sacrificed its reputation in its pursuit of bigger profits. In the beer business, if a company loses its resources and money, but retains its reputation, it can always be rebuilt. But if it loses its reputation, no amount of money and resources will bring it back."

SOME OBSERVATIONS

A remarkable aspect of this story is that the loss of perceived quality turned out to be irreversible. Correcting the product was not enough to affect the changed perceptions, despite the spending of enormous sums on advertising developed by competent agencies. Some consumers were simply impossible to convince. An effort to make a small improvement in margins cost $1 billion in brand equity!

Note also that the decay of the brand did not happen immediately but occurred over a period of 10 years. There are several possible explanations: First, the effort to "correct" the quality problem resulted in an annual (and sometimes semiannual) advertising campaign. The result was an ineffective hodgepodge reaching the consumer. Further, it replaced the successful "Gusto" thrust that had been consistently run for 15 years. Second, the "word" about Schlitz probably took years to diffuse through the population. Third, people are reluctant to change; there is a lot of inertia in the marketplace. What really happened is that the brand was weakened and made vulnerable to the efforts of competing brands. Over time it just could not survive.

WHAT IS PERCEIVED QUALITY?

Perceived quality can be defined as the customer's perception of the overall quality or superiority of a product or service with respect to its intended purpose, relative to alternatives.[2] Perceived quality is, first, a perception by customers. It thus differs from several related concepts, such as:

- Actual or objective quality—the extent to which the product or service delivers superior service
- Product-based quality—the nature and quantity of ingredients, features, or services included
- Manufacturing quality—conformance to specification, the "zero defect" goal

Perceived quality cannot necessarily be objectively determined, in part because it is a perception and also because judgments about what is important to customers are involved. An evaluation of washing machines by a *Consumer Report* expert may be competent and unbiased, but it must make judgments about the relative importance of features, cleaning action, types of clothes to be washed, and so on that may not match those of all customers. After all, customers differ sharply in their personalities, needs, and preferences.

Perceived quality is defined relative to an intended purpose and a set of alternatives. Thus, it is very different for Target stores than for Nordstrom or Bloomingdale's. Because Target does not deliver the same level of personal service, the same quality merchandise, and the same store ambience as Nordstrom does not mean that it will have lower perceived quality. It will simply be judged by a different set of criteria— perhaps ease of parking, waiting time at check-outs, courtesy of the check-out people, and whether desired items are in stock.

Perceived quality differs from satisfaction. A customer can be satisfied because he or she had *low* expectations about the performance level. High perceived quality is not consistent with low expectations. It also differs from attitude: A positive attitude could be generated because a product of inferior quality is very inexpensive. Conversely, a person could have a negative attitude toward a high-quality product that is overpriced.

Perceived quality is an intangible, overall feeling about a brand. However, it usually will be based on underlying dimensions which include characteristics of the products to which the brand is attached such as reliability and performance. To understand perceived quality, the identification and measurement of the underlying dimensions will be useful, but the perceived quality itself is a summary, global construct.

HOW PERCEIVED
QUALITY GENERATES VALUE

As Figure 4–3 suggests, perceived quality provides value in several ways.

FIGURE 4–3 The Value of Perceived Quality

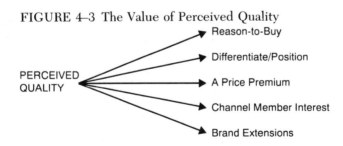

REASON-TO-BUY

The Schlitz story, which vividly illustrates the role that perceived quality can play, is not such an isolated example. In many contexts, perceived quality of a brand provides a pivotal reason-to-buy, influencing which brands are included and excluded from consideration, and the brand that is to be selected.

A customer often will lack the motivation to obtain and sort out the information that might lead to an objective determination of quality in a given application. Or the information may simply be unavailable. Or the customer may not have the ability or resources to obtain or process it. In any case, perceived quality becomes central.

Because the perceived quality is linked to purchase decisions, it can make all elements of the marketing program more effective. If the perceived quality is high, the job of advertising and promotion is more likely to be effective. By contrast, a perceived quality problem such as the one discussed in the Schlitz case is difficult to overcome.

DIFFERENTIATE/POSITION

A principal positioning characteristic of a brand—whether a car, a computer, or a cheese—is its position on the perceived quality dimension. Is it a super premium, premium, value, or economy entry? Further, with respect to a perceived quality category, is the brand the best, or is it only competitive with others in the class? The discussion in Chapter 5 will elaborate.

A PRICE PREMIUM

A perceived quality advantage provides the option of charging a premium price. The price premium can increase profits, and/or provide resources with which to reinvest in the brand. These resources can be used in such brand-building activities as enhancing awareness or associations, or in R&D activities to improve the product. A price premium not only provides resources, but can also reinforce the perceived quality. The "you get what you pay for" belief is especially important in the case of goods and services for which objective information is not readily available.

Instead of a price premium, the customer may be offered a superior value at a competitive price. This added value *should* result in a larger customer base, higher brand loyalty, and more effective and efficient marketing programs.

CHANNEL MEMBER INTEREST

Perceived quality can also be meaningful to retailers, distributors, and other channel members, and thus aid in gaining distribution. We know that the image of a channel member is affected by the products or services included in its line—stocking "quality products" *can* matter. In addition, a retailer or other channel member can offer a high perceived quality product at an attractive price, to draw traffic. In any case, the channel members are motivated to carry brands that are well-regarded, that customers want.

BRAND EXTENSIONS

In addition, the perceived quality can be exploited by introducing brand extensions, using the brand name to enter new product categories. A strong brand with respect to perceived quality will be able to extend further, and will find a higher success probability than a weaker brand. A study of 18 proposed extensions of six brand names, including Vuarnet and Crest, found that perceived quality of the brand name was a significant predictor of the evaluation of the extensions.[3] The material in Chapter 9 will elaborate.

THE PIMS FINDINGS

The PIMS database includes information on dozens of variables such as ROI, perceived quality, market share, and relative price for over 3,000 businesses, some of which have supplied information since 1970. Hundreds of studies, most trying to find clues to strategic success have used this database. Perhaps the most definitive finding from this research is the role of product quality. Robert Buzzell and Bradley Gale, in their book *The PIMS Principles*, conclude: "In the long run, the most important single factor affecting a business unit's performance is the [relative perceived] quality of its products and service, relative to those of competitors."[4]

Figure 4–4 summarizes the overall effect of relative perceived quality by showing the ROI and ROS (return on sales) as a function of the quality position. Thus the lowest-20-percentile businesses had around a 17% ROI, whereas those in the top-20-percentile earned nearly twice as much.

A detailed examination of the relationship of perceived quality and other key strategic variables in addition to ROI, by Jacobson and Aaker, provides insights on how perceived quality does create profitability:[5]

1. Perceived quality affects market share. After controlling for other factors, products of higher quality are favored and will receive a higher share of the market.

2. Perceived quality affects price. Higher perceived quality allows a business to charge a higher price. The higher price can directly improve profitability or allow the business to improve quality further to create higher competitive barriers. Further, a higher price tends to enhance perceived quality by acting as a quality cue.

3. Perceived quality has a direct impact on profitability in addition to its effect on market share and price. Improved perceived quality will, on average, increase profitability even when price and market share are not affected. Perhaps the cost of retaining existing customers declines less with higher quality, or competitive pressures are reduced when quality is improved. In any case, there is a direct link between quality and ROI.

4. Perceived quality does not affect cost negatively. In fact, it doesn't affect costs at all. The image that there is a natural association between a quality/prestige niche strategy and high cost is not reflected in the

FIGURE 4–4   Relative Perceived Quality and ROI

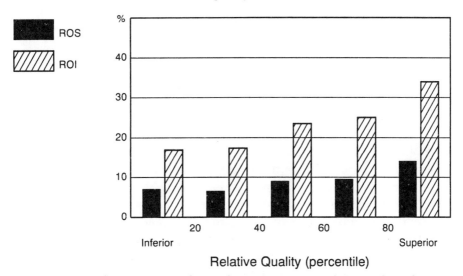

SOURCE: From *The PIMS Principles: Linking Strategy to Performance* by Robert D. Buzzell and Bradley T. Gale, p. 107. Copyright © 1987 by The Free Press, a Division of Macmillan, Inc. Reproduced by permission of the publisher.

data. The concept that "quality is free" may be in part the reason—enhanced quality leads to reduced defects and lowered manufacturing costs.

As the search for alternatives to short-term financials proceeds, there is a need to make alternative measures credible by quantifying their value. The PIMS database is important because it is a vehicle with which to show the value of an important brand equity dimension, relative perceived quality.

PERCEIVED QUALITY AND BUSINESS PERFORMANCE

Another perspective on the importance of perceived quality in the competitive area emerged from a study of 248 different businesses. A key manager from each business was asked to identify the sustainable competitive advantage (SCA) of the business.[6] The resulting list of SCAs was topped by a "reputation for high quality," named by 105 (over 40%) of the managers. The next most mentioned SCA, "customer service/product support," received only 78 mentions. When the sample was divided into 68 high-tech firms, 113 service firms, and 67 manufacturing firms, perceived quality was the most frequently mentioned SCA in each set. Clearly, perceived quality is regarded as important to long-run business success.

A side note: The third most frequently mentioned sustainable competitive advantage was another dimension of brand equity, name recognition/high profile. And the tenth most mentioned was the installed customer base—still another dimension of brand equity.

WHAT INFLUENCES PERCEIVED QUALITY?

If perceived quality is to be understood and managed, it is necessary to consider what influences it. Why do some customers believe that the quality is high or low? How could perceived quality be improved? What attributes do customers use to make overall quality judgements?

The dimensions that underlie a perceived quality judgment will depend upon the context. For a lawn mower it might include cutting quality, reliability, availability of maintenance, and cost of maintenance. To learn relevant dimensions in a given context, it is usually useful to conduct some exploratory research. For example, customers can be asked why some brands have higher quality than others, and why pairs of brands

FIGURE 4–5 Quality Dimensions

Product Quality

1. Performance: How well does a washing machine clean clothes?
2. Features: Does a toothpaste have a convenient dispenser?
3. Conformance with specifications: What is the incidence of defects?
4. Reliability: Will the lawn mower work properly each time it is used?
5. Durability: How long will the lawn mower last?
6. Serviceability: Is the service system efficient, competent, and convenient?
7. Fit and finish: Does the product look and feel like a quality product?

Service Quality

1. Tangibles: Do the physical facilities, equipment, and appearance of personnel imply quality?
2. Reliability: Will the accounting work be performed dependably and accurately?
3. Competence: Does the repair shop staff have the knowledge and skill to get the job done right? Do they convey trust and confidence?
4. Responsiveness: Is the sales staff willing to help customers and provide prompt service?
5. Empathy: Does the bank provide caring, individualized attention to its customers?

differ in quality. Then the relative importance of the emerging dimensions needs to be assessed.

Two efforts to generate a set of dimensions which will apply across several product classes illustrate the complexity of the "perceived quality" concept and provide a useful point of departure when developing scales in a given context.

DIMENSIONS OF PERCEIVED QUALITY: THE PRODUCT CONTEXT

With respect to product quality, Harvard's David A. Garvin suggests seven product-quality dimensions, as summarized in Figure 4–5.[7] The first, *performance*, involves the primary operating characteristics of the product. For an automobile, these could include acceleration, handling, cruising speed, and comfort. Thus, there are dimensions within dimensions. Further, customers often will differ in their attitude toward performance attributes. Fast acceleration would be highly valued by some, but considered irrelevant (or even a liability) by others more concerned with economy and comfort.

The second, *features,* are secondary elements of products, such as the type of VCR remote control, or the inclusion of a map light in an automobile. In addition to being important tie-breakers when two products seem similar, features can also provide signals that the firm understands the needs of product users.

The third, *conformance with specifications* (the absence of defects), is a traditional, manufacturing-oriented view of quality. Reducing the percentage of defects, especially at the customer site, has been one of the reasons for the success of Japanese automakers in the past.

The fourth, *reliability*, is the consistency of performance from each

---

Redefining Quality in Automobiles

Throughout the 1970s and 1980s the primary quality objective was to be defect free—the J. D. Power rating based upon customer experience provided a credible measure.[8] By this measure the Japanese cars were far superior to competitors. However, in the late 1980s, U.S. cars begin to catch up—to the point that the differences were of reduced consequence. The problem for U.S. car makers is that the Japanese car makers changed the quality game.

The new quality concept is called *miryokuteki hinshitsu* (literally meaning "things gone right")—it now takes for granted defect-free manufacturing and changes the focus to making cars that fascinate and delight. The idea is to engineer extraordinary levels of look, sound, and feel into cars, the cumulative effect of which will alter the personality of the car. The whole concept is implemented with the *kaisen* (continuous improvement) philosophy, a research-based concern with customer desires and strong conceptualizations of what a car's personality should be.

Examples of refinements and improvements intended to affect quality are not hard to find. Nissan developed the first computer-driven "active suspension" to smooth the ride of the Infiniti without compromising handling and placed a counterbalanced lid on its Maxima to help people juggling groceries. Lexus developed its soft, comfortable feel based upon extensive human engineering. The Miata was designed to have the look and feel of classic sports cars. Honda developed the same feel for all the buttons and a system to reduce vibration. Of course, by themselves each of these innovations are modest. However, together with many other improvements, they can really change the totality of the product.

purchase to the next, and the "up time"—the percentage of time that the product delivers an acceptable performance. Tandem Computers developed the concept of several computers working in tandem so that if one failed, the only impact would be the slowing of low-priority tasks. Tandem enjoyed having a unique product because IBM was committed to an operating system which could not be easily adapted to the Tandem concept. Tandem's marketing effort focuses on large-scale users of computers for which system down time is particularly undesirable, such as on-line banking terminals, stock exchanges, and retail on-line computer operations.

The fifth characteristic, *durability*, reflects the economic life of the product: How long will it last? Volvo has long positioned its cars as durable—it once showed pictures of 10-year-old Volvos still running well.

Garvin's sixth characteristic, *serviceability*, reflects the ability to service the product. Caterpillar Tractor created a strong point of differentiation with its parts-and-service organization, together with a service culture. The firm's goal was "24-hour parts service anywhere in the world." Its competitive advantage in service was sustainable in that competitors had neither the dealer network nor the scale (total sales volume), even if they did invest to create the systems technology and organizational culture.

The seventh characteristic is *fit and finish*, which refers to the appearance or feel of quality. For automobiles it might be reflected by the paint job and fit of the doors. "Fit and finish" is important because it is a dimension which customers can judge. The assumption usually is that if the business cannot produce good "fit and finish" products, the products probably will not have the other, more important, quality attributes.

DIMENSIONS OF PERCEIVED QUALITY:
THE SERVICE CONTEXT

Different dimensions emerge in service businesses. One series of studies of customer perceptions of service quality by Parasuraman, Zeithaml, and Berry, involving industries such as appliance repair, retail banking, long-distance telephone, securities brokerage, and credit cards resulted in the identification of several service dimensions which included the eight shown in Figure 4–5.[9]

Several of the dimensions are similar to those in the product context. The *competence* of the service people roughly corresponds to the *per-*

formance dimensions in product quality, as it concerns the delivery of the basic function being sought by the customer. The *tangibles* dimension is similar to *fit and finish* in product quality, in that their importance is in large part their role in acting as signals of competence/performance.

Reliability takes on a different flavor in a service context because of the people involved. The service necessarily changes with the specific service person, customer, or day involved. Standardizing a service operation provides an effective approach to achieving reliability that often is easily communicated to customers. Consider the operations of fast-food and hotel chains. The most successful ones have relied upon a very standardized facility and operating system.

The other five dimensions relate to the personal interface between the service firm and the customer. Including *responsiveness*, *empathy*, *credibility*, *trustworthiness*, and *courtesy*, they center mainly around the nature of the interaction between the customer and the service people. Was the customer treated with respect? Did the firm show that it really cared about the customer?

DELIVERING HIGH QUALITY

The first step toward improving perceived quality is to develop the capability of delivering high-quality levels. It usually is wasteful to attempt to convince customers that quality is high when it is not. Unless the use experience of customers is consistent with the quality position, the image cannot be maintained.

Of course, the delivery of high quality will depend upon the context. The key at Xerox when they turned around the quality of their firm in the late 1970s was product design—designing products which were inherently more reliable (even if turbo speed was sacrificed). In contrast, a bank improved quality by focusing upon the interaction of its people with the customers. In studies done on achieving quality, the following seem constantly to appear.

Commitment to Quality. Achieving and maintaining quality over time is difficult. If quality is not elevated to a top priority for the organization, it is impossible to achieve. The mission of Nordstrom, Federal Express, and Honda, as reflected in what they say and what they do, is to deliver quality. It is not just given lip service. They do not compromise.

A Quality Culture. The quality commitment needs to be reflected in the culture of the organization, its norms of behavior, its symbols, and

Quality at Sheraton

A team of two dozen people developed a service-improvement program at Sheraton labeled The Sheraton Guest Satisfaction System.[10] The system involves:

- **Employee Goals:** Be friendly, acknowledge guests' presence, answer guests' questions, and anticipate guests' problems and needs.
- **Hiring:** Responses to videos of incidents help select people who really empathize with others.
- **Training:** A series of training programs include role-playing to help trainees learn to handle situations of various sorts.
- **Measurement:** Quarterly reports are based on guest questionnaires which rate factors (such as bed comfort and lighting) as well as interactions with employees.
- **Ongoing meetings:** Performance is assessed, problems are corrected, and improvements are developed.
- **Rewards:** Ten percent of the top-performing and most-improved hotels each quarter become members of the Sheraton's Chairman's Club and are eligible for prizes. In addition, each hotel has its own employee-recognition programs.

Sheraton continued its advertising theme "Little things mean a lot" while the program was taking hold. Only when it feels that the service quality has achieved a sufficient level of performance and reliability will it go ahead with plans to announce the "new" Sheraton.

its values. When there is a trade-off to be made between quality and cost, quality wins. It is an easy decision. There are plenty of role models in the organization and its heritage to show the way.

Customer Input. Customers ultimately define quality. Managers too often are mistaken in their assumptions about what customers believe is important. At General Electric, appliance division managers overestimated the importance of workmanship and features to consumers, and underestimated the importance of the ease of cleaning and appearance. And credit-card customers were much more concerned with security features and liability for lost cards than managers thought.

The need is to obtain accurate and current customer input. The exposure of managers to customers on a regular basis is one approach. IBM assigns top managers to accounts, Radio Shack has an "adopt a store" policy which requires that executives spend time in a retail outlet, and Disneyland has it managers go on stage in the park on a regular basis.

Another approach is to employ focus groups, surveys, and experiments. L. L. Bean, the famous mail-order purveyor of outdoor apparel and equipment, conducts regular customer-satisfaction surveys, and holds group interviews, to track customer perceptions of the quality of its own and its competitors' products and services. The company also tracks all customer complaints, and asks customers to fill out a short, coded questionnaire to explain reasons for returning merchandise. Too, a major Japanese bank has a person with the responsibility of providing a summary each day of problems that customers encountered and complained about.

Measurement/Goals/Standards. The difference between paying lip service to quality and actually achieving it is often to have goals which are measureable and tied into the reward system. If the quality goal is too general, it can too easily become ineffectual. The resulting goals and standards should be understandable and prioritized. Too many goals without a set of priorities can be as self-defeating as no goals at all.

Allow Employee Initiative. The Japanese have shown that employees, working in teams, provide a very effective approach to quality improvement. Employee groups not only are sensitive to problems, but also are in a position to implement and support solutions.

Another perspective comes from the Zeithaml et al. research stream.[11] A key finding of theirs was that service quality problems often were caused by employees' lack of control over the delivery of service quality. Some felt, for example, that they lacked flexibility in dealing with customers, and thus blamed problems on the system rather than on themselves. Firms would attempt to regulate quality via a "by-the-book" approach rather than through a "by-the-customer" approach.

Customer Expectations. Perceived quality can also be deficient because expectations are too high. Holiday Inn developed a "No surprises" advertising campaign after learning that customers really valued consistent quality with no unpleasant surprises. The problem was that (as operations managers correctly predicted) a zero-defect operation simply is unattainable. The campaign served to raise customer expectations above those delivered.

SIGNALS OF HIGH QUALITY

Achieving high quality is not enough; actual quality must be translated into *perceived* quality. In most situations the dimensions of quality that are most critical also are the most difficult to judge. A car buyer may feel that durability is a key attribute, but will not have a good way to judge durability. With effort, information might be garnered from *Consumer Reports,* or from users, about experience with the firm's product in prior years. But for many the time and effort required might be a barrier, and the value of knowing about last year's model may not prove relevant. The solution is to look for some signal or indicator of that dimension. For example, if a model has offered a longer warranty, the customer can reason that the firm must have such confidence in the product that they are willing to stand behind it.

In the service-quality set of dimensions the most important to a customer usually will be the competence of the service provider. A surgeon, automobile mechanic, loan officer, lawyer, carpet layer, or check-out person should first be competent. Mistakes in judgment or in execution can cause inconvenience, or even injury. However, the customer lacks the ability to judge competence. As a result, seemingly trivial but observable characteristics are relied on. The neatness of the waiting room and number of patients might suggest the quality of a physician. Likewise, the appearance of service personnel can be an indicator of their professionalism. Note the advertisement for Bekins shown in Figure 4–6. Who would you select as your mover?

A consumer products company developed a "better" window cleaner which was essentially colorless. However, in use tests this "improved" product did not do well against the established cleaner—until the new product was tinted blue. Its evaluation then increased markedly, and the firm had a winner. The color of the product made the difference: A colorless product lacked credibility.

Research has shown that in many product classes a key dimension which is visible can be pivotable in affecting perceptions about more "important" dimensions which are difficult, if not impossible to judge. For example:

- Stereo speakers: Larger size means better sound.
- Detergents: Suds mean cleaning effectiveness.
- Tomato juice: Thickness means quality (though not in fruit-flavored children's drinks).
- Cleaners: A scent such as lemon can signal cleaning power.

FIGURE 4–6 Signaling Quality

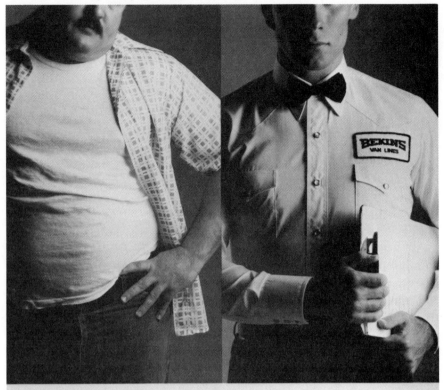

Which outfit would you trust to move your exhibit?

You wouldn't choose a carrier strictly on the appearance of its people. Yet, it is a good indication of a carrier's attitude toward service, its expectations of its people and its understanding of your needs.

At Bekins we do everything possible to put your mind at ease. Neat, uniformed trade show handlers are just the beginning.

Only experienced display and exhibit specialists get to wear the Bekins uniform. They're professionals who understand the concerns, constraints and logistics involved in managing an exhibit.

Bekins' trade show experts will handle the entire job. They'll arrange scheduling, pick-up and delivery, storage between shows, and help you comply with local regulations and drayage rules anywhere in the U.S. or the world.

Our people will also be on the site to supervise. And they'll stay there until you're satisfied.

Even our trade show fleet is different. It's used exclusively for transporting exhibits and displays, unlike most other carriers.

Bekins' trade show experts can also help you plan an entire year's program in advance, including scheduling and a firm annual budget. We'll even custom engineer a system to meet your specific needs.

There are a lot more reasons why Bekins looks better than all other carriers, and why we should be your choice. Let us custom design a proposal for you. Send for our free trade show Logistics Analysis Kit. Write: Bekins Trade Show Service, High Technologies Division, P.O. Box 109, La Grange, IL 60525. Or call toll free: **1-800-451-3989.** In Illinois: **1-312-547-3113.**

BEKINS
High Technologies Division

Courtesy of Bekins, High Technology Division.

- Supermarkets: Produce freshness means overall quality.
- Cars: A solid door-closure sound implies good workmanship and a solid, safe body.
- Orange juice: Fresh is better than refrigerated, which is better than bottled. Bottled is followed by frozen, canned, and (finally) dry product forms.

In addition to information about a brand's product features (termed *intrinsic cues*) there are a host of other brand associations—such as the amount of advertising used, the brand name, or the price (termed *extrinsic cues*)—that can influence perceived quality.

The amount of advertising supporting a brand can signal that the firm is backing the brand, which logically implies it must be a superior product. One laboratory study of athletic shoes and refrigerated entrees found that the perceived quality of newly introduced brands was influenced by a knowledge that heavy advertising was supporting the new entry.[12]

Another signal is the brand name. The discussion here has focused on the impact of perceived quality upon the brand name. However, there also is a link in the reverse direction: Customers have been shown to develop perceptions of quality based on the brand name. Brand-extension research clearly shows that a brand name can affect quality perceptions when that brand name is attached to a different product class.

The Radisson Hotel found that pizza, offered as part of room service, was not a popular room-service item. However, it observed a large quantity of pizza boxes in the trash, indicating that their guests were going outside for pizza. When they put a card in the rooms indicating that guests could order "Neapolitan" pizza, and gave a telephone number different from room service, sales took off. Hotel room service obviously was a signal for inferior pizza, whereas an Italian name, which distanced it from the hotel, made a big difference even though (or maybe because) it was not an established pizza name.

PRICE AS A QUALITY CUE

One variable that can be an important quality cue is price. An analysis of 36 studies, most of which involved frequently purchased, relatively low-priced consumer products, showed that price was consistently found to be a strong quality cue, nearly as strong as the brand name.[13] The classic story is that Chivas Regal was a struggling brand until it decided to raise its price to be dramatically higher than competitors'. Its sales then took off. Price clearly became a quality cue, as the product itself was not changed.

The relevance of price as a quality cue will depend on other cues available, the individual, and the product involved. Price will tend to be relied on as a quality cue when other cues are not available. When intrinsic cues (such as speaker size or a car-door slam) are available, or extrinsic cues (such as a brand name), people will be less likely to rely on price.

Individuals differ in their reliance on price as a quality cue. If a person lacks the ability or motivation to evaluate the quality of a product, price will be more relevant. Consider a raincoat, for example. Some will be knowledgeable enough to detect differences in material and tailoring. Others will tend to rely upon other cues, including price. Individuals also differ with respect to their value of quality. Some will consider the prestige or worth of a high-priced brand to be of value, and others will not.

The use of price as a quality cue will differ across product classes. Product classes which are difficult to evaluate are more likely to have price as a quality cue. For example, research has shown that price tends to signal quality in wine, perfume, and durables. Further, product classes with little price variation provide correspondingly few quality signals. A customer will not attribute much quality difference from a few cents' difference in price.

Price will be more relevant as a quality cue when there are more differences in perceived quality across product classes. In a classic study, Leavitt asked respondents to select between pairs of brands in four low-priced consumer product categories when the only information was the price.[14] Two involved product classes, cooking sherry and moth flakes, were considered to have far fewer quality differences between brands than razor blades and floor wax. The percentage of respondents that selected the higher-priced brand was related to the perceived difference in quality. It was 57% and 30% for the two heterogeneous product classes, and 24% and 21% for the others.

PIMS research shows that the relationship between relative perceived quality and relative price association is a two-way street.[15] A higher price, on average, leads to higher relative perceived quality. This relationship is consistent with the notion that, in the absence of complete information, price is used as a signal of quality. Another explanation, however, is that firms able to charge a higher price are more willing and/or able to take the steps to improve product quality—be they costly, risky, or involving high initial expenditures.

Making Perceptions Match Actual Quality

It can be frustrating to realize that achieving high levels of quality is not enough. Customer perceptions must be created or changed—but how? How can enhanced quality be communicated? One way is to manage signals of quality, such as price levels, or the presentability of employees or facilities. Each one of these can provide cues to customers.

Another way is to simply communicate a quality message. The problem in this case is that customers are used to hearing people say "We are the best." In fact, in most cases this claim is considered by the law and customers alike as harmless puffery. It takes, for example, five years in the automobile industry for quality changes to be so perceived as to be reflected in purchases. The challenge is how to add credibility by, say, explaining why quality is superior; by offering guarantees; or by using external measures.

A quality claim will be more credible if customers know on what it is based. Thus, an insurance firm can explain how a computer system enables them to respond faster and more accurately to customer needs. A machine tool firm can explain how a new plant enables them to generate equipment with higher tolerances, and how a testing program clearly makes sure that the process will generate good quality. But the argument must be understandable and persuasive.

A meaningful guarantee can provide convincing support for a quality claim. Thus, a restaurant serves lunch within 10 minutes, or the meal is free. The "Bugs" Burger Bug Killers will refund the fee if there is dissatisfaction (or a recurrence) during a 12-month period. Further, in the case of hotel clients, if a guest spots a pest, the firm will pay the guest's current bill, and a future one. An effective guarantee should be:

- Unconditional: Nordstrom department stores are legendary for taking back items that they never carried.
- Easy to understand: It should be clear.
- Easy to invoke: The Procedure should be simple and require a minimum of effort.
- Meaningful: It is of little help to get a small postage fee back if an important piece of mail gets lost.

FIGURE 4–7 Exploiting an Independent Survey

LOOK WHAT HAPPENS WHEN YOU PUT THE CUSTOMER FIRST.

J.D. Power & Associates	J.D. Power & Associates	J.D. Power & Associates
1987	**1988**	**1989**
CUSTOMER SATISFACTION INDEX™	CUSTOMER SATISFACTION INDEX™	CUSTOMER SATISFACTION INDEX™
1. Acura	1. Acura	1. Acura
2. Honda	2. Mercedes	2. Mercedes
3. Mercedes	3. Honda	3. Honda
4. Toyota	4. Cadillac	4. Toyota
5. Mazda	5. Toyota	5. Cadillac
6. Subaru	6. Lincoln	6. Nissan
7. Cadillac	7. BMW	7. Subaru
8. Nissan	8. Volvo	8. Mazda
8. Jaguar	9. Mazda	8. BMW
10. Mercury	9. Audi	10. Buick
11. BMW	11. Subaru	11. Plymouth
11. Lincoln	12. Nissan	12. Audi
		12. Volvo

Since we first introduced Acura automobiles three years ago, we've kept one simple philosophy: put the customer first. An idea whose time has obviously come again. Because, for the third year in a row, Acura automobiles and dealers have been ranked the most satisfying in America, among all automakers, by the people most qualified to judge them...their owners. Which brings us to another old saying...the customer is always right.

ACURA
Precision crafted performance.

An effective guarantee not only provides customer credibility, but can set clear standards to employees and encourage a customer-focus culture. It can also provide feedback: At least a small percentage of customers inevitably will be dissatisfied and invoke the guarantee. Thus, a meaningful measure over time can be obtained of not only the quantity of complaints but their nature.

An outside, unbiased confirmation of quality claims also can provide needed credibility. Hewlett-Packard advertised its No. 1 standing in the Datapro customer independent surveys over five years. The survey measures customer perceptions of computer manufacturers regarding six key service and support categories, including maintenance effectiveness, maintenance responsiveness, troubleshooting, documentation, education, and software support.

An influential measure in the automobile industry is the J. D. Power survey of automobile buyers one year after they have taken delivery. The incidence of repair is determined. Admittedly this is only one dimension of quality, but, because the statistics are comparable across models, it becomes very influential—and (as Figure 4–7 illustrates) firms that score well are quick to advertise that fact.

QUESTIONS TO CONSIDER

1. Is perceived quality measured? How has it changed over time? Why? How does it compare to competition? How might it be strengthened.

2. Upon what is perceived quality based in your organization? What are the dimensions that are important to the customer?

3. What are the important cues that signal quality to customers? Are they managed so that they deliver the right signal? Could other cues be created?

4. Is the delivered quality adequate? If so, how can that fact be credibly communicated?

5

·

Brand Associations
The Positioning Decision

Apple produced a good computer, the Apple II, but created a great distinction. It made using a computer a "friendly," unintimidating process. Everything at Apple, from its logo to its down-to-earth founders, underscores its uniqueness.

Tom Peters

THE WEIGHT WATCHERS STORY

In 1978 the H. J. Heinz Company bought the Weight Watchers International for $71 million, and Foodways National, which made and marketed Weight Watchers frozen entrees, for $50 million.[1] Two years later they purchased Camargo Foods, a Weight Watchers licensee for nonfrozen foods. In 1989 the Weight Watchers division of Heinz had revenues of $1.3 billion and its operating income was over $100 million, close to the total acquisition price of the three companies. Further, Heinz called the Weight Watchers line its "growth engine for the 1990s."

The acquisition of the Weight Watchers name was an effort to capitalize upon a heightened concern with health and fitness by obtaining a strong association with weight control. The health-and-fitness trend turned out to be a good bet, as it was one of the growth areas of the eighties. Close to 60 million people in the U.S. try to lose weight each year. Further, as the population gets older, the concern for weight control increases.

The Weight Watchers program, founded in 1963, provided a core group of people who attended and/or now attend Weight Watchers classes. In 1988, an average of a million people attended Weight Watchers classes each week in some 24 countries. They spent $500 million in fees and bought nearly one-third of Weight Watchers' frozen-food entrees. Over 850,000 people subscribe to the Weight Watchers magazine. A large percentage of Americans have general knowledge of the system, which includes weekly meetings wherein participants weigh-in and hear lectures on cooking, shopping, and exercise. Most American non-members know someone who has been through the Weight Watchers program.

Of interest to Heinz was not only the program but the weight-control associations that went with the name, along with the health and nutrition links created by the weight-control dietary program. During the 1980s, Heinz exploited these associations by extending the name relentlessly to new products.

They successfully introduced lines of Weight Watchers frozen novelties which grew out of the Chocolate Treat Bar introduced in 1982. The brand was then extended to salad dressings, spaghetti sauces, turkey-based meat products, yogurt, frozen desserts, breads, and snack packets made from dehydrated fruit. Even pizza, ice cream, and Mexican food were not off-limits. By 1989 they had 60 frozen-food items and over 150 non-frozen-food items. Each extension not only took advantage of the Weight Watchers name and associations but reinforced its associations and name awareness as well.

In most of the food categories, notably frozen entrees, the two salient dimensions in the low calorie/health segment in which Weight Watchers was competing were taste and weight control. Gaining a strong, convincing position on either dimension was difficult. Weight Watchers had a lock on the top position of the weight-control dimension against rivals such as Stouffer's Lean Cuisine, Campbell Soup's Le Menu, Armour Food's Classic Lites, and Banquet Foods' Light & Elegant. In the words of Anthony O'Reilly, the CEO of Heinz since 1979: "You can say light and you can say very light and you can say extra light and trimline or slimline, but at the end of the day, Weight Watchers has an authority about it, and a cogency and a simplicity in that if the product is good and tastes good, the consumer will take it."[2]

The problem was that, in the early 1980s, Weight Watchers also had a lock on the *bottom* of the taste dimension—in part because of its association with hard-core dieting and also because its products were of

FIGURE 5–1 A "Feeling Guilty" Ad

PIZZA WITHOUT GUILT

NOW YOU DON'T HAVE TO RESTRAIN YOURSELF FROM EATING THE FOOD YOU LOVE WHEN YOU'RE ON A DIET.

It's here. The last thing you ever thought you could eat on a diet. The food people call "junk." The one they hate to love. It's *pizza.* The hot bubbly kind you

have to tilt your head back to eat. The kind worth burning your mouth for. And since it's made by Weight Watchers, you can eat a whole one *without*

feeling guilty.

Like all 28 of our meals, we make our pizza pie so it will fit into *any* sensible weight loss program.

We twirl our dough thin and crispy instead of thick and soggy.

We don't use a drop of olive oil and no one misses it.

We give you herbs and spices that taste delicious. Instead of cornstarch and fillers that don't do a thing for the flavor. Or the figure. And surprise of surprises, Weight Watchers Frozen Pizza is actually *good* for you. Fresh mozzarella and romano cheese are a natural source of calcium, Vitamin D and protein. The tomatoes in our sauce are ripe with Vitamin C.

Now. The next time you're walking down the street and you happen to get a warm whiff of hot cheesy pizza and your tastebuds start to tingle, what do you do? Do you give in? Do you buy a slice? Do you suffer that bizarre paradox of remorse and enjoyment as you eat it?

No.

You keep walking.

And you don't stop till you get to your freezer.

WEIGHT WATCHERS® FROZEN MEALS. THE TEMPTATION YOU DON'T HAVE TO RESIST.

WEIGHT WATCHERS IS THE REGISTERED TRADEMARK OF WEIGHT WATCHERS INTERNATIONAL, INC. © WEIGHT WATCHERS INTERNATIONAL, INC. 1980

Courtesy of Weight Watchers International, Inc.

inferior taste. Further, since taste was (as ever) subjective, it was difficult to convince buyers that Weight Watchers had improved, especially in the face of a competitor (Stouffer's Lean Cuisine), which had both "Stouffer's" and the upscale term "cuisine" embedded in its name. In contrast, a competitor could attack Weight Watchers with the more objective claim of a "below 300 calorie dinner."

Weight Watchers addressed the perceived taste problem in several stages. First, they improved the product dramatically over the first half of the 1980s by investing in R&D and product testing. As a result, the entire product line gradually became broader and more interesting and, more importantly, of better quality. The quality difference between it and Lean Cuisine shrank noticeably.

Second, the original advertising (illustrated in Figure 5–1) poked fun at dieters who "cheated," and emphasized guilt and failure. It was neither positive nor compatible with a quality food product. A new campaign (see Figure 5–2) proved uplifting and positive. Lynn Redgrave, who had successfully lost weight through Weight Watchers, was featured. The tag line "This is Living" was added.

Third, they changed the package several times, striving to achieve a more high-quality/classy package while still retaining enough of the familiar to maintain the Weight Watchers association. The package that emerged had a red banner with a Weight Watchers signature, and a picture of a food dish on a clean white background. It had a more upscale tone to it and worked better in displays. The old and new packages are shown in the two figures.

Fourth, the successful introduction of frozen desserts in 1983, and other "splurge" products later, helped to neutralize the "hard-core dieter" image of Weight Watchers. It showed that Weight Watchers was not above having fun and enjoying desserts.

The efforts paid off. In 1988, Weight Watchers passed Lean Cuisine, to become the top-selling low-calorie frozen-entree line. A remarkable achievement! Weight Watchers may have benefited from Stouffer's decision to attach the Stouffer name to Lean Cuisine. Lean Cuisine might have been a more credible low-calorie entry *without* the maker's name— which is associated with the Stouffer "red box" line featuring heavier food, often with creamy sauces.

Interestingly, in 1986, Weight Watchers introduced a new line of frozen entrees positioned as the best-quality low-calorie frozen food. It was introduced under the Candle Lite Dinners name, with the Weight Watchers name present on the front of the box but clearly de-emphasized. That line, with entrees like Cordon Bleu, was priced higher than Le

FIGURE 5–2 A "This Is Living" Ad

Courtesy of Weight Watchers International, Inc.

Menu, previously the highest priced low-calorie frozen dinner. Thus the name, the price, and the entree selection all signaled top quality. The theory was that the Weight Watchers name would still provide low-calorie credibility.

The Candle Lite line did not succeed and was withdrawn. The hypothesized reason was that the price was too high for frozen dinners. However, it may be that going that far upscale with the Weight Watchers line was too much of a stretch. Customers were willing to buy into a good-quality, competitively priced entry from Weight Watchers, but perhaps not one so upscale.

Weight Watchers is an example of a brand with strong associations—weight control plus health and nutrition—which were dominant dimensions of a growing, crowded market. Heinz had a vision in 1978 that these associations could be the basis of a sustainable competitive advantage not only in the core frozen-entrees area but in numerous extensions as well. In fact, Heinz plans to triple Weight Watchers' business in the first half of the 1990s, in part by "bringing the Weight Watchers brand to every nutritional event from breakfast to bedtime, both here and abroad."[3]

ASSOCIATIONS, IMAGE, AND POSITIONING

A brand association is anything "linked" in memory to a brand. Thus, McDonald's could be linked to a character such as Ronald McDonald, a consumer segment such as kids, a feeling such as having fun, a product characteristic such as service, a symbol such as the Golden Arches, a life-style such as harried, an object such as a car, or an activity such as going to a movie theater next to a McDonald's. Recall Figure 3–5 showing the McDonald's anchor attached to its associations.

The association not only exists but has a level of strength. A link to a brand will be stronger when it is based on many experiences or exposures to communications, rather than few. It will also be stronger when it is supported by a network of other links. Thus, if the link between kids and McDonald's were based only on some ads showing kids at McDonald's, it would be much weaker than if the link involved a complex mental network involving birthday-party experiences at McDonald's, Ronald McDonald, McDonald's games, and McDonald's dolls and toys. Again recall Figure 3–5 and imagine links connecting the boats that were chained to the anchor.

A brand image is a *set* of associations, usually organized in some meaningful way. Thus, McDonald's is not just a set of 20 strong associations and 30 weaker ones. Rather, the associations are organized into groups that have meaning. There might be a kids' cluster, a service cluster, and a type of food cluster. There might also be one or more visual images, mental pictures that come to mind when McDonald's is mentioned, such as the Golden Arches, Ronald McDonald, or (inevitably) hamburgers and fries.

An association and an image both represent perceptions which may or may not reflect objective reality. Whereas the stage coach often is associated with Wells Fargo, that does not necessarily mean that Wells Fargo is logically or physically any more western than is the Bank of America. An image of competence may be based upon the appearance of a doctor's office and the manner of the staff rather than on an objective measure of the health of former patients.

Positioning is closely related to the association and image concepts except that it implies a frame of reference, the reference point usually being competition. Thus, the Bank of California is positioned as being smaller and friendlier than the Bank of America. The focus is thus on an association or image defined in the context of an attribute (friendliness) and a competitor (Bank of America).

A well-positioned brand will have a competitively attractive position supported by strong associations. It will rate high on a desirable attribute like friendly service, or occupy a position distinct from that of competitors—such as being the only store that offers home delivery.

A "brand position" does reflect how people perceive a brand. However, "positioning" or a "positioning strategy" can also be used to reflect how a firm is trying to be perceived. Thus, "Cadillac is positioned as an upscale car competitive to Mercedes" could mean that Cadillac is trying to be so perceived, and not necessarily that it has succeeded.

HOW BRAND ASSOCIATIONS CREATE VALUE

The underlying value of a brand name often is its set of associations—its meaning to people. Associations represent bases for purchase decisions and for brand loyalty. There are a host of possible associations, and a variety of ways they can provide value. Among the ways in which associations create value to the firm and its customers are: helping to process/retrieve information, differentiating the brand, generating a reason to buy, creating positive attitudes/feelings, and providing a basis for extensions (see Figure 5–3).

FIGURE 5–3 The Value of Brand Associations

Help Process/Retrieve Information

Associations can serve to summarize a set of facts and specifications that otherwise would be difficult for the customer to process and access, and expensive for the firm to communicate. An association can create a compact information chunk for the customer which provides a way to cope. A set of hundreds of facts and incidents about Nordstrom can be summarized by a strong position relative to competitors of Nordstrom on a service dimension, for example.

Associations can also influence the interpretation of facts. A visual image such as the Benedictine monk used to introduce a Xerox copier ("It's a miracle!") provides a context that helps ensure that the desired interpretation is achieved. A high-technology position (HP products are technically advanced) can influence the interpretation of a long list of specifications.

Further, associations can influence the recall of information, especially during decision-making. For example, a symbol such as the Travelers umbrella or the Wells Fargo stage coach will trigger thoughts about the brand or experiences with it that would not be precipitated in its absence.

Differentiate

An association can provide an important basis for differentiation. In some product classes such as wines, perfumes, and clothes the various brands are not distinguishable by most consumers. Associations of the brand name can then play a critical role in separating one brand from another. The personality of Cher, for example, provides a point of differentiation for her line of perfumes. Because the personality of Cher is unique, so ostensibly is the brand that bears her name.

A differentiating association can be a key competitive advantage. If a brand is well positioned (with respect to competitors) upon a key attribute in the product class, such as Nordstrom on service, or upon an application, such as Gatorade and athletics, competitors will find it hard to attack. If a frontal assault is attempted by claiming superiority upon that dimension, there will be a credibility issue. For instance, it would be difficult for a competing department store to make credible a claim that it has surpassed, or even matched, Nordstrom on service. A competitor to Gatorade, for all practical purposes, may have to find an application other than athletic competition. Thus, an association can be a formidable barrier to competitors.

REASON-TO-BUY

Many brand associations involve product attributes or customer benefits that provide a specific reason to buy and use the brand. They represent a basis for purchase decisions and brand loyalty. Thus, Crest is a cavity-prevention toothpaste; Colgate provides clean, white teeth; and Close-Up generates fresh breath as well as serving its more pedestrian purpose. "Miller time" provides a reason-to-buy for Miller beer: a well-deserved reward. Bloomingdale's is fun, and sells high-fashion goods. Mercedes and the American Express Gold card add status to the user.

Some associations influence purchase decisions by providing credibility and confidence in the brand. If a Wimbledon champion uses a certain tennis racket, or a professional hair stylist uses a particular hair-coloring product, consumers will feel more comfortable with those brands. An Italian name and the accompanying Italian associations will lend credence to a pizza maker.

CREATE POSITIVE ATTITUDES/FEELINGS

Some associations are liked and stimulate positive feelings that get transferred to the brand. Celebrities like Bill Cosby, symbols such as the Jolly Green Giant, or slogans such as "Reach out and touch someone" can all, in the right context, be likable and stimulate feelings. The associations and their companion feelings then become linked to the brand. One of the roles of the Charlie Brown characters, now used as the spokespersons for Metropolitan Life, is to soften an otherwise large, impersonal organization and a serious message by linking Metropolitan with Charles Schultz's well-liked characters and the warm, positive feelings that go along with them.

Likeable symbols can also serve to reduce the incidence of counter-arguing where the audience argues against the logic of an advertisement. For example, Chevron, during the oil crises of the seventies, successfully battled the resentment against oil companies only when they told their story using cute cartoon dinosaurs accompanied by cheerful, fun music. It's hard to get mad at cute, funky symbols of the firm and its message.

Some associations create positive feelings during the use experience, serving to transform it into something different than it would otherwise be. Advertising, for one thing, can make the experience of drinking Pepsi seem more fun and driving a Bronco more adventuresome than it would be without the advertising.

BASIS FOR EXTENSIONS

An association can provide the basis for an extension by creating a sense of fit between the brand name and a new product, or by providing a reason to buy the extension. Thus, Honda's experience in small motors makes extensions from motorcycles to outboard motors and lawn mowers plausible. Similarly, Sunkist has an association with healthy outdoor activities as well as oranges that has helped make the brand name fit a variety of products—including fruit bars, soft drinks, and vitamin C tablets. The Weight Watchers story provides another example. In Chapter 9, extensions will be discussed in more detail.

TYPES OF ASSOCIATIONS

What does Sears mean to you? Or IBM? Or the Bank of America? Or Levi Strauss? A considerable number of associations could be relevant to just about anyone. For one person, Sears might mean a trip to the store with Grandfather in an old Chevrolet with a rattling hood. To another, Sears may be associated with a first bicycle and the sense of freedom it generated. To yet another, Sears usually means tires and auto parts and a place that delivers value.

Of course, the manager of a brand will not be equally interested in *all* associations. Rather, he or she will be primarily interested in those associations that directly or indirectly affect buying behavior. Management's interest is in not only the identity of brand associations but also whether they are strong and shared by many, or weak and differ from person to person. A diffuse image involves a very different context from that of a firm image consistent across people.

In the Weight Watchers story, taste and weight control, which could be labeled either product attributes or customer benefits, were the dominant perceptual dimensions. How brands were positioned on these two dimensions became pivotal to brand choice. Developing the associations that drove those positions was the management challenge. Product attributes or customer benefits are an important class of associations, but there are others that can also be important in some contexts. Some will reflect the fact that products are used to express life-styles, social positions, and professional roles. Still others will reflect associations involving product applications, types of people who might use the product, stores that carry the product, or salespeople who handle it. The name, symbol, and slogan are indicators of the brand but also can be important associations as well. They are discussed in Chapter 8.

Eleven types of associations, shown in Figure 5–4, will be discussed in the balance of this chapter: (1) product attributes, (2) intangibles, (3) customer benefits, (4) relative price, (5) use/application, (6) user/customer, (7) celebrity/person, (8) life-style/personality, (9) product class, (10) competitors, and (12) country/geographic area.

PRODUCT ATTRIBUTES

Probably the most used positioning strategy is to associate an object with a product attribute or characteristic. Developing such associations is effective because when the attribute is meaningful, the association can directly translate into reasons to buy or not buy a brand. Crest became the leader in toothpaste by obtaining a strong association with cavity control in part created by an endorsement by the American Dental Association. This association directly drove a market position which hovered around 40% for years.

In many product classes different brands will be associated with different attributes. For example, Volvo has stressed durability, showing "crash tests," and telling how long their cars last. (A discovery that a crash test was rigged was damaging as it went to the core of their association.) BMW, in contrast, talks of performance and handling with the tag line: "The ultimate driving machine." Jaguar, "A blending of art and machine," offers performance and an elegant style. Mercedes, "The ultimate engineered car," emphasizes engineering excellence in a luxury car. Hyundai, "Cars that make sense," provides the price advantage. Thus, all have selected a different attribute/benefit on which to base their positioning.

FIGURE 5–4 Brand Associations

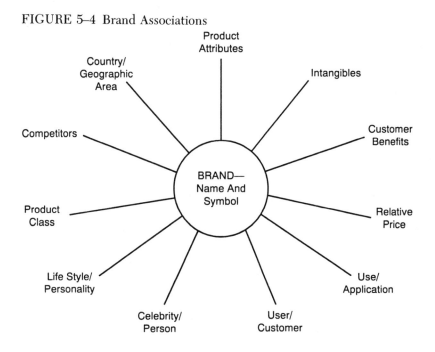

The positioning problem is usually to find an attribute important to a major segment and not already claimed by a competitor. The identification of an unmet customer problem can sometimes lead to an attribute previously ignored by competitors. Brands of paper towels had emphasized absorbency until Viva was successfully introduced stressing durability, customers were irritated with towels that disintegrated when wet. Viva's demonstrations showed their product's durability and supported the claim that Viva "Keeps on working."

It is always tempting to try to associate a brand with several attributes, so that no selling argument or market segment is ignored. However, a positioning strategy which involves too many product attributes can result in a fuzzy, and sometimes contradictory, confused image. In part, the problem is that the motivation and ability of the audience to process a message involving multiple attributes is limited.

The use of several attributes can work well when they support each other. Saratoga Water is blessed with tiny bubbles that consumers early on said made the brand easier to drink. Saratoga packaged these unique globules in a light plastic bottle, to help position the water as a light drink: "Tiny bubbles make Saratoga light. The new plastic bottle makes it even lighter." When the attributes are inconsistent such as Weight

Watchers faced in dealing with taste as well as weight control, the task can be especially difficult.

INTANGIBLES

Companies love to make brand comparisons. Brands engage in shouting matches, attempting to convince others of the superiority of their brand along a key dimension or two. Bayer is faster-acting. Texas Instruments has a faster chip. Lean Cuisine has fewer calories. Volvo has a longer life. Bran One has more fiber than other cereals. A word processor compares its capabilities against competitors' along a list of 30 attributes.

There are several problems with such specmanship. First, a position based upon a specification is vulnerable to innovation. There will always be a competitor suddenly a bit faster, or having more fiber or less calories, or whatever.

Second, when firms start a specification shouting match, they all eventually lose credibility. After a while nobody believes an aspirin firm that claims to be the most effective or the fastest-acting. There have been so many conflicting claims that eventually all have become discounted.

Third, people do not always make decisions based upon a particular specfication anyway. They may feel that small differences on some attribute are not important. Or they may simply lack the motivation or ability to attempt to process information at a detailed level.

Regis McKenna, an advisor to Silicon Valley firms, points out that intangible factors are more effective associations to develop than specific attributes. An intangible factor is a general attribute, such as perceived quality (the subject of Chapter 4), technological leadership, perceived value, or healthy food, which serves to summarize sets of more-objective attributes.[4] Consider, for example, technological leadership. Zeiss sunglasses sell for a large price premium because of the reputation of the firm as a leader in optics technology. This reputation is based upon the activities and opinions of its management, its product line, and its product development over a long time period. Customers perceived Zeiss as a technological leader without knowing the specs of specific models or exactly in what way they are superior.

A laboratory study of cameras demonstrated the power of an intangible attribute.[5] Customers were shown two camera brands. One was positioned as being more technically sophisticated, and the other as easier to use. Detailed specifications of each brand, also given, clearly showed that the easier-to-use brand had the superior technology. When subjects

General Motors Returns to Its Roots

Alfred Sloan had a segmentation vision for General Motors nearly 70 years ago: Five brand names would each focus upon a different segment with a distinct product offering.[6] In the last few decades, this vision has become blurred. Each one of the models has tried to cover all segments. Thus Chevrolet has offered upscale cars, and Cadillac the small, lower-priced Cimmaron. In fact, during the mid–1980s, the five brands were accused of being virtually identical. This lack of differentiation was blamed by some for the loss of market share.

General Motors brought in advertising executive Shirley Young in 1988, in part to lead a return to the basic concept of Sloan. Her prescription was to identify the historical associations of the brand, the heritage, and then create products and advertising which represent contemporary but consistent versions of that heritage. According to Young a brand is a friend, and you don't tamper with what it means to people. Rather than throwing away the established associations, you simply update them.

Each GM brand searched its history to rediscover what it stood for—what differentiated it. Thus, simply put, Chevrolet is to build lower-priced quality cars; Pontiac is to concentrate on performance and a younger market; Oldsmobile should excel in innovative technology; Buick should focus on highway comfort; and Cadillac is to be the standard of luxury worldwide.

The new focus has influenced the GM offering—there is evidence that the strategies of the brands are more distinct. The Chevrolet "Heartbeat of America" campaign is consistent with the heritage of Chevrolet. Buick is focusing upon older customers and emphasizing "distinctive, substantial, powerful, and mature" cars with the theme "Premium American motorcars." Pontiac is offering all-wheel drive, and features excitement. Oldsmobile will offer a new engineering development that projects dashboard readings onto the lower windshield. Cadillac is more consistently upscale, aimed for the older driver.

were shown both brands together, the easier-to-use brand was rated superior on technology by 94% of the subjects. However, when the easy-to-use brand was shown two days after the other was exposed to the subjects, only 36% felt that the easier-to-use brand had the best technology. With the actual specifications blurring after two days, most subjects relied upon the high technology positioning to make their judgment.

Unlike more concrete attributes, an "intangible attribute" such as technology, health, or nutrition is more difficult to counter. If Life cereal is well-positioned on nutrition, it is not as vulnerable as a competitor that provides 10% of daily vitamin needs (who can be upstaged by another providing 20%). Further, a consumer is not burdened with learning and processing detailed information about calories, fiber, and vitamins. The perception that Life cereal is "healthy" is all that he or she wants to know about it, unless something happens to stimulate a review of that perception.

A company name like GE, SONY, H-P, IBM, or Ford is used to cover a wide variety of products and thus does not gain product-specific associations. However, it still can develop such intangible associations as innovation or perceived quality, which can help products (and even brands) under its umbrella. The development of such associations can be tricky, given the product-level associations over which the firm may have limited control.

CUSTOMER BENEFITS

Because most product attributes provide customer benefits, there usually is a one-to-one correspondence between the two. Thus, cavity control is both a product characteristic of Crest, and a customer benefit. Likewise, BMW is good-handling (a product characteristic) providing the customer driving satisfaction (a customer benefit). However, whether the *dominant* association is a product attribute or a customer benefit can sometimes be pivotal. When Crest comes to mind, does the customer think of an ingredient like fluoride and how it works, or is the dominant thought a happy dentist finding no cavities after a child's checkup? When BMW is mentioned, is the visual image that of a car or of a satisfied driver? The difference is important in the development of associations.

It is useful to distinguish between a rational benefit and a psychological benefit. A rational benefit is closely linked to a product attribute and would be part of a "rational" decision process. A psychological benefit, often extremely consequential in the attitude-formation process, relates to what feelings are engendered when buying and/or using the brand.

Snickers is an example of a brand which extended its associations from a candy bar with caramel, nuts, and chocolate to reward at the end of the day, a psychological benefit. Similarly, "Miller time" has been used to associate Miller's beer with a well-deserved break after a day on a construction (or similar) job. Thus, the association of a product class with all its links to calories, sugar, or alcohol is replaced by the concept of a reward for work well done which is linked to positive activities and people.

Table 5–1 shows several examples of how psychological benefits follow from rational benefits but are very different. A research study used the table's examples to test the power of psychological associations.[7] A new-product concept was put forth to respondents with either two rational benefits, two psycholgoical benefits, or one rational and one psychological benefit. The experiment was repeated for computers, banking, and shampoos. For example, a shampoo concept using both benefits was presented as:

> When it comes to shampoo, a man's needs are different than a woman's. That's why now there's Avanti—the first shampoo designed specially for men. Avanti is made with a blend of three essential proteins a man's hair needs most. And its unique formulation has conditioners that are built right in. So now with Avanti:
>
> • Your hair will be thick, full of body [the rational benefit].
> • You'll look and feel terrific [the psychological benefit].

In all three tests the brand concepts were evaluated in terms of the percentage of users who named the brand concept as one of the top three brands. In all cases the pure rational appeal was better than the pure psychological, but also in all cases the combination of one rational and one psychological benefit was significantly and meaningfully superior (average rating of 81% versus 64% and 55%).

In a follow-on study, 168 television commercials were obtained for which a standardized commercial laboratory test had been conducted, and persuasion or effectiveness scores were available. All 168 commercials were judged to incorporate a rational benefit, but only 47 were judged to also contain a psychological benefit. These 47, providing both benefits, had a higher effectiveness index (136 versus 86) than those that relied only on rational appeals.

A conclusion from these studies is that a psychological benefit can be a powerful type of association, even for products like computers. Further,

TABLE 5–1 Psychological Benefits

Product	Feature	Rational Benefit	Psychological Benefit
Computer	Bubble memory	Can't lose your work	Job safety/security
Computer	Touch-screen entry	Easy to use	Feeling professional
Banking	High-yield IRA	Make high return	Financial security/ independence
Banking	Personal banker	Personal service	Confidence/self-image enhancement
Shampoo	Built-in conditioner	Full, thick hair	Confidence about looks
Shampoo	Natural protein	Safe to use every day	Exciting/sexy

SOURCE: Stuart Agres, *Emotion in Advertising: An Agency's View,* The Marschalk Company, 1986.

a psychological benefit will be more effective if it is accompanied by a rational benefit.

RELATIVE PRICE

One product attribute, relative price, is so useful and pervasive that it is appropriate to consider it separately. In some product classes there are five well-developed price levels. The evaluation of a brand in these product classes will start by determining where it stands with respect to one or two of these price levels.

For example, in the beer market there are mainstream premium beers such as Budweiser, Coors, and Miller. The super-premium category, which includes Michelob, Lowenbrau, and Coors Gold, is intended to be perceived as being of higher quality, meriting a higher price. The highest category would include such prestige beers as Henry Weinhard, Herman Joseph, Anchor Steam, Samuel Adams, and some imports, and would have a still higher expected price and quality level. The economy or "price brand" category, including Anheuser–Busch's Busch Bavarian, Stroh's Old Milwaukee, and Miller's Milwaukee's Best, have a substantially lower price, and lack the advertising support of the other brands. At the lowest end are the store brands, such as Brown Derby.

Among general-merchandise stores, the premium ones would be Saks Fifth Avenue, Neiman Marcus, and Bloomingdale's, followed by department stores such as Macy's, Robinson's, Bullocks, Rich's, Filene's,

Dayton's, Hudson's, and so on. Stores like Sears, Montgomery Ward, and J. C. Penney are positioned below the department stores but above such discount stores as K-Mart. Table 5–2 shows a profile of the market entrees in the hospitality industry.

Positioning with respect to relative price can be complex. The brand usually needs to be clearly in only one of the price categories. The job then is to position its offering away from others at the same price point. One way is to relate its offering to a higher price level. For example, Suave is a line of "economy" shampoos which Helene Curtis has successfully marketed at a price substantially lower than competitors'. It attempts to position its quality with the premium shampoos by showing a model saying "When Suave makes my hair look this good, paying more just doesn't make sense." Budget Gourmet shows an attractive entree on a gold plate with the tag line "If price is no object, why not spend a little less?" And Isuzu claims it offers an economy car which performs

TABLE 5–2 Hotels Segmented by Price/Quality

Quality Segment	Competitors	Typical Bath Amenities
Budget	Motel 6 Econolodge McSleep	Two small bars of soap, plastic or paper cups, two towels
Economy	Days Inn Hampton Comfort	Medium bars of soap, plastic cups, shampoo
Midrange	Courtyard Ramada Holiday Inn	Plush towels, some individual toilets
Luxury	Marriott Renaissance Clarion	Baskets with bath gel, body gel, body cream, mouthwash, shoe and sewing equipment, shower caps; oversize towels; some hair dryers
Super Luxury	Four Seasons Hyatt Regency Westin Hotels	Fresh flowers, potpourri, designer soap, glass tumblers, lighted makeup mirrors, terry robes, retractable clothesline, telephone and TV, marble fixtures, heating lamps
Luxury Suites	Clarion Suites Embassy Suites Guest Quarters	Additional sink and vanity in bedroom; suite accommodations

SOURCE: In part drawn from Faye Rice, "Hotels Fight for Business Guests," *Fortune*, April 23, 1990, pp. 265–274.

like a racing car, demonstrating this on a skid pad much as does Porsche with its 944. The positioning is thus against another price point.

Positioning against brands with a higher relative price by upgrading a brand can be tricky. Sears, for example, periodically has attempted to offer more upbeat fashion clothing featuring designer labels. But advertising upscale fashions invariably adversely affects their core-value image: Customers wonder whether they are still the value store. Attempting to offer merchandise competitive with a department store's runs the risk that customers will suspect that Sears *has become* a department store. Worse, the conclusion may be that Sears is an *inferior* department store, rather than the desired conclusion that Sears remains (as usual) a superior-value store.

The premium segment is enticing in many markets because it often represents an area with high growth and high margins somewhat protected from the murderous cost–price squeeze from offshore firms. To be a part of the premium category, a brand has to offer a credible case either that it is superior with respect to quality, or that it indeed can deliver status worth a price premium. One vehicle to help accomplish that positioning is a brand name having "premium" connotations. Thus, the makers of Old Spice licensed the right to use the Pierre Cardin name in order to provide a premium line of fragrances.

Attempts to elevate an existing brand name, such as the Reserve Cellars of Ernest & Julio Gallo, Coors Gold, Maxwell Master Blends, or Candle Lite by Weight Watchers, is difficult. The name itself *means* a lower relative price. Thus, the case that suddenly there also is premium quality or status is just that much harder to make. It is much easier to move a brand down than up. Moving down, however, creates the risk of damaging the existing quality association.

USE/APPLICATION

Another approach is to associate the brand with a use or application. Campbell's soup for many years positioned itself as a lunchtime product and used noontime radio extensively. More recently it has been repositioned as a complete meal. The Bell Telephone Company has associated long-distance calling with communicating with loved ones, in its "Reach out and touch someone" campaign. Coors Beer associates its product with the outdoors, mountains, and hiking, whereas Lowenbrau associates its beer with good friends in a warm social setting.

A study of the coffee market revealed that there were nine relevant use contexts for coffee:[8]

1. To start the day
2. Between meals alone
3. Between meals with others
4. With lunch
5. With supper
6. At dinner with guests
7. In the evening
8. To keep awake in the evening
9. On weekends

In this study there were sharp differences in brand profiles across use occasion (Hills Brothers had a 7% share of breakfast use but only a 1.5% share of the remainder of the day). The major differences were found between AM and PM coffee drinkers.

Products can, of course, have multiple positioning strategies, although increasing the number involves obvious difficulties and risks. Often a positioning-by-use strategy represents a second or third position for the brand, a position that deliberately attempts to expand the brand's market. Thus, Gatorade (a beverage for athletes who, particularly in the summer, need to replace body fluids) has attempted to develop a positioning strategy for the winter months. The concept is to use Gatorade when flu attacks and the doctor says "Drink plenty of fluids." Similarly, Quaker Oats has attempted to position their hot cereal product as a natural whole-grain ingredient for recipes, in addition to its accustomed breakfast-food role.

USER/CUSTOMER

Another positioning approach is to associate a brand with a type of product user or customer. When it works, a user positioning strategy is effective because it can match positioning with a segmentation strategy. Identifying a brand with its target segment often is a good way to appeal to that segment.

The role of a user position can be illustrated by the cosmetics industry in the late 1980s.[9] The dominant firm featured Noxell's Cover Girl line, which, with just over 20% of the market, had a sharply defined image as the makeup for the girl next door. Cover Girl was firmly established as *the* product for wholesome, healthy (and usually blonde) women. Revlon garnered around 15% of the market by being associated with presumably more-sophisticated women. In contrast, Schering–Plough's Maybelline held just under 20% of the market, but was slipping in part because it lacked a strong image. It had relied upon mass marketing—drug stores and discount chains, low price, trade promotion, and new-product innovation in order to maintain their market position. To firm up the brand, it was repositioned as the cosmetic line for the "style leader," putting forth an image of a fashion-forward company with a host of products for chic women. Using the theme "Smart, beautiful, Maybelline," ads showed fashionable women, suggesting what sort of assets their cosmetics truly are —a far cry from the old ads describing the bright colors and chemical composition of its eyeshadow.

Another example of a firm which attempts to find neglected users is Cadbury, with its Canada Dry ginger ale, soda, and seltzer products, and its Schweppes line.[10] Cadbury has targeted the adult soft-drink market, leaving the teen-age market to Coke and Pepsi. Canada Dry ginger ale got a new, cleaner green-and-gold package and the advertising tag line "For when your tastes grow up." The logic is that as people mature, they begin to want a drink that is less sweet—like ginger ale. A raspberry ginger ale was added, to provide an alternative to fruit-flavored seltzers. And Schweppes tonic water benefited from those who might want a nonalcoholic cocktail.

A classic example of a successful user association was the decision by Miller's to position Miller Lite as a beer for the "heavy" beer drinker—the one who wants to drink a lot but dislikes that filled-up feeling. In contrast, previous efforts by others to introduce low-calorie beers were dismal failures, partly because they emphasized the low-calorie aspect. One even claimed its beer had fewer calories than skim milk, and another featured a thin light-beer personality.

A problem with a strong association, particularly a strong user association, is that it limits the ability of a brand to expand its market. For example, Club Med caters to couples—in fact, the average age of its guests is 37.[11] Further, six Club Med villages are oriented to kids and even have baby clubs. Yet the Club Med image is of a resort for physically fit singles wanting to meet other young singles. The task of expanding the customer base requires convincing those intimidated from exploring that type of resort that it is an appropriate destination for people with children. Thus, their strong image is both a strength and a limitation.

CELEBRITY/PERSON

A celebrity often has strong associations. Linking a celebrity with a brand can transfer those associations to the brand. One characteristic important for a brand to develop is technological competence, the ability to design and manufacture a product. In tennis rackets, for example, a key element of marketing strategy is to obtain endorsements from leading tournament players. Especially in the case of a new racket, the endorsement of a name player is crucial. Prince, now the leading racket company, started with an unusually oversized racket in 1975. The racket did not really become a viable mainstream competitor until Pam Shriver, a prominent touring pro, started using it.

It is most difficult to convince people that your product, whether it be Prince rackets or Nike basketball shoes, is superior in design and manufacture to those of your competitors. The challenge is not only to create a credible argument, but also to get people to listen to it and believe it in the face of similar competitive claims. By contrast, it is relatively easy for people to believe that Pam Shriver uses Prince. She says she does, and in fact since she plays in public the word would get out if she did *not* do what she claims. Further, since so much is riding on her performance, it is obvious that she would not use Prince unless it was superior in her eyes. Of course, the more successful Pam Shriver is, the greater will be her credibility.

In the mid-eighties, Nike faced a challenge from Reebok, who had exploited the aerobics craze to take over first place in the athletic-shoe market.[12] Nike came back with Air Jordans, basketball shoes using air-cushioning technology featuring patented pressurized-gas pockets in the soles ("Pump it up!"). The shoe was a smash success, with first-year sales of over $100 million. Its key was the endorsement of the apparently gravity-defying basketball player Michael Jordan bolstered by his electrifying demonstrations in the Nike advertising.

A person attached to the brand need not be a celebrity. The fabled man in the Hathaway shirt wearing an eyepatch, Betty Crocker, Juan Valdez (Colombian coffee), Mrs. Paul, Mr. Whipple, Mr. Goodwrench, the Maytag repair man, and the Marlboro man have strong identities and characteristics that have become important brand associations. The person need not even be real. It can be a cartoon symbol such as Mr. Clean, the Pillsbury Doughboy, the Keebler elves, or the Michelin tire giant.

There is more control over the associations of a fictional character like Betty Crocker than a real person who will age and change over time. It is much more feasible to have the Marlboro man retain the same associations over a long time period than someone like Bill Cosby, M. C. Hammer, or Jane Fonda. Of course, some symbols like Sara Lee, Colonel Sanders, Laura Scudder, and Famous Amos have become detached from the real people they represent.

LIFE-STYLES/PERSONALITY

If your car were suddenly to become a human being, what kind of person would you expect it to be? Great to have around? Hard to live with? Every person, of course, possesses a personality and a life-style that is rich, complex, and vivid and distinctive as well. But a brand— even a machine such as a car—can be imbued by customers with a number of very similar personality and life-style characteristics.

A study of Betty Crocker illustrates.[13] Research, involving more than 3,000 women, focused not only upon the Betty Crocker image but also upon women's feelings about desserts in general. They found that 90% of the women polled were familiar with the Betty Crocker name. In general, Betty Crocker was viewed as a company that was:

Honest and dependable
Friendly and concerned about consumers
A specialist in baked goods

—but also:

Out-of-date
Old and traditional
A manufacturer of "old standby" products
Not particularly contemporary or innovative

The conclusion was that the Betty Crocker image needed to be strengthened to become more modern and innovative, and less old and stodgy.

Research by Pepsi reported by Pepsi's president Rodger Enrico, involving 17 groups of loyal drinkers of either Pepsi or Coke, provided insights into the personalities of the two brands.[14] Generally, Coke projected a Norman Rockwell–type image of family and flag, and a solid, rural America. Pepsi, by contrast, was considered exciting, innovative, and fast-growing—albeit somewhat brash and pushy. Building on this research, Pepsi decided to exploit and reinforce its image. It therefore moved away from the Pepsi challenge taste-test and returned to the Pepsi generation with a campaign featuring Michael Jackson.

PRODUCT CLASS

Some brands need to make critical positioning decisions that involve product-class associations. For example, Maxim freeze-dried coffee needed to position itself with respect to both regular and instant coffees. Some margarines position themselves with respect to butter. Dried-milk makers came out with instant breakfast positioned as a breakfast substitute, and a virtually identical product positioned as a dietary meal substitute. The hand soap Caress by Lever Brothers positioned itself apart from the soap category, toward a bath-oil product.

Wasa Crispbread was positioned as a high-fiber, low-calorie alternative to rice cakes, Ry-Crisp, and similar products. In order to expand their business, they repositioned as an alternative to bread. Ad campaigns showed the product being used as an open-faced sandwich with attractive toppings.

The soft drink 7-Up was for a long time perceived as a mixer beverage, despite efforts to emphasize its "fresh, clean taste" and "thirst-quenching" properties. An effort was made to reposition the brand as a soft drink, as a logical alternative to the "colas" but with a better taste. The successful Uncola campaign was the result.

COMPETITORS

In most positioning strategies, the frame of reference, whether explicit or implicit, is one or more competitor(s). In some cases the reference competitor(s) can be the dominant aspect of the positioning strategy. It is useful to consider positioning with respect to a competitor for two reasons. First, the competitor may have a firm, well-crystallized image, developed over many years, which can be used as a bridge to help communicate another image referenced to it. If someone wants to know where a particular address is, it is easier to say it is next to the Bank of America building than to describe the various streets to take to get there. Second, sometimes it is not important how good customers think you are; it is just important that they believe you are better than (or perhaps as good as) a given competitor.

Perhaps the most famous positioning strategy of this second type was the Avis "We're number two, we try harder" campaign. The message was that the Hertz company was so big that they did not need to work hard. The strategy was to position Avis with Hertz as major car-rental options, and therefore to position Avis away from National, which at the time was a close third to Avis.

Positioning with respect to a competitor can be an excellent way to create a position with respect to a product characteristic, especially price–quality. Thus, products that are difficult to evaluate, such as liquor products, often will use an established competitor to help the position task. For example, Sabroso (a coffee liqueur) positioned itself with the established brand, Kahlua, with respect to both quality and the type of liqueur. Its print advertisement showed the two bottles side-by-side and used the heading "Two great imported coffee liqueurs. One with a great price."

Positioning with respect to a competitor can be accomplished by comparative advertising—advertising in which a competitior is explicitly named and compared on one or more product characteristics. Pontiac has used this approach to position some of their domestically produced cars as being comparable in gas mileage and price to leading imported cars. Pontiac could attempt to position itself as having improved gas mileage without mentioning the competition, but it would be a more difficult task. By comparing Pontiac to a competitor which has a well-defined economy image, like a Volkswagen Rabbit, and using factual information such as EPA gas ratings, the communication task becomes easier.

COUNTRY OR GEOGRAPHIC AREA

A country can be a strong symbol, as it has close connections with products, materials, and capabilities. Thus, Germany is associated with beer and upscale automobiles, Italy with shoes and leather goods, and France with fashions and perfume. These associations can be exploited by associating a brand with a country.

The fastest-growing segment of the liquor market, imported vodka, is largely driven by country connections. The leading brand, Stolichnaya, has a Russia association. Other competitors have an association with Finland (Finlandia), Sweden (Absolut), and Iceland (Icy). The connection with such countries provides a fresh, crisp, frosty image. The Icy product was embarrassed when word got out that some of the ingredients came from the corn fields of the Midwest.

There can be sharp differences between countries with respect to people's perceptions. A study of TV sets and automobiles conducted in a mid-America city in the mid–1980s illustrates.[15] Respondents were asked to rate models described as being made in one of four countries. For both products, Japan was rated highest on economy, workmanship, and technology, while the U.S. was highest on service, and Germany on prestige. There were differences among the products. U.S. products were higher than German with respect to technology in TV sets, but the reverse was true in automobiles. The U.S. service edge over Germany was much higher in TV sets than in automobiles.

Another study involving 13 products, 21 perceptual dimensions, and 5 countries suggests that the impact of a country will vary sharply, depending upon the context.[16] For example, the French were much more sensitive to country of origin than were Canadians. The French regarded products from France, Japan, and the U.S. as generally superior to those from Canada and Sweden. U.S. products were held in higher regard in Canada and France than in Britain. The impact of the country of origin receded among those who had visited there and thus had firsthand experience. Issues about country associations can get both complex and important as countries attempt to develop global strategies.

QUESTIONS TO CONSIDER

1. Who are the major competitors for your brand, by segment? How is each actually perceived? Identify the two most important competitive dimensions—i.e., taste and weight control for frozen dinners. Graphically place each competitive brand in a two-dimensional chart. Where is each brand attempting to be positioned? Note on the chart differences between positioning strategies and actual positions.

2. Does your brand have any associations that should be exploited, either by solidifying a position in the current product class or by extending into a new product class? Weight Watchers started with weight control and added health and nutrition associations. Are there any associations that should be added to your brand? Consider the 12 types of associations discussed as a starting point.

3. Some associations like the Wells Fargo stage coach serve as a link to other, more useful, associations like reliability and independence. Does your brand now have, or does it need to obtain, such linking associations?

6

The Measurement
of Brand Associations

Far better an approximate answer to the right question, which is often vague, than an exact answer to the wrong question, which can always be made precise.

John Tukey
[Statistician]

THE FORD TAURUS STORY

In December of 1985, Ford launched its Taurus automobile.[1] As shown in Figure 6–1, it had a rounded, aerodynamic look and "feel." This design was a radical departure from the norm, and thus a major risk for Ford.

The car was a smashing success in the upper-middle car segment, which included the Chevrolet Celebrity, the Oldsmobile Ciera, the Pontiac 6000, the Chrysler LeBaron, the Audi 4000, the Nissan Maxima, the Toyota Cressida, and the car that the Taurus replaced, the Ford LTD. During its second year, Taurus's sales hovered around 100,000 units per quarter. In contrast, its prime competitor, the Chevrolet Celebrity, saw its sales, which had been over 100,000 per quarter, fall to 60,000–70,000 per quarter. Clearly, the risk had paid off.

During the early life of Taurus, Ford conducted extensive periodic research on the associations of the model. A description of this research

FIGURE 6–1 A Ford Taurus Ad

Courtesy of Ford Motor Co.

provides insights into how the Taurus won the day. It also suggests how association research can work.

A marketing research firm, Allison–Fisher, maintains a panel of 200,000 nationally representative homes whose occupants are compensated for filling out questionnaires periodically. A subsample of this panel who are both planning to purchase a car in the next six months and are familiar with the cars in the segment are contacted. The perceptions of each car in the segment are obtained from each sample member. For each of the segment cars, the respondent is asked to check those attributes which are descriptive of that car.

Figure 6–2 shows the resulting profile for the Ford LTD in June of 1985, the Taurus six months later, just after it was introduced, and the Taurus again in December of 1987. Clearly, the image of the Taurus was sharply different from that of the LTD from the outset. In contrast to the LTD, the Taurus was regarded as being technologically advanced, sporty, likely to get excellent gas mileage, and designed with young people in mind. However, the Taurus also clearly had major problems. It was regarded less favorably with respect to being a family car, quality, interior room (int room) being a car that will last a long time (lastlong)

FIGURE 6–2 Ford LTD and Taurus Image Profiles

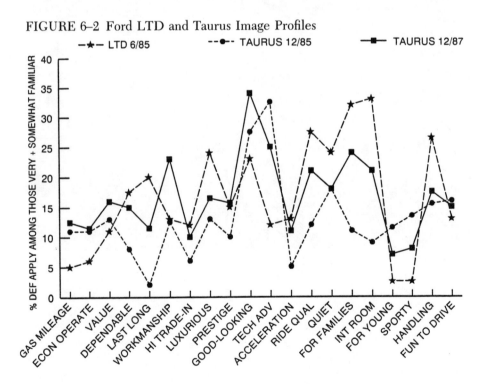

and handling. Clearly these perceived liabilities needed to be addressed.

During its first two years, the Taurus advertising stressed quality *and* workmanship, and attempted to provide facts to demonstrate that the car *did* have interior room and *was* suitable for families. Notice how the disparity between the Taurus and the old LTD position changed during those two years. The Taurus image on "for families," "interior room," "workmanship," "ride quality," "long lasting," and notably "good-look-ing" increased dramatically. On the other hand, the car was perceived as being less "technologically advanced" as it had been at the outset—probably a good omen for Ford.

The Figure 6–2 data are somewhat hard to process as-is, and would be more so were numbers from seven other cars to be added. A solution, termed multidimensional scaling, is to position the cars and the attributes in a two- or three-dimensional space (termed a perceptual map) providing a representation with the following two characteristics: (1) Cars that have similar profiles are positioned close together, and cars that have dissimilar profiles are positioned far apart. (2) Cars that rate high on an attribute are placed close to that attribute, and cars that are rated low on an attribute are placed far away from that attribute.

Obviously the result is not as complete or accurate a portrayal as the profile shown in Figure 6–2. However, especially when several of the attributes are closely related (excellent gas mileage, economical to op-erate, and good value), a two- or three-dimensional representation can be helpful.

Figure 6–3 shows a three-dimensional portrayal of the market prior to the introduction of the Taurus. Each car is represented and located via a triangle, on the floor of the space, attached by a vertical line to a floating name-plate, or "balloon," showing its height. The locations of the cars and their attributes suggest the dimension labels: Prestige/Economy, Import/Domestic, and Unproven/Dependable. Note that the imports, which are all high on workmanship, are clustered together near the Workmanship attribute. They differ, however, on Prestige, which displays a distinct ordering of first Audi, then Maxima, and then Cressida. Note also that the LTD has an extreme position on the Family, Room-iness, Domestic side of the space.

Figure 6–4 shows graphically where the Taurus was positioned both in 1985 and two years later. As was said earlier, when the Taurus entered the market it occupied a very distinct position. After two years it became more of a domestic Family car that was Good-looking but still was con-sidered Sporty and Technologically advanced.

Of interest is the relationship of the Taurus to its competitors. In fact,

FIGURE 6–3 The Upper Middle Segment Before Taurus

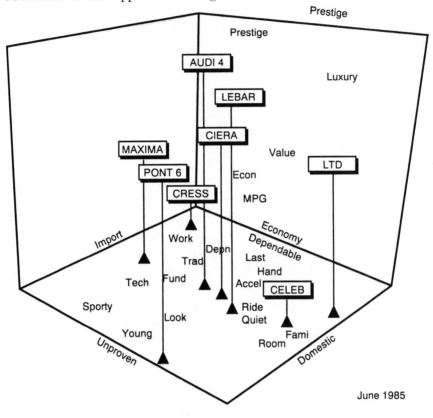

the imports were largely unaffected by the Taurus; they maintained Workmanship and Younger images. However, the new Ford had a substantial impact on the images of the GM cars. Prior to the Taurus's arrival the Celebrity, the Ciera, and the Pontiac 6000 were spread out comfortably throughout the space. Thus, they avoided head-on competition with each other, and appealed collectively to a broad portion of the segment. The Taurus, however, pushed the GM cars closer together, toward the Family and Roominess position. The Pontiac 6000 was particularly hurt.

The Ford Taurus example demonstrates the role of association research, as illustrated by Figures 6–2, 6–3, and 6–4, in developing and implementing positioning strategies. Of course, Ford can afford to spend much more on association research than most firms, because the market in which it is engaged is so huge. However, many of the basic issues of

FIGURE 6–4 The Impact of the Taurus upon GM

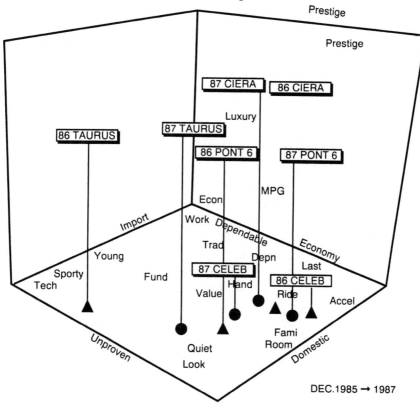

association measurement appear in the Ford example, and thus it should be instructive to others as well. Attributes need to be identified. The perceptions of brands and their competitors need to be obtained. And the position of the brands with respect to attributes and competitors needs to be analyzed.

WHAT DOES THIS BRAND MEAN TO YOU?

The Ford example illustrates the structured scaling approach to determining perceptions of a brand and its competitors. Issues concerning, and techniques for implementing, scaling approaches will be considered shortly. However, first we shall consider less-structured approaches useful for providing a rich, insightful picture of how a brand is perceived.

An obviously direct way to find out what a brand means to people is to ask them. An in-depth discussion of a brand, either with individual customers or with focus groups of up to 10 participants, can be quite helpful. Among questions to be pursued are: What brands are used? Why? What brand associations exist? What feelings are associated with the brand use? What people?

INDIRECT APPROACHES

Although direct approaches toward learning perceptions can be useful, often it is worthwhile to consider more-indirect methods—even some that might appear a bit offbeat. The indirect approaches often are motivated by the assumption that respondents may be either unwilling or unable to reveal feelings, thoughts, and attitudes when asked direct questions.

Respondents may be *unwilling* because they feel the information is embarrassing or private. For example, they may realize that *their* reason for using designer jeans is that the jeans make them feel socially accepted—"in style." They may cope either by not answering or (more frequently) by providing rationalizations that appear logical: They might focus upon quality of workmanship, fit, price, and/or style, even though such considerations are in fact secondary.

Alternatively, respondents may simply be *unable* to provide information as to why they buy certain items because they don't know the real reasons. For example, they simply may not be consciously aware that a feeling of social acceptance was a dominant feeling and motivation. The actual feelings may have been suppressed via a defense mechanism, or might never have arisen—simply because there has never before been a reason to think the matter through.

Many of the approaches to be presented are termed *projective methods*. They address the two aforementioned problems, in part by allowing the respondent to project him- or herself into a context which bypasses the inhibitions or limitations of more-direct questioning. In projection research the goal usually is disguised. Thus, instead of focusing on the brand, the discussion centers upon the use experience, the decision process, the brand user, or off-the-wall perspectives such as considering the brand to be a person or an animal. Another characteristic of projection research is the use of ambiguous stimuli, wherewith there is freedom to project experiences, attitudes, and perceptions. The questions and procedures used tend not to be confining.

Anyone responsible for a brand should seriously consider employing indirect approaches to help understand what a brand means to people. In many cases they should be replicated through time, and across segments as well and should be followed by more structured scaling approaches. It is inexcusable to have to guess at people's perception of a brand. There are many indirect approaches to understanding brand associations. Figure 6–5 shows nine we will here discuss.

FREE ASSOCIATION

Word association is an effort to bypass the inhibiting thinking process of the respondent. The procedure is to have a list of objects consisting of, or including, brand names. The respondent is asked to provide the first set of words that come to mind. The key is to avoid thinking or evaluating but rather to generate words and thoughts as fast as they arrive. Although these can be written down by the respondent, an oral response is often better at capturing spontaneous thoughts. The word

FIGURE 6–5 Determining Brand Meanings

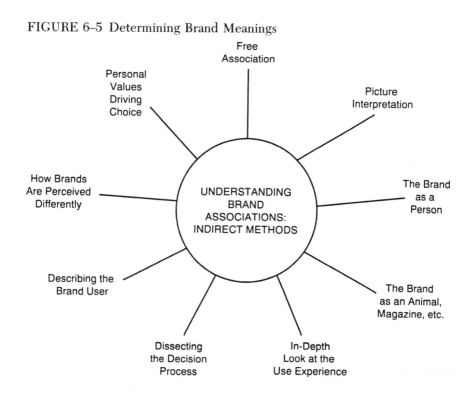

association task can be followed with a discussion of why a certain association emerged.

This technique is particularly good for getting reactions to potential brand names and slogans. For example, Bell Telephone found that "The System Is the Solution" triggered negative "Big Brother is watching you" reactions among some people.

The result of a word association task often is hundreds of words and ideas. To evaluate quantitatively the relative importance of each, a representative set of the target segment can be asked to rate on a five-point scale how well the word fits the brand, from "fits extremely well" to "fits not well at all."

For perspective, it is useful to conduct the same associative research on competitive brands. When such a scaling task was performed on words generated from a word association task for McDonald's, the strongest associations were with the words Big Macs, Golden Arches, Ronald, Chicken McNugget, Egg McMuffin, everywhere, familiar, greasy, clean, food, cheap, kids, well-known, French fries, fast, hamburgers, and fat. In the same study, Jack-in-the-Box had much-lower associations with the words everywhere, familiar, greasy, and clean, and much-higher associations with tacos, variety, fun, and nutritious.

A variant of word association is sentence completion. The respondent is asked to complete a partial sentence such as:

- "People like the Mazda Miata because. . . ."
- "Burger King is symbolized by. . . ."
- "A friend of yours has just bought his first car. He asks you what he should do about getting insurance for it. You reply—"You should. . . ."[2]

Here again the respondent is encouraged to respond with the first thought that comes to mind.

PICTURE INTERPRETATION

Another approach is to have respondents interpret a scene presented in which the product or brand is playing a role. For example, in one study respondents were shown the view of a highway from the driver's perspective behind the wheel of a particular car, and asked to put themselves in the scene. Other respondents did the same for another brand. In both cases the picture had the capacity to elicit feelings associated with driving, such as showing assertiveness, power, or social status. In yet another study, a sketch was shown of a man reading a particular catalog, his wife standing nearby and making a remark. The respondent was asked to indicate what comment the wife was making.

Still another study gave respondents two scenarios.[3] One involved a break after a daytime hike on a mountain, while the other was during a small evening barbecue with close friends. During the scene the beer served was either Coors or Lowenbrau. Respondents were asked to project themselves into the scene and indicate on a five-point scale the extent to which they would feel "warm," "friendly," "healthy," and "wholesome." The study was designed to test whether the advertising of Coors and Lowenbrau had established associations with their use contexts—Coors with hiking, wholesomeness, and health, and Lowenbrau with a barbecue-type setting, friends, and warmth. The results showed that Coors was evaluated higher in the mountain setting and Lowenbrau in the barbecue setting, as expected, but that the other (word) associations were not sensitive (related) to the setting. Coors, for example, in the hiking context was higher on the "warm" and "friendly" dimensions, as well as on "healthy" and "wholesome."

The use of a picture is one way to allow respondents to express how they really feel by using the characters in the scene as vehicles to communicate their own attitudes and feelings. It might be awkward to admit feeling a sense of power or prestige when driving a BMW, but there is no problem in attributing these feelings and attitudes to an ambiguous, unnamed character. Further, attitudes and feelings might emerge of which a respondent was not consciously aware.

IF THIS BRAND WERE A PERSON

Joseph Plummer, a former research director of Young & Rubicam, indicates that there are three components to a brand image: product attributes (Tang is an orange-flavored powder, containing vitamin C, that comes in a jar), consumer benefits ("lemon-fresh" Pledge polishes furniture and repels dust), and brand personality.[4] A brand might be characterized as being modern or old-fashioned, lively or dull, conventional or exotic. He argues that for many product classes brand personality is a key element in understanding brand choice.

In one study conducted by Y&R, respondents were asked to select from a set of 50 "personality related" words and phrases those they would use to describe each of a set of brands. One test of this technique demonstrated that various brands were perceived very differently. A total of 39% said that Holiday Inn was "cheerful," whereas only 6% said that Birds Eye was. Forty-two percent applied the "youthful" descriptor to Atari; only 3% applied it to Holiday Inn. Thirty-nine percent described Oil of Olay as "gentle," while no one applied it to Miller High Life. In profile, Holiday Inn was described as cheerful, friendly, ordinary, practical, modern, reliable, and honest, whereas Oil of Olay was described as gentle, sophisticated, mature, exotic, mysterious, and down to earth.

Using research, Y&R developed a campaign for a Swedish insurance company, whose product has associations with accidents and injuries— outcomes to be avoided. A series of humorous commercials showed that most accidents could happen to anyone, and actually are humorous, or at least not really so tragic, if looked at from the "right" perspective. The advertising created a personality of a firm that was approachable, warm, and (most of all) human. Somewhat similarly, Dr. Pepper made great sales progress during the 1970s by creating for itself the personality of an original, fun, offbeat underdog.

Ernest Dichter, the father of qualitative research, routinely used a psychodrama wherein he asked people to act out a product: "You are Ivory soap. How old are you? Are you masculine or feminine? What type of personality do you have? What magazines do you read?"[5] The result can be a rich picture of a brand's associations.

McCann–Erickson has respondents draw figures of typical brand users.[6] In one case, they asked 50 people to draw figures which would represent two brands of cake mix, Pillsbury and Duncan Hines. Pillsbury users were consistently portrayed as apron-clad, grandmotherly types. By contrast, Duncan Hines's purchasers were shown as slender, contemporary women. In another study, McCann asked consumers to write obituaries for two competing food companies. One firm, perceived as female, elicited warm responses: "She'll be missed and can never be replaced." The other was depicted as colder, less accessible, and male: "If we only knew him better."

ANIMALS, ACTIVITIES, AND MAGAZINES

Sometimes, when discussing a brand, people have difficulty in articulating their perceptions. They tend to use obvious, mundane descriptors because that is what they are accustomed to using. A Ford Taurus might be described in terms of obvious characteristics—having an aerodynamic shape and driven by families with young children. But the challenge is to enhance the richness of the responses.

A useful approach is to ask customers to relate brands to other kinds of objects—such as animals, cars, magazines, trees, movies, or books. Questions might be used, such as:

- If Clorox bleach or Tide detergent were animals, what kind of animals would they be? Why? What characteristics of the animals reminds you of the brands?
- If CitiBank and Bank of America were cars, what models would they be?
- If United Airlines, American Airlines, and Delta were magazines, what would they be?

Y&R is an advertising agency which has productively used this indirect approach.[7] In one study, Y&R gave respondents a list of 29 animals and said: "If each of these brands was an animal, what one animal would it be?" They asked similar questions for 25 different activities, 17 fabrics, 35 occupations, 20 nationalities, and 21 magazines. The goal was to obtain customer-created symbols of brands.

The average symbols that emerged were instructive. Oil of Olay was associated with mink, France, secretaries, silk, swimming, and *Vogue*. Kentucky Fried Chicken, by contrast, was associated with Puerto Rico, a zebra (recall the stripes on a Kentucky Fried Chicken bucket), a housewife dressed in denim, camping, and reading *TV Guide*. The result was a rich description of the brand that suggested some associations to be developed and others to be avoided.

THE USE EXPERIENCE

Instead of asking which brand respondents are using, and why, the discussion might focus on the use experience. A discussion of specific past-use experiences can allow respondents to open up, to recall and communicate feelings and contexts that were part of their use experiences. A picture of a brand can thus emerge which is not filtered or summarized.

Ernest Dichter tells about the first assignment that he conducted for Ivory soap decades ago.[8] Instead of asking why they were using a particular brand of soap, he engaged 100 customers in depth interviews, letting them talk in a free associative way about their bathing habits. One finding was that young women would take an unusually thorough bath before going out on a date. This observation and others led him to believe that the pre-date bath had a rituralistic kind of meaning and was associated, in an anthropological sense, with cleansing oneself of past attitudes and feelings. These insights resulted in the theme: "Be smart, get a fresh start with Ivory soap."

Another classic example of insights obtained from a focus upon the use context is the study of people's attitudes toward Saran Wrap, a plastic food-wrap. When Saran Wrap was first introduced in the mid-fifties it was very thin and clingy, which meant it was extremely effective at sealing but also difficult and frustrating to use. The product, which often would stick to itself, engendered a dislike from some so intense that it could not be explained by any rational reaction to the frustration associated with the use difficulty.

A series of depth interviews focusing upon the brand and its use suggested that a segment of the homemaker population hated the role of keeping house and cooking. At that time, prior to the emergence of the women's movement, it was not acceptable to verbalize this intense dislike—indeed, women were even inhibited from admitting it to themselves. Lacking an outlet for expressing themselves, women transferred these feelings onto Saran Wrap. The frustrations with the product came to symbolize their frustrations with their role and life-style. As a result of this study, the product was made thicker and less clingy.

THE DECISION PROCESS

Another approach could be to track a person's decision process. When a decision process is dissected, the influence of brand associations often emerges that may not be a part of someone's summary picture of a brand. The associations might be subtle, such as the use experience of a grandfather, or indirect, such as the nature of who recommended the brand.

Consider the search for a second personal computer for use at home by a user of an IBM personal computer. It starts by finding which clone would be cheapest. A concern with service and back-up leads to mail-order brands (such as Dell) that offer on-site service. An article about the convenience of a portable stimulates the consideration of Toshiba and Zenith. A friend has a Toshiba, while the Zenith is used extensively by the U.S. government. A concern for product obsolescence leads to considering buying a new IBM or Compaq and using the existing computer as a back-up. However, if the primary computer is to be upgraded, then maybe an Apple should be considered, since its graphics capability and ease of use match the application. This process can lead to some deep insights into the perceptions of Dell, Toshiba, Zenith, IBM, Compaq, and Apple.

What Is the Brand User Like?

Joel Axelrod, a prominent market researcher who has been involved in many hundreds of brand-research studies, has said that his experience and experiments have shown that only two questions need to be asked in order to understand customer preference.[9] One, focusing on the brand user, asks how the user of one brand or product differs from the user of another. In particular, how do the needs and motivations of the users of the two brands differ? When the brand user (rather than the brand) is spotlighted, respondents are more likely to provide responses that go beyond a logical rationale for their brand choice. (The second question will be discussed shortly).

The basic question can be framed in many ways, and can involve both open-ended and scaled measures. Respondents can be given a shopping list (including the brand of interest), or a description of activities of a person (including the use of the brand), and asked to describe the person in more detail than provided. The shopping list for one set of people could include one brand or product, and another set of people would get the same list but with another brand. The differences in the profile of the person can be very revealing.

A classic study, conducted when instant coffee was somewhat new and not entirely acceptable, involved a seven-item shopping list.[10] For one group, Maxwell House drip-grind coffee appeared while Nescafé instant coffee was on the companion list. The profiles of the two women were very different. The instant-coffee buyer was perceived as being lazy, a bad homemaker, and slovenly, whereas the woman buying the drip-grind coffee was industrious, a good homemaker, and orderly.

Sometimes richer insight can be obtained by a study of the use of product type rather than brand. In one such study people were shown a crude picture of two women shopping in a supermarket (see Figure 6–6), each pushing a shopping cart.[11] Told that one woman is purchasing a dry soup mix, they were asked to tell a story about her and to describe what she is saying to the second woman (who has never tried a dry soup). They were also asked to tell what the second woman is like. Projected into the stories by the respondents were four main-user profiles or types:

1. *The creative woman:* "The dry-soup user is the good cook, what you call a creative cook, and she creates miracles with these package soups. By adding it to hamburger you can create meat loaf that is extraordinary. The other one just doesn't know the magic some dry soups can create in your cooking."

FIGURE 6–6 Two Women Shopping

SOURCE: From "Dreams, Fairy Tales, Animals and Cars," by Sidney J. Levy, in *Psychology and Marketing* 2, Summer 1985, pp. 67–81, copyright © 1985 by John Wiley & Sons, Inc.

2. *The practical, modern woman:* "This one is a young mother with small children who likes the convenience of dry soup to make easy meals. It's easier to store than cans because she can buy more of it and it offers greater variety in flavors. . . . She is younger, more apt to try new products and experiment."

3. *The lazy or indifferent woman:* "The one on the outside is looking at dry soups because they are easy to reach, easier to carry home from the store than canned. She feels they are easier to fix. She is lazy and bored and takes the easy way out when she is cooking. She likes to shop and get away from the kids. She has five or six that get on her nerves. She is just going to get envelopes and fix a big batch for them."

4. *The underprivileged woman:* "She has to buy it because she has a very large family and these are more economical—the dried are lower in price, three to four cents a serving. The dry-soup buyer says the dry soup is just as good in taste and nutritional value."

WHAT DISTINGUISHES BRANDS FROM ONE ANOTHER?

Recall that Joel Axelrod claimed that two questions provide the key to understanding preference—the first being how brand users differ.[12] The second question involved learning how a brand or product differed from other brands or products. It could be that a perceived difference between brands is the color of the package. Few respondents would say that the package is important to their purchasing decisions. However, it may be a factor nevertheless, and focusing upon the differences between brands allows the respondent to talk about such seemingly irrelevant elements.

One approach is to give the respondent pairs of brands, and ask how they differ. Another approach that is particularly good at generating customer-driven vocabulary is to give the respondent three brand names from a set of brands familiar to him or her. The respondent is asked to identify the two brands that are most similar, and to describe why those two brands are both similar to and different from the third. The exercise could be applied to a second and third group of three brands. The more direct approach would be to ask which brand of a set of two or three is preferred, and why.

FROM PRODUCT ATTRIBUTES TO BENEFITS TO PERSONAL VALUES

The means–end chain model suggests that it is useful to push respondents beyond product attributes and toward consumer benefits and personal values.[13] The concept is that personal values represent the desired end state and should be included. Personal values can be externally oriented ("feeling important" or "feeling accepted"), or can relate to how one views oneself ("self-esteem," "happiness," "security," "neatness"). Product attributes such as "miles per gallon" or "strong flavor," and consumer benefits such as "saves money" or "don't have to wash hair so frequently" represent the means that can be used to achieve the desired ends.

One approach to eliciting a means–end chain can be illustrated by using an airline example. The process begins with a exercise in which consumers are asked to state why one airline is preferred. Consumers are then asked why an attribute such as "wide-body" is preferred. One response might be "physical comfort." The consumer is then asked why "physical comfort" is desired. The answer could be "to get more done." Another "why" question yields a value, "feel better about self." Similarly, the "ground service" attribute leads to "save time," "reduce tension," "in control," and "feeling secure."

An advertising campaign based on the ground-service attribute would then address the consequences ("save time," "reduce tension," and "in control") and value ("feeling secure") dimensions. A mother traveling with children and needing personal service might be presented. The theme is "in control," being able to cope with the situation. The result is a feeling of security that would become a key brand association.

INTERPRETING QUALITATIVE MARKETING RESEARCH

Much of what has thus far been described is qualitative research, often involving projective techniques and small samples. Because it is fast, relatively cheap, and involving to the respondent, it can put managers in close contact with customers vividly and efficiently. Most of all, it provides the possibility of obtaining nonintuitive insights which can lead to improved brand strategy. The key is the interpretation of the research. The following can help guide the interpretation process:

- Be thinking of the bottom line all the time: What is the essence of the brand? Try to find what Dichter calls the soul of the product: What really drives decisions to buy and rebuy?
- Do not constrain the responses. Let them flow. Use ambiguous stimuli.
- Look for what the brand signals. Some foods, for example, signal sophistication, and others blue-collar.
- Look for symbols: What symbolizes the brand? What visual image does the brand generate?
- Look for contrasts. For example, one brand is associated with older men and another with younger women.
- Look at connections. One useful outcome of qualitative research is that one thought can lead to another, sometimes uncovering links which stimulate hypotheses about how preferences are formed.
- As association/positioning ideas emerge, test them by getting reactions from respondents.

SCALING BRAND PERCEPTIONS

A more direct way to measure associations is to scale the brands upon a set of dimensions, as was done in the Ford Taurus example. Scaling approaches are more objective and reliable than qualitative approaches. Less vulnerable to subjective interpretation, they can be based upon a representative sample of customers; the incidence of associations and the relationships among them can thus be quantified.[14]

As the Ford example illustrated, scaling perceptions involves determining perceptual dimensions, identifying the target segment, specifying the competitive set, presenting and interpreting the brand profiles, and presenting and (finally) interpreting a two- or three-dimensional spatial representation of the perceptions. The example also illustrated the value of monitoring the perceptions over time, and of looking at the dynamics—especially when a new brand has been introduced.

There are some additional considerations that go into providing quantitative pictures of a brand image. Several of these issues, assumptions, considerations, and caveats will now be considered.

BEYOND ATTRIBUTES AND BENEFITS

Of course, perceptual dimensions need not be limited to attributes and benefits. Suppose a respondent was asked to express his or her agreement or disagreement on a seven-point scale with statements regarding the attributes of the American Express travel card. For example:
I would consider the American Express card to be:

Widely accepted at top retail outlets
Widely accepted in Europe
Prestigious

The scale could also be applied to obtain profiles of the user of the brand, or for use situations:
I would expect the typical American Express card user to be:

Over 50
Wealthy
Independent
Intelligent

The American Express card is very appropriate for:

Traveling in Europe
Travel-related transactions
Shopping
Dining

WHO ARE THE RELEVANT COMPETITORS?

A basic input to most scaling tasks is a list of relevant competitors.[15] How many should be included? Which ones should be considered beyond the set of clearly identified, close competitors? The answers to two questions often help address this issue.

First, which competitors are considered by customers making purchase decisions? For example, a sample of Mazda convertible buyers could be asked which other cars they considered, and perhaps which other showrooms they actually visited. A Diet Pepsi buyer might be asked to recall his or her last purchase of Diet Pepsi, and whether any alternatives went through his or her mind. Alternatively, the respondent could be asked which brand would have been purchased had Diet Pepsi been out of stock. The resulting analysis would identify the primary and secondary groups of competitive products.

Second, which competitors are associated with the major use situations? A large set of products and use contexts can be obtained by asking respondents to recall the use contexts for Pepsi, for example. One might be with an afternoon snack. The respondent could then be asked to name beverages appropriate to drink with an afternoon snack. For each beverage so identified, the respondent could be asked to identify appropriate use contexts so that the list of them would be more complete. This process would continue for perhaps 20 or 30 respondents, until a large list of use contexts and beverages was generated.

Another group of respondents would then be asked to make a judgment, perhaps on a seven-point scale, as to how appropriate each beverage would be for each use situation. Then, groups of beverages could be clustered, based on their similarity in terms of appropriate use situations. Thus, if Pepsi was regarded as appropriate with snacks, it would compete primarily with other beverages similarly regarded. The same approach would work with an industrial product such as computers, which might be used in several rather distinct applications.

Removing Redundancy:
Identifying Underlying Dimensions

A very large set of relevant scales can emerge from qualitative research. A technique such as factor analysis is used to reduce this set to a few underlying factors or dimensions by combining the words or phrases whose meanings are similar: A brand that is scaled high on one of the "redundant" scales will tend to be rated high on the others as well.

For example, a car dealership might be perceived to differ by the efficiency of repair, the cleanliness of the shop, the friendliness of the service contact person, and the ease of making appointments. When a shop is perceived to be high on one of those four attributes, it will tend also to be high on the others. In that sense, they are redundant and might be combined by a summary construct that might be labeled as "repair service quality."

Identifying the Important
Perceptual Dimensions

Of concern in any scaling study is identifying the most important perceptual dimensions. One direct way of obtaining this information is asking respondents how important each attribute or benefit is to their choice of brands. The problem here is that many respondents claim that *all* dimensions are important to them.

A second approach is identifying which attributes discriminate between buyers and nonbuyers. One study of snack food found that although nutrition and convenience were the attributes rated most important by mothers, "taste" and "kids like it" were better predictors of purchase.

A third way (discussed in Chapter 1 in the context of placing a value upon a brand name) is asking trade-off questions: If you had to sacrifice a low price, high reliability, or a particular feature, which would you give up? Termed trade-off (or conjoint) analysis, this technique provides a sensitive measure of dimension importance to a customer.

A consideration is whether the perceptual dimensions discriminate between brands. If an attribute really discriminates, sets one brand off against another, it might be worth retaining even though it does not seem important according to other measures. There may be something hidden that makes it more influential than it appears it should be. Conversely, if an attribute or benefit patently appears to be important (such as airline safety) but does not discriminate between brands, then it may be of only marginal usefulness.

Natural Groupings

Research International, a major international marketing-research firm, uses a technique (termed "natural grouping") which combines elements of both quantitative and qualitative research. They start with a set of brands or products. Respondents are asked to divide the set successively into subsets. At each split the respondent is asked to describe the subgroups in his or her own words.

Suppose that five insurance firms were to be evaluated by a respondent. (See Figure 6–7.) The group is first divided into two subsets, and reasons are given as to the rationale therefor. Each subset is divided further, until there is no reason to make additional divisions.

FIGURE 6–7 Grouping Insurance Firms

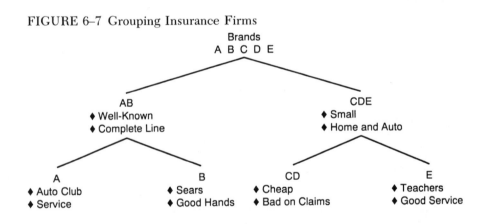

A two- or three-dimensional perceptual map of the population can be obtained from the data: Brands most often grouped together will be close to one another in the space, and brands not frequently in the same group will be relatively far apart. The technique is called correspondence analysis. Further, the associations with each brand can be obtained, and positioned in the space with the pertinent brand (as in Figure 6–3).

THE SCALING TASK

There is always a concern with the validity of the scaling task. Can a respondent actually position beers on an "aged a long time" dimension? There could be several problems. One, a possible unfamiliarity with one or more of the brands, can be handled by asking the respondent to evaluate only familiar brands (although even the degree to which a respondent is familiar with a brand might still be an issue). Another potential problem is the respondent's ability to understand operationally what "aged" means, or how to evaluate a brand on this dimension. Any ambiguity in the scale, or inability of a respondent to use the scale, will affect the validity and reliability of the results.

Yet another concern is with the nature of the scale used. Customers can be asked to simply check whether a certain item is associated with a brand. A relatively easy task, this can lend itself to a large number of dimensions and telephone interviewing. Rank-order data (which brand is the highest on this dimension, the second highest, etc.) generates very sensitive information, but also can exaggerate small differences. A five- or seven-point scale is an alternative that taps the information of the respondent most completely.

DETERMINING PERCEPTIONS BY SEGMENT

Perceptual measurement needs to be done with respect to a specified segment within the context of a competitive set of brands. In the Ford Taurus case the upper middle market segment defined both the set of competitors and the segment.

Much of the time the scaling task should be done for multiple segments. Any relevant segment defined by age, life-style, attitude, or usage may well have different perceptions from others'. For example, the user and nonuser groups quite often differ in their brand perceptions. And these are the very differences that often drive preference and purchase. Thus, in the Ford Taurus case it might be worthwhile to look at the differences between those who are considering or have bought the Taurus and those who have not.

BEYOND PERCEPTIONS

Interest is not only in the associations with the brand, and the position of the brand on the perceptual dimensions, but also on:

1. *Association strength.* How confident are customers about the associations with the brand?

2. *Clarity of the image.* Do customers agree upon the associations with a brand (a clear, sharp image often means a strong, differentiated brand)? Or does the image differ across people? The task of sharpening a diffused image is quite different from the task of changing a very tight, established one. Sometimes, of course, a brand like Pepsi will *want* ambiguity on some attributes—such as the type of people who drink the product. If the Pepsi drinker were too tightly defined, some segments might be alienated.

QUESTIONS TO CONSIDER

1. What does your brand mean to each major segment? What are the word associations? If your brand were an animal, what animal would it be? Similarly, which magazine, car, tree, person, or book? What is really going on in the use experience? What is the soul of your brand—its inner meaning? Which types of people are thought to use your brand? Which ages, gender, and life-styles? How do perceptions of your brand differ from competitors' brands? What values are influenced by your brand (i.e., security, control, self-assurance, etc.)?

2. Who are the competitors of your brand? What is the profile of your brand on the most relevant perceptual dimensions, and how does it differ from the profile of competitor brands? Using what you feel are the two most important perceptual dimensions, position the major competitors in a two-dimensional space. Would it be useful to conduct a quantitative study to confirm that the space is actually as you have drawn it?

7

Selecting, Creating, and Maintaining Associations

A man is known by the company he keeps.

Anonymous

I think of advertising as the engine pulling a train. If you take away the engine the train will roll along for a while, but eventually the train will slow.

Pierre Ferrari
Coca-Cola Foods

THE DOVE STORY

A by-product of World War II was the discovery of a soap-like product, later named the Dove "beauty bar" by Lever Brothers. The product, made from a soap-like molecule without the potentially irritating alkaline element, is a ph-neutral, mild cleansing product. It generates a noticeably different "feel" to the skin when used regularly.

Dove was introduced nationally in 1957. It was positioned as a beauty bar (not a soap) with one-fourth cleansing cream that "creams" skin while washing. The cleansing cream was shown being poured into the beauty bar. The message was that whereas soap dries your skin, Dove creams your skin while you wash. This original positioning with the association of cream is still being used, virtually unchanged since 1957. The claim has been buttressed by a face-test testimonial approach (introduced in

1969), by a seven-day test (1979), and by the replacement of the word "cleansing cream" with "moisturizer cream" (also 1979). However, the basic position remains.

One measure of the strength of the Dove equity is the relative price that it maintains. In 1987 its market share was 9%, but its dollar share was 13.8%, reflecting the premium price that it commanded.

A common belief is that a strong association can be developed in people's minds within a period of years, or even months, especially if a healthy advertising campaign is available. The Dove story illustrates the power of sustained, consistent communication efforts. Dove enjoyed over three decades of advertising showing moisturizing cream being poured into the beauty bar, and testimonials affirming its moisturizer potency. There are many customers who have seen a Dove ad 600 times over 30 years and have had those exposures reinforced through product usage by themselves and others familiar to them. Think of the difficulty of a competitor product trying to take over the moisturizer position: It would be very difficult, even with a breakthrough product.

Dove did introduce a brand extension in the 1960s, a dishwasher detergent to compete with Ivory. The extension has survived, but may have been a mistake. The creamy association of Dove did not help the dishwasher product. Further, although the detergent did provide name recognition over the years, it could not have been helpful to the associations important to the beauty bar.

THE HONEYWELL STORY[1]

Honeywell is a $7 billion firm which has long been a leader in providing solutions to control and automation problems for buildings, industrial process applications, aircraft, and other settings. In most areas it is considered the premium high-quality option.

Honeywell developed an image problem caused by its attempt to be "The Other Computer Company." A commitment was made to computers in the 1960s, in part because computer technology was believed to be important to a core part of their control and automation businesses, and in part because it looked attractive. The effort failed: They could not develop a presence with a critical mass in computers, and in 1986 they began to divest themselves of the business.

The highly visible computer and information systems dominated the image of Honeywell, clouding their association with control and automation. Rather than as a leader in control and automation, they were perceived as emphasizing computers, and computer applications such as information systems and office automation. Further, their computer operation was at best always in the shadow of IBM, and at worst an organization struggling to stay alive. The image of a struggling firm nibbled at the traditional concept of being the premium supplier of control and automation solutions.

By 1982 Honeywell had decided to de-emphasize computers. The advertising campaign that ran from 1982 to 1987 stressed problem solving: "Together we can find the answers." Although not emphasizing computers, this new approach did little to weaken the associations created by the computer business.

In 1988 a campaign was launched to return to the firm's associations with its core—controls. The new slogan, used in a worldwide campaign was "Helping you control your world." A key means for reasserting the control associations was bringing them alive using interesting, vivid applications such as the use of Honeywell control systems to:

- Protect the historic "Treasures of Tutankhamen" exhibits.
- Provide reliable performance, even in space: Four Honeywell components of a control-system module operating in a space satellite for six years were operating perfectly.
- Make airplane cockpits better, safer, and more efficient.
- Control environments from penguins in a zoo to an operating room.
- Control an elevator system.

The thrust toward controls was very different from that of the computer business. The hope was that the link of the Honeywell name with the unsuccessful computer business would be *weakened*.

For Honeywell France, the implementation of the 1988 "back to basics" positioning effort involved a considerable publicity effort. Honeywell had received a contract to provide the advanced and innovative control systems for the Opera of the Bastille, a very visible and controversial project which François Mitterrand proudly inaugurated on July 13, 1989. "Honeywell at the Opera" was exploited with a technical press release aimed at the construction and management press, a general-interest press release, and the entertaining of 50 clients and/or prospects at a special event at the opera.

The Honeywell story illustrates how apparently useful associations with computers and thus advanced technology backfired, resulting instead in weakening the basic association with "top-of-the-line" controls. As we have seen, the solution was to return to the basic associations of control. The use of the opera assignment to gain publicity well illustrates that advertising is not the only approach to managing associations.

WHICH ASSOCIATIONS?

In Chapter 5 a variety of associations which could provide the basis for a brand position were described. In Chapter 6, methods of determining the brand associations were developed. In this chapter, several issues will be addressed: First, which associations? How should a brand be positioned? Second, how can associates be created? Third, some guidelines on maintaining associations are discussed followed by a section on managing disasters.

The selection of the associations will drive all elements of the marketing effort. The importance is particularly relevant in the context of a new product or service. Let us assume that we have a new service concept, a video store which will deliver and pick up videos from a special mailbox attached to the customers' home. Among the possible associations are such attributes as home-delivery convenience, speed, movie selection, catalogue selection, and friendly operators. Which should be the primary and which the secondary associations? Answers are needed to generate the name and symbol, and to design the details of the operations.

Such positioning decisions will likely determine not only short-term success but also long-term viability, because associations need to support competitive advantages which will be sustainable and convincing. For example, in the long run a "friendly, funky" culture may be more difficult to duplicate than home delivery.

The positioning decision for an established brand is complicated by the set of associations already in place. As a result, consideration needs to be given as to which associations should be weakened or eliminated, as well as which should be created or enhanced.

The selection is based upon an economic decision involving the market response to the associations, and the investment and marginal cost associated with them. Basically, a position is needed that will attract a worthwhile market—which could mean either a small part of a large market or a large part of a small market—at a cost that will result in attractive returns over an appropriate time frame. The problem is, of course, that it is not easy to forecast the sales and cost streams that will be associated with any specific positioning decision.

There are guidelines that can help, however: Figure 7–1 summarizes

FIGURE 7–1 The Positioning Decision

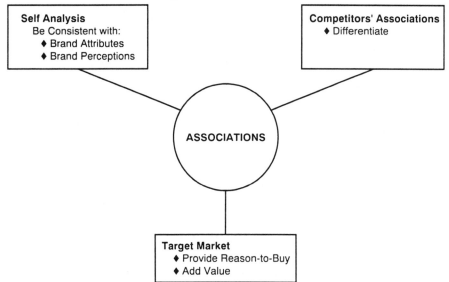

three considerations that can be helpful in analyzing the positioning decision.

SELF-ANALYSIS

Don't try to be something you are not. Before positioning a brand, it is important to conduct in-home blind-taste tests or in-office use tests which ensure both that the brand can deliver what it promises and that it is compatible with a proposed image. To create a position different from that which the brand delivers is extremely wasteful. It is also strategically damaging, as it will undermine the basic equity of the brand: Consumers will be skeptical about future claims.

Brand perceptions can in fact be more important than the physical product itself, especially if they are strong because of a name, or past advertising. It is thus important to make sure that the nature and strength of existing associations are known. Altering existing associations, especially strong ones, usually is very difficult. In general, it is best to build upon existing associations, or even to create new ones, rather than to change or neutralize existing ones.

Hamburger Helper, introduced in the 1970s as an add-to-meat product which would generate a good-tasting, economical, skillet-type dinner, illustrates. It did well early in the decade, when meat prices were high, but in the mid–1970s homemakers switched back to more exotic, expensive foods. Reacting to the resulting drop in sales, the manufacturer attempted to make Hamburger Helper more exotic by positioning it as a base for casseroles. However, the product—at least in consumers' minds—could not deliver. They continued to view it only as an economical, reliable convenience food. Furthermore, making casseroles was not a problem area for which anyone's help was needed. In a personality test, in which women were asked to view the product as though it were a person, the most prevalent complimentary characteristic ascribed to the product was "helpful."

If a repositioning task is involved, does the organization have the will and ability to exert the effort to implement it? It is tempting but naive, and usually fatal, to decide on a positioning strategy which exploits a market need or opportunity but assumes that your brand is something it is not, or that your organization can deliver on a difficult repositioning task.

COMPETITORS' ASSOCIATIONS

Knowing the competitors' associations is a second key to the positioning decision. For most brands in most contexts, it is imperative to develop associations that represent points of difference with competitors. If there is nothing different about your brand, there is no reason for customers to select it over another, or even to notice it. Studies of new-product introductions have shown that the single best predictor of both new-product success and its ability to gain awareness is having a point of difference. The fatal error is to be a "me too" entry.

In the paint product class most brands are very similar; they generally emphasize quality based upon the experience of the firm or some brand attribute.[2] Dutch Boy attempted to differentiate by focusing upon the look that will result, and the associated feelings of pride and satisfaction with "The Look that gets the Look" tag line. A New Age soundtrack added to the TV appeal to the younger target audience—those who had not become "used" to a given brand. The emphasis is thus on feelings rather than the product.

Sometimes it is useful to develop several common associations with only one point of difference. An example would be IBM PC (personal computer) clones which emphasize that they are identical to IBM models in all important performance characteristics, but less expensive (or faster, or smaller). The co-opting of the major associations of the competitors is necessary for two reasons. First, these associations are critical to the user. Without them, the customer would not consider a brand. Second, the communication of the associations can be very easy. Instead of communicating the operating systems, the specifications, the size, and so on, the only task is to say that the product is identical to IBM, except. . . .

An attribute can be so central that it needs to be emphasized even though there is a competitor who has preempted it. An example is Caress soap by Lever Brothers. It is positioned as a soap creating soft skin—very similar to the creamy skin position of Dove. However, unlike Dove's $\frac{1}{4}$ moisturizer and testimonials, it has developed associations with soft skin, demonstrated by means of elegant models and "soft light, soft colors, soft kisses." Thus, it *has* a point of difference, a different set of associations, even though they are supporting a similar product attribute (soft skin) to that of Dove (creamy skin).

When your brand is the dominant brand and has control of distribution outlets, it is less important to be different. In fact, competitors perceived as similar to you will likely lose out because they lack your recognition and distribution. Salem menthol cigarettes, for example, developed associations with refreshing greenery and streams. Competitor cigarettes using similar associations saw their advertising registering as Salem exposures actually reinforcing the Salem associations. There was no incentive for Salem to worry about appearing different from their competitors.

There are successful brands, it should be noted, which have avoided strong associations, relying instead upon recognition and strong customer loyalty. The associations are deliberately made weak so as to avoid excluding any customer group. Pictures of bottles of Coca-Cola with the words "It's the real thing," or Budweiser's claim that Bud is "the king of beers," or "Somebody still cares about quality" illustrate such a strategy.

TARGET MARKET

The third dimension of analysis involves the target market. The name of the game is to develop associations that build or develop brand strengths and attributes, that provide a point of difference, and to which the target market will respond. Just being different will help recognition, but a much stronger position will be one that provides a reason-to-buy or adds value to the product.

An Association That Provides a Reason-to-Buy. One role of an association is to provide a reason-to-buy the brand. Thus, associations with attributes often provide an explicit reason-to-buy:

- Finlanda vodka has the icy, refreshing cold of Finland.
- NutraSweet tastes better.
- Maytag has reliability: The serviceman gets bored.
- Sharp's FAX machine is No. 1 in sales because they offer superior value.

The reason-to-buy needs to be influential enough to really be attractive to buyers. Some associations, even attribute associations, do not work because customers do not value them—or, worse, find the associations detracting or even offensive.

The value to customers of an association providing a reason-to-buy can be determined by talking to customers through focus groups, one-on-one interviews, surveys, and/or market tests. A survey of 1,250 consumers indicated that the initial thrust of 7-Up into the noncaffeine soft-drink market (which stimulated the introduction of noncaffeine colas) did tap a sizable segment.[3] A total of 28% of those sampled said that it makes a great deal of difference to them if their soft drink has caffeine. In the same survey, over 40% mentioned 7-Up when asked which non-caffeine soft drink first comes to mind—over four times greater than Pepsi Free.

The concept of a unique selling proposition (USP), developed and used by Rosser Reeves, one of the creative giants of the advertising profession, had a reason-to-buy focus. A USP involves a specific and unique product benefit important enough to affect consumer purchases. Examples are "M&M's melt in your mouth, not in your hand," "Colgate cleans your breath while it cleans your teeth," and "Better skin with Palmolive." Reeves preferred a USP based on experiments so that the proposition would be more believable, defensible, and sustainable. "Better skin from Palmolive," for example, was supported by tests involving people washing their face regularly with test soaps.

Another tenet of Reeves' was that when a good USP is found, it should be retained indefinitely. One client, Anacin, spent over $85 million in a 10-year period by repeatedly showing an original commercial which had cost $8,200 to produce. Reeves was once asked by a client what his 700 agency people did while they kept running the same ad for a decade.

He replied that they were engaged in keeping the client from changing the advertising.

An Association That Adds Value. An association can "hit" indirectly, not by explicitly providing a reason to buy but by creating an association that adds value. The association does not necessarily have to generate a rational reason to buy which could be easily verbalized. Rather, it can involve the association of a feeling with the brand and its use experience. The association might be created by advertising, by providing a vicarious use experience, or by showing that others have that feeling during the use experience. In any case the feeling, which may be subconscious in that a person may have difficulty verbalizing it, provides added value.

Consider the gift of a Tiffany bracelet. For most, opening a Tiffany package will feel different from opening a Macy's package—the feeling will be more intense, more special. Further, the wearing of a Tiffany bracelet may even make the wearer feel more attractive and confident than if that same bracelet had been purchased at a department store. The associations of prestige and quality are hypothesized to actually change the use experience, to add value to the brand.

The Tiffany associations that add value were generated over a long time-period. Involved were store location, store ambiance, type of store personnel, product selection, and advertising. Figure 7–2 illustrates. Note the copy: "The vision with which Tiffany opened its doors has not changed in 153 years. . . . Classic beauty. That's what ties together everything Tiffany creates. . . ."

Some advertising is designed to associate feelings with the brand and its use experience. For example, advertising has been created that generates the feelings of:

- *Being elegant and stylish.* A perfume ad showed a sophisticated woman preparing for a ball. A BMW ad showed a stylish, elegant woman slowly entering a car.
- *Prestige, success, and being someone.* American Express ads show celebrities who have been card holders for years.
- *Excitement.* An ad for a motorcycle shows a driver careening around and over objects on a motorcycle in a risk-filled ride. A camera safari ad shows a dangerous incident in which a photographer is experiencing intense adventure.
- *Warmth.* The telephone ad "Reach out and touch someone" shows very warm, tender scenes of two friends or relatives having

FIGURE 7–2 Tiffany—Classic Beauty

Courtesy of Tiffany & Co.

a special phone conversation because one of them cared to make the effort to call. Lowenbrau has run a "Something special" series of ads. In one, a happy dinner scene involving a proud father and a son who just passed his bar exam shows warmth, pride, and love.

Determining associations that add value can come from basic marketing research about product use.[4] A decision to reposition Betty Crocker desserts around ideas of family bonds, love, and good times was based upon research about people's feelings about desserts. The research showed that desserts are viewed as a way to show others you care, and are associated with happy family moments. One respondent said that desserts are a "fun, social" event, and another recalled experiencing closeness, and laughing. The result was the "Bake someone happy" campaign.

Transformational Advertising. Advertising which creates brand associations that change the use experience is termed "transformational advertising" by William Wells of BBD Needham. Transformational advertising transforms the use experience making the brand user feel (for example) more elegant, adventuresome, or warm, thereby potentially adding value to the customer. Thus, the "Reach out and touch someone" AT&T campaign made some telephoning experiences different—it created an enhanced feeling of warmth. Wells set forth several guidelines for successful transformational advertising that shed light upon the task of creating associations that add value.

Successful transformational advertising must be able to make and maintain associations among the feelings (such as warmth), the brand (AT&T long distance), and the use experience (calling a loved one). This means an adequate advertising budget is required that will permit frequent exposures, the discipline and patience to run advertising that is consistent (that continues to develop the same feelings associated with the same use experience), and the development of advertising that will clearly associate the brand with the feelings and use experiences.

Transformational advertising works best when there is a positive product, so that the advertising can make the experience richer, warmer, and more enjoyable. However, transformational advertising has also been used to mitigate unpleasant experiences. For example, some of the transformational airline advertising has probably helped some face the anxieties of flying. Also, the "People use our money to make the most out of life" campaign for Household Finance Corporation (HFC) may have now and again reduced the unpleasantness of applying for a loan.

Transformational advertising must be believable, or at least have the ring of truth to it, so people do not consider it silly or even ridiculous. It will not be effective if it is disconfirmed by real-life experiences with the product. No amount of "Ride the friendly rails" would transform the experience of riding the New York subway.

A Segmentation Commitment.   Positioning usually implies a segmentation commitment—an overt decision to ignore large parts of the market and concentrate only on certain segments, namely those interested in the associations selected for the brand. Such an approach requires commitment and discipline, because it is not easy to turn your back on potential buyers. Yet the effect of generating a distinct, meaningful position is to focus on the target segments and not be constrained by the reaction of other segments.

CREATING ASSOCIATIONS

Associations are created by anything linked to the brand. Of course, the features and benefits of the product or service, together with its package and distribution channel, are central to a brand image. Further, the brand's name, symbol, and slogan are among the most important positioning tools (and will be considered in more detail in the following chapter). Certainly the advertising effort is a direct contributor. However, the wide variety of other approaches to the generation of associations should also be considered. Some, like promotion and publicity, are visible as well as important. Others, more subtle and complex, require an understanding of what signals are used by customers to form perceptions.

IDENTIFYING AND MANAGING SIGNALS

Customers often discount or disbelieve factual information. Worse, they usually lack the interest and ability to process it, and, thus, never really even get exposed to it. They cope by using signals or indicators—one attribute or association can imply others.

A health-conscious consumer, for example, may not be willing or able to digest the nutritional information on a cereal box. Instead, the consumer looks for signals that allow the creation of perceptions without detailed processing of information. A signal for a healthy cereal, for example, might be its oat bran content, or 100% of average daily nutritional requirements, or the absence of sugar. Thus, the inclusion of oat bran, for some consumers, may not be important per se, but provides a signal that the manufacturer is concerned about making the product healthier.

It is important to know which associations are to be created. However, it is also necessary to address this question:

What are the key signals of the associations that are to be formed— how can the perceptions be influenced?

In Chapter 3, signals of high quality were discussed. Consumers generally lack the ability to evaluate the actual quality of many products. As a result, signals of quality become important—the size of stereo speakers, the sound of a car door, the thickness of tomato juice, the price of the product. Services are particularly hard to evaluate. Here again consumers look for signals—the appearance of furniture movers, the neatness of a doctor's office, the demeanor of a bank teller.

Perceived quality is not the only association influenced by signals. The classical pianist at a Nordstrom signals a host of associations including a relaxed, low-pressure shopping atmosphere and a store with a set of unique and special extras. The 48-hour parts delivery guarantee of Caterpillar signals a commitment to the customer, and a worldwide distribution network. The pink cast added to Cherry 7-Up, which affected the acceptance of the product, signals "refreshing" as well as "cherry taste." Similarly, the cleanliness of the cabin of an aircraft can affect perceptions of the safety of the plane. Tom Peters tells of an airline that was convinced that a stain on the seat of a plane is a strong erroneous signal of a poor safety record of the pilot and aircraft.

Providing Credibility in the High-Tech World. A new high-technology product, especially from a firm without a track record, needs to develop associations which will provide credibility both that the product is worthwhile and that the firm will survive and remain committed to the product.[5] The backers of such a new firm can signal credibility: Venture capitalist Ben Rosen brought instant credibility to both Compaq and Lotus. An alliance with IBM brought the image of an established organization to both Sytek and Microsoft. Obtaining a key customer can mean all the difference, too. If Safeway has bought a computer system after analysis and comparison, a buyer for another retail store will enjoy reduced uncertainty. And the print media, especially via product reviews, can be a shot in the arm: An article in *PC Magazine* can make more of an impact than 20 ads in the same publication.

Categorizing Brands. Instead of making a detailed "piecemeal" evaluation of a brand, customers often use signals to associate a brand with a certain product category. The premise is that people often divide the world of objects around them into categories as an efficient way to organize information.

Mita Sujan, a consumer behavior researcher, explored categorization using a "110 camera" and a "35-mm single-lens reflex camera" as comparison stimuli.[6] Each camera was described in detail along five dimensions. For example, the reflex camera had "great versatility—the range of shutter speeds and aperture settings allowed for perfectly exposed pictures in very low light or bright sunlight," and the 110 camera was "very easy to load [and unload]—the film cartridge only had to be dropped into the camera, thus eliminating any chance of misloading."

Respondents tended to evaluate the cameras based upon the name. The 35-mm single-lens reflex label signaled a high-quality camera, part of the 35-mm category. In contrast, the 110 label signaled a lower-quality camera—part of a lesser-quality category. This categorization occurred even when the descriptions for the two cameras were reversed—when the 110 camera description was attached to the 35-mm camera. This study showed that the power of these labels to signal a product category even when the detailed factual information was clear.

UNDERSTANDING UNANTICIPATED SIGNALS

Sometimes attributes that represent significant utility to the customer and are emphasized as product advantages by the firm turn out to have negative connotations which provide unanticipated signals of negative associations. It is critical to understand sometimes-subtle interpretations of brand associations. Thus, a second question is:

What unanticipated signals may be generated by brand associations?

For example, when Pringle's was introduced in 1968, P&G was planning to gain a major share (over 30%) of the fragmented U.S. potato-chip industry. They had what they considered a breakthrough product which had taste parity, was consistent in shape and quality, never burned, would stack, and could be packaged in a compact cylindrical container that would protect the chips from damage. All of these elements represented real customer advantages. They also provided the basis for P&G

to engage in national advertising and distribution, thereby generating enormous economies of scale.

However, these product elements in combination provided signals of "artificial," "made from inferior ingredients," "processed," and "having inferior taste." Taste is after all the key bottom-line attribute, and customers thought that the product did not deliver even though in blind-taste tests, the product was judged just as good as competitive products. Why then the taste problem? Because in the market, the customers were not exposed to the product "blind." In the context of the other brand characteristics emphasized in the chips' introduction, the taste was deemed inferior. The brand's performance was very disappointing. The advertising support was eventually withdrawn, and Pringle's became a relatively small-niche player.

The Pringle's case is reminiscent of the initial efforts to launch a certain diet beer that failed because of perceived taste problems. When Miller Lite, however, introduced the *same* product positioned as a beer for macho, heavy beer drinkers interested in great-tasting beer that is less filling, it was an enormous success. The associations with low calorie, diet products was avoided.

THE ROLE OF PROMOTIONS

A sales promotion provides a short-term incentive to make a purchase decision. As was discussed in Chapter 1, promotions often are effective at impacting sales, but run the risk of increasing price sensitivity and reducing brand loyalty. Promotions which simply offer a discount or rebate are the most likely to cheapen the brand and thus adversely affect the brand image.

There are ways to engage in promotions to enhance rather than tarnish brand equity. A key is to include in the criteria for developing promotions a brand-equity component plus a constraint that no promotion will be allowed which will damage equity in the brand. In contrast, the normal practice is to assume that promotions have their own agenda—to stimulate sales, and thus to select and evaluate them accordingly.

Strengthening Associations and Brand Awareness. One way that promotions can enhance equity is to reinforce and strengthen key associations and brand awareness. Consider the leather-strapped luggage tags that American Express gives to its card members, the terrycloth robe Ralph Lauren offers to buyers of its Polo cologne, the Western accessories offered by Wells Fargo, or the Levi's accessories (such as belts and handbags) offered as promotional items by Levi's retailers. In each case the promotional items both reinforce associations and brand awareness.

Figure 7–3 shows an Ivory promotion in which $100,000 is given to the consumer who finds one of the sinkable Ivory bars in circulation. This simple idea reenforces the floating attribute of Ivory that is itself a signal for the purity position.

This Ivory cash promotion has the potential of being far more effective than a contest with (say) a Hawaiian trip as a prize. Here the Ivory user is offered a potential reward just for using the product—participation in

FIGURE 7–3 Ivory Floats!

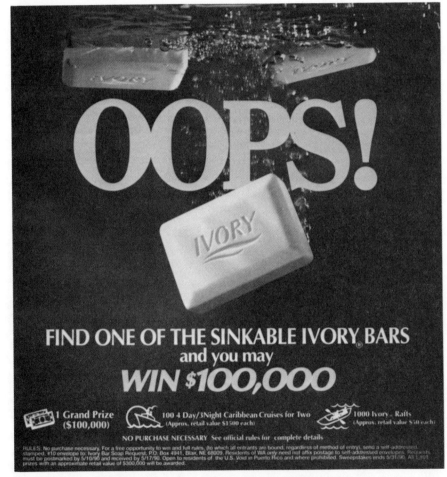

© The Procter & Gamble Company. Used with permission.

an enjoyable contest with a sense of humor. The whole concept should engender positive feelings that can only help the brand. Further, the Ivory user is automatically involved in the contest; no extra effort (such as puzzles, paperwork, mailing, etc.) is required. The Ivory nonuser or underuser thus has an incentive to try the brand. Finally, the key attribute of the product is reenforced in an unusual message that may well stimulate attention in the face of considerable category-advertising clutter.

Branding Promotions

Viewing the promotion as a brand is helpful. Like a brand, a promotion needs to develop awareness and associations, including a link to the brand. For example, consider a promotion to win a Hawaiian vacation for a product with no link to Hawaii or travel. Only those who participate will be likely to recall which brand is involved. Compare with the Pillsbury Bake-Off, which has been run annually for over 30 years. This contest has high awareness, and association with the Dough-Boy (Green Giant has recently been integrated into the promotion). The promotion has brand-enhancing power, even for those who do not participate. Further, promotion awareness and association-building do not have to start from ground zero each year.

A promotion that is tightly linked to the brand and its symbol or primary associations avoids the identity problem of a more generic promotion which can be attributed to any brand. In effect, it is useful to brand a promotion so that it will not be attributed to another brand.

The rash of auto rebates is a good example of equity-jeopardizing activities.[7] Instead of a dollar rebate, suppose that the Chrysler New Yorker could offer an all-expenses-paid weekend in New York, including Broadway shows. Or that the Sterling automobile would include a set of silverware with a car purchase. Or Jeep Wagoneer would provide a package of outdoor gear and two mountain bicycles with each purchase. In each case, the promotion would potentially provide a powerful reinforcement of a key association.

Promotions to Enhance Loyalty. Promotions can be used to reward your existing customers and thus increase loyalty. Look at promotions as a way to strengthen the core customer as well as to attract new ones. A promotion that gives a free ice-cream cone to someone who buys on 10 occasions will reward the existing customer. VISA Gold ran a promotion in which users were provided with the possibility that their next purchase could be free.

Promotions to Enhance Perceived Quality. Sometimes a relatively inexpensive way to upgrade a brand's image is to use an upscale promotion that has strong associations compatible with a high perceived quality product. A "quality" promotion presented in an appropriate manner will suggest a quality product. By contrast, a quality brand is expected to avoid "cheap" promotions.

One of the few studies relating promotions to the evaluation of the brand provided evidence that the quality of the promotion *can* matter.[8] The study involved a video-tape premium for a VCR, and a calculator premium for a typewriter. Subjects were asked to evaluate a product/ premium combination. The quality of the VCR was either low ($200 Goldstar), medium ($250 Toshiba), or high ($350 JVC). Similarly, the quality of the three-tape premiums was low ($6 K-Mart), medium ($12 Scotch), or high ($18 Maxell). Remarkably, the premium quality was as important as the brand quality in consumers' evaluations of the promotional package, even though the objective worth of the premium was a small fraction of the total package.

Add Value. Promotions offering premiums that add value to the product are more likely to avoid damaging the brand than those that simply provide a price discount. Thus BMW, instead of engaging in price rebates, might include a telephone in the car. A bicycle manufacturer might include an air pump or helmet with the bike. Given that the premium is of appropriate quality, the image of the brand should be enhanced.

What type of premium should be selected? A study conducted by J. Walter Thompson researchers in the early 1970s compared premiums related to the product class to those that were unrelated.[9] For soap products the related premium (kitchen gloves) was more effective than the unrelated (a briar pipe). The briar pipe would not often be used by the buyers, who were predominantly female; and, in addition, it may have suggested stains. However, milk-product and shampoo-related premiums (a drinking mug and a hairbrush) were less effective than unrelated premiums (eyelashes and garden seeds). In these cases the unrelated items might have been more desirable because they were something of an extravagance (relative to mugs and hairbrushes), while the related premiums may have been uninteresting. Thus, the nature of the premiums that work best may be difficult to predict when using simple rules like how related they are to the brand.

Obviously a specialized promotion designed to add value (such as including a telephone with a new car purchase) will not always appeal to a wide audience. One solution is to offer several choices, perhaps including a dollar discount. If the promotion features the association-enhancing choices, it should still serve to add value, and perhaps strengthen associations.

THE ROLE OF PUBLICITY

Creating associations and recognition need not be expensive. In fact, paid advertising sometimes is extremely difficult and expensive because it lacks both credibility and interest value. Well-conceived publicity can provide both. Patagonia sportswear occasionally is worn by models on the covers of such key magazines as *Ski* and *Sports Illustrated.* To reinforce photographers who happen to select their product, they send them a thank-you note and a small financial token. They also find ways to call attention to the cover—by using point-of-purchase material, for example.

For publicity to be most effective, there should be an event or action that is newsworthy, perhaps because it is unusual. Ben and Jerry's ice cream sponsored a colorful, funky "cowmobile" which crossed the U.S. passing out free ice cream. Local media found it irresistible. In addition to helping recognition, it also helped reinforce the concept that this ice cream is made by two real people who put their name on the product and stand behind it.

INVOLVING THE CUSTOMER

The strongest associations are those that can involve the customer to the point of becoming interwoven with his or her life. For example, for many small wineries, wine tours are the heart of their effort to build brands. Those experiencing a tour and/or taste session not only gain firsthand exposure to the product, together with credible information about what is behind it, but also have an interesting, enjoyable experience which will become part of the various associations.

CHANGING ASSOCIATIONS

Changing associations (repositioning a brand) often is a delicate job because of the existing associations. The easiest case is where the change is not inconsistent with existing associations. For example, annual tracking studies indicated that All-Temperature Cheer was a product whose principal attribute was gradually becoming obsolete as fewer customers changed water temperature. They thus started a new campaign with the promise that "Nothing goes better in cold." The new claim was not inconsistent with the old; there was just a different spin to it.

However, when an existing association *is* inconsistent with the repositioning, two concerns arise. First, the existing associations can inhibit the repositioning effort. Second, they may well be important to a worthwhile segment who could be potentially alienated by the repositioning. Consider the effort of J. C. Penney to move its image upscale, away from its traditional Sears/Ward's positioning.[10] They have increased the use of national brands like Van Heusen, stocked more-fashionable merchandise, used trendy black-and-white ads, emulated Bloomingdale's with event days, reduced the number of sale days, improved the location of changing-rooms, and installed fashion consultants. Clearly a substantial, expensive effort involving all phases of the operation was needed to counter the strong associations that Penney's had generated over the years.

The need by J. C. Penney to be sensitive to the traditional customer base influenced the change effort. First, they learned that it was important not only to continue to stock traditional lines, but to make sure that these got aisle space so that they did not get lost in the store. Second, they doubled the use of direct mail, an advertising medium that allowed them to treat the traditional customer more properly. Third, they found that the catalogue needed to be toned down so that it didn't offend.

MAINTAINING ASSOCIATIONS

Often it is more difficult to maintain associations than to create them, in the face of demands upon the marketing program and of external forces alike. Among the guidelines are to: (1) be consistent over time, (2) be consistent over the marketing program, and (3) manage disasters in order to minimize their damage.

BE CONSISTENT OVER TIME

It is certainly possible, and indeed sometimes seems (and is) desirable, to change associations. However, it should be recognized that such a task often is wasteful as well as difficult and expensive.

Changing associations is wasteful when associations that have been nurtured over a long time-period are allowed to dissipate when a new association is emphasized. Consider the investment and value of the Dove association with moisturizers. Suppose Dove decided that moisturizing was insufficient and that another association (such as glamorous hands) was to be the new message. The moisturizer association, a huge asset, would then be gradually lost.

In many respects the set of associations is the result of all the accumulated marketing efforts behind the brand. In particular if the advertising, promotion, and packaging has supported a consistent positioning strategy over time, the brand is likely to be strong. Consider the consistency of the message of such brands as Dove, Marlboro, American Express Travelers Checks, Maytag, and McDonald's. Conversely, if the positioning changes, the advertising investment that preceded the change loses much of its value.

If the advertising is working, stick with it. An advertiser often will get tired of a positioning strategy and the advertising used to implement it, and will consider making a change. However, the personality or image of a brand, like that of a person, evolves over many years, and the value of consistency through time cannot be overestimated. Some of the very successful, big-budget campaigns have run for 10, 20, or even 30 years. Some of the most ineffective have generated a new campaign annually.

A common mistake is to underestimate the task of creating a new set of associations. Another is to believe that customers are bored with the current advertising, and even the positioning, and that a change is needed to freshen it all up.

BE CONSISTENT OVER ELEMENTS
OF THE MARKETING PROGRAM

One of the dangers of making alterations is that a change in the marketing program or the product line that makes perfect sense in isolation can affect the association. A good example is E. J. Korvette, a pioneer discounter.[11]

Eugene Ferfauf started Korvette's in 1948 with a tiny luggage shop one flight up on East 46th Street in Manhattan. Soon he was also selling appliances at a $10 markup. Customers lined up to buy. By the end of 1951 he had moved to the street level, and opened a second branch. During the next 15 years 27 stores were opened as far away as Chicago and St. Louis, credit was offered, and the line was expanded to include soft goods and fashion merchandise, furniture, carpets, and even food.

By 1965, Korvette's had grown to over $700 million and Ferfauf was named by a famous professor of retailing as one of the six greatest merchants in U.S. history. But then the story changed dramatically. Sales fell, losses mounted, and the firm began decades of futile efforts to find a profitable niche in the retailing scene. There were many causes of Korvette's rapid decline, including the inability to manage a firm that was spread out geographically, growing too rapidly, and moving into too many different types of merchandise. However, a major problem was the impact of the changing firm upon its image.

During the early fifties a clear image of Korvette's was created by a host of signals besides the dramatically low prices. The product line was focused, there were few services, the store was bareboned, the location oozed of cheap, and the customers clearly were bargain hunters. There was a definite Korvette "feel." But then the changes took away that feel—and more. Upgrading the stores and adding services created inconsistencies with the old image. The new products blurred the image of hard goods and demonstrable bargains. The store became, and felt, very different from the original concept that was so attractive to customers.

The message is: Be consistent. Changes at the margin can be tolerated, but an image usually has difficulties in dealing with inconsistencies. The customer will need to resolve them by adjusting perceptions.

USE THE ORGANIZATION TO PROTECT BRAND EQUITY

Often there is enormous pressure on managers to generate short-term results, even at the expense of firm assets such as brand equity. Promotional activity and distribution alternatives are particular threats. Sharp short-term improvements often can be obtained by engaging in very visible promotions, such as a two-for-one offer for a hair cream, or a dinner discount with a purchase of a symphony ticket. Levi Strauss once ran a promotion involving the sponsorship of a rock group's tour involving displays and T-shirts that tied in. However, after this experience it was decided not to engage in a similar promotion again, in part because of the nature of the rock group associations that were involved.

Expanding distribution to broaden the sales base is another method used to dramatically increase sales. Adding a large chain of convenience stores or drug stores can dramatically add sales to a brand that has relied upon department or specialty stores. However, the new channel also can create associations that are damaging enough to weaken associations on which the brand equity is based.

One approach to protecting equity is identifying certain activities that will not be permissible. For example, Gatorade might have a policy that the brand is to be a premium-priced entry and that no price program, including promotions, should ever run counter to a premium-price position. They could also specify types of promotions that would be permissible and those that would not. Thus, they might decide that Gatorade is to have a macho image and so should be associated with football and hockey, but not with golf or baseball. Sunkist could have a policy that the only acceptable promotions would be those that would reinforce associations of sun and health.

A procedure could be in place to supplement or to support such policies. Thus, any new promotion should itself be tested to see what its associations are by itself and, if possible, what impact it will have upon the brand associations. Ideally, there would be a set of standard procedures to measure the brand's association on a regular basis. These same procedures could then be applied to the promotion: Only if the promotion would have solely desirable associations would it be considered.

There is, of course, a distinction between a set of associations of a promotion and the transfer of some of these promotions to the brand. A rock group may have some associations that are isolated from a sponsor, and thus may do little harm or good. A judgment needs to be made if the transfer is likely to occur. An association test of the brand in the context of a promotion might not be sensitive enough because it cannot reflect the intensity of exposure that the promotion might receive. A more sensitive test would be to link a fictitious brand name to the promotion, and compare its associations to that of another fictitious brand name not linked to the promotion.

Organizational Considerations. Many firms are set up so that the brand manager is under intense pressure to generate short-term financial performance. Such "fast track" managers often are promoted or moved after only a few years if their brand's financial performance is high. Thus their time frame is only one or two years—and in some cases only months.

The mechanism used within most firms to *protect* brand-damaging short-term pressures is *oversight* by top management. By regularly reviewing brand plans, those initiatives that are risky for the long-term health of the brand can be modified or killed. Such oversight presents two problems. *First,* the top managers are often also pressing for short-term financial results, and thus an aggressive brand-defense posture can undercut their motivational relationship with the brand managers. It is (to say the least) awkward first to press for improvements in sales, share, and profits, and then to kill a promotion on the basis of a judgment that it might weaken some associations. *Second,* oversight tends to be ad hoc: It offers no guarantee that all programs and plans will be reviewed in a timely manner.

One partial solution, which has been implemented by several firms including Colgate–Palmolive and Canada Dry, is to have a brand-equity manager. Such a position could focus on protecting the brand equity. He or she would have responsibility for measuring brand equity periodically, in order both to detect signals that the equity was being eroded, and to approve various programs, proposed by brand managers, that would have the potential to affect the brand associations.

MANAGING DISASTERS

The most dramatic damage facing a brand is a disaster affecting its image, and thus its equity. There is no shortage of examples. Consider the cases of the Audi 5000, the Suzuki Samurai, Chrysler, Tylenol, Nestlē, and AT&T. In each the approach used to control the damage is instructive.

AUDI 5000

Audi 5000 cars built after 1978 were alleged to have "sudden acceleration" problems that resulted in adverse publicity culminating with a feature on CBS's "60 Minutes" in November of 1986. Audi's response, which was to blame American drivers, did little to defuse the situation, and Audi sales plummeted from 74,000 in 1985 to around 21,000 in 1989. Audi did redesign the car so the problem disappeared. However, the fact that they never admitted that the original design was defective (indeed it may *not* have been defective) made their fix less credible.

In 1989 there was some evidence that the sales decline was slowing, in part due to two programs offered by Audi to reduce the risk of owning a tainted car: the "three-year test drive," involving a three-year lease structured with low monthly payments; and the "guaranteed resale value," in which a two-year resale value was guaranteed to be the equal of comparable BMW, Mercedes, and Volvo models. Both were expensive, reflecting the damage to the brand caused by the "sudden acceleration" controversy.

Suzuki Samurai

Suzuki's successful sport–utility vehicle, the Samurai, was assailed at a June 1986 press conference by *Consumer Reports* because of an alleged tendency to tip over, even though its competitors had the same problem.[12] Within days Samurai ran ads with testimonials from 10 auto magazines, offered a $2,000 rebate, showed a tape of other vehicles tipping over in the "Samurai test" done by *Consumer Reports,* and accused *Consumer Reports* of grandstanding in order to advance their decade-long effort to promulgate rollover standards. Two months later sales, which had slumped badly, recovered—although the damage will certainly linger for years.

Working in Suzuki's favor was the fact that its customers were (or wanted to feel) young and fun-loving. Their ads under the theme "For drivers who 'won't grow up' " would show harried people getting away in a Samurai, perhaps to a fishing hole. The background slogan asked: "Aren't there enough hours in the day when you have to be a grown-up?"

Chrysler

Chrysler was caught setting back odometers on cars driven by company executives. Lee Iacocca immediately pronounced in ads "We blew it," and that customers would be compensated and the practice discontinued.

Tylenol

Someone injected some poison into containers of Tylenol capsules. Johnson & Johnson immediately recalled *all* the product, and relaunched only after redesigning the packages to make them tamper-resistant thereby providing a visible fix to the problem. They also supported the relaunch with aggressive advertising and promotions. Six months after the incident, they had recovered 95% of their market share.

NESTLĒ

In 1975, complaints against Nestlē's marketing of baby-food formula to Third World counties culminated with a book, published in Germany, calling Nestlē "the baby killer."[13] Nestlē won a law-suit battle against the publisher, but lost the war despite an aggressive public-relations campaign to convince people that they were doing good and not harm. The result was a widespread boycott lasting some five years, until Nestlē finally made major adjustments in their marketing program.

Critics objected to Nestlē associating their product with health by using nurses to market it, by giving away free samples in hospitals, and by generally associating the product with doctors and hospitals. They further believed that Nestlē discouraged breast feeding by ignoring or de-emphasizing it in all their promotions, including their baby booklets. The sad reality was that a subset of consumers used the product with bad water and unsterilized bottles, a combination which sometimes was fatal to infants. Many of the affected consumers could (and should) have used breast feeding. Of course, for many others, the infant formula was entirely appropriate.

AT&T

AT&T, while competing with a quality-and-reliability theme under the slogan "The right choice," had a computer software breakdown. As a result their customers failed to make half of their long-distance calls during a one-day period. AT&T admitted the problem, apologized to customers, explained the problem and its fix, and provided a discount day for their customers. Competitors, of course, were quick to capitalize—running such ads as "If you have problems with your long-distance supplier. . . ."

RESPONDING TO DISASTERS

Clearly, all firms are vulnerable both to accidents and to those who are motivated to exploit bad luck. But there are ways to mitigate (if not avoid) both disasters and the rapacity of business vultures. The best approach to handling a disaster (besides being lucky) usually is to avoid it. Toward this end, it is useful to create worst-case scenarios about what could happen if a product were misused or a promotion misinterpreted. With scenarios in place, action can be taken to reduce the probability of such occurrences. For example, the instability of the Samurai is well-known. Better design could have ensured that the car would be less vulnerable to mishaps than its competition (in fact it was about the same). A mechanism such as a booklet might have encouraged drivers to be aware of the risks, and drive more appropriately.

A second line of defense is to detect the problem early and do something about it before it blows up. Both Nestlé and Audi had plenty of warning; the disaster in each case simmered for years before it broke. If their ultimate actions had been taken early on, they would have avoided the damage.

When adverse publicity does break, the goal is to reduce its duration. The key is to admit the problem, then remedy it as convincingly and quickly as possible. Tylenol is an excellent example of how prompt action can control a real disaster. If the firm insists that it is right, as Audi and Nestlé did, that action inevitably precipitates a prolonged public argument even if they *are* right. If, however, fault is immediately admitted (as Chrysler did), critics simply have nothing to talk about.

In some cases the right approach is to take the critics on and attempt to convince customers that the problem is phony, as was done in the Samurai case. It is important to be quick and strong—Samurai responded in just days with vivid evidence that competitors had the same problem even though *Consumer Reports* implied otherwise. However, the "take them on" strategy has grave risks. Somewhat peculiarly, if it is effective enough to reach and impact upon people, there is more than an even chance that many will remember (as with Samurai) only the problem, not the rejoinder.

Certainly Nestlé, even though they had solid arguments, made a blunder by fighting the issue against such opponents as the American Federation of Teachers, and the American Federation of Churches. In fact, in the first six months of 1981 *The Washington Post* published 91 articles critical of Nestlé. This torrent of criticism occurred after four years of sophisticated public-relations and educational efforts by Nestlé, but only token efforts to change their marketing policies. The Nestlé case shows that public-relations efforts not only can be ineffective but can actually fan the flames.

QUESTIONS TO CONSIDER

1. What are the primary and secondary associations that your brand should develop? Are they consistent with each other, with the brand attributes, and with the established perceptions of the brand? Do they represent a point of differentiation? Do they provide a reason-to-buy for the customer? Do they add value by transforming the use experience? Are all really useful?

2. What signals are important for each of the desired associations? Do unanticipated and undesired signals exist? What can be done to establish and reinforce desired associations? What about publicity, image-reenforcing promotions, licensing, or linking to people, places, or events?

3. Are the programs that affect associations consistent over time? Over elements of the marketing program?

4. What promotions would enhance brand equity? Is there anything associated with the brand that is newsworthy and would support a publicity effort?

5. Who in the organization is charged with developing and protecting brand equity? Does that person have any conflicting goals? Are there systems in place to protect brands against promotions or other activities which could damage brand equity? Should a manager of brand equity be established?

6. What disaster scenarios can be created? What programs might reduce their probability of occurring, or minimize their damage?

8
The Name, Symbol, and Slogan

What's in a name? That which we call a rose by any other name would smell as sweet.

William Shakespeare

Shakespeare was wrong. A rose by any other name would not smell as sweet . . . which is why the single most important decision in the marketing of perfume is the name.

Al Ries and Jack Trout

An idea, in the highest sense of that word, cannot be conveyed but by a symbol.

Samuel Taylor Coleridge

THE VOLKSWAGEN STORY

In 1968 the VW Beetle (or Bug) sold 423,000 units in the U.S.—more than any other single automobile model had ever sold. That record, which still stands, was to be the high-water mark for the remarkable little German import, a car that sold more units than the Model-T Ford.

The Beetle had become perhaps the most successful symbol in U.S. business history. The distinctive shape had persisted for nearly 20 years in advertising, in the culture, and on the road. In contrast with virtually

[*181*]

all other models that had come and gone, it was easily recognizable and had a rich set of associations.[1]

THE BEETLE IMAGE

During the 1950s the Beetle became known as a tough, reliable, economical car—in large part because it was a well-designed, well-made automobile supported by an excellent service and parts system. The early sales were stimulated by GIs who had experienced versions of the Beetle in postwar Germany. By the late fifties annual sales passed 100,000, based in large part on "Volkslore" stories, spread by word-of-mouth, of incredible durability and/or performance. The unique ability of the car to float led to water races/contests and more stories. Eventually two intrepid drivers attempted to cross the English Channel in a Bug. This however proved a bit too much of a challenge, practically mandating a tunnel-enclosed roadway between Great Britain and the Continent.

The Beetle was perceived as a sharp counterpoint to the excesses of

FIGURE 8–1 A Pair of Classic VW Ads

FIGURE 8–1 Continued

The advertisements have been copyrighted by, and are reproduced with the permission of, Volkswagen of America, Inc.

the Detroit model of what a car should be—large, powerful, expensive to buy and maintain, gas-guzzling, and either luxurious or macho. In sharp contrast, the Beetle was small, simple, economical, reliable, and (except to VW addicts) ugly.

In the 1960s the Beetle came to represent, especially to an owner, a type of person and life-style. The Beetle owner was someone who was not into materialism and status symbols. Rather, he or she was willing to make a statement by driving an ugly, funky car, thereby demonstrating independence—a willingness to go against the grain, irreverence for convention, being young (or young in spirit), admitting to a sense of humor, and possessing a logical, practical mind. At one point, VW car owners would honk at each other, signaling their membership in their "club."

The Beetle culture of the sixties was largely due to the remarkable advertising created by Doyle Dane Bernbach (DDB). Their print ads, first run in 1960, would typically show a large picture of the car above a provocative headline. One advertisement showed steam coming out of a nonexistent radiator (the Beetle has an air-cooled, rear-mounted engine) with the caption "Impossible." A headline under a picture of a flat tire read "Nobody's perfect." Several advantages of the car were listed under the headline "Ugly is only skin-deep." The two real classics were "Think Small" and "Lemon." Two such ads are shown in Figure 8–1, including "Think Small."

Many of the advertisements took the novel approach of directly disparaging the product. "Lemon" was extreme, even for VW. The copy noted that the car shown had a blemish (on the chrome strip on the glove compartment) which was caught by one of the 3,389 inspectors at their factory. The ad closed by explaining that inspection is one reason that a VW lasts longer and requires less maintenance than other cars.

The campaign went into television with the same irreverent, humorous, self-deprecating style. In one of the early television ads the camera looks through the windshield of a car traveling on a dark, snow-covered country road during a heavy snowstorm. The viewer asks: "Who is driving, and where?" Finally the car stops, and the driver gets out, opens the door of a large building, starts a huge snowplow. The announcer asks: "Have you ever wondered how the man who drives the snowplow drives to the snowplow? This one drives a Volkswagen."

The Beetle culture had an active life outside of advertising. There were bumper stickers ("Student Porsche Driver"), savings bonds given to babies born in Beetles (about 20 per year), and student contests on how many bodies could be transported by a Beetle (the record was 103). A "Concerto for Yellow Volkswagen and Orchestra" (complete with door slams and engine starts) was written. There were countless Beetle jokes. (One owner peers under the front hood and exclaims that the motor is missing. His friend says: "Are you in luck! They gave me a spare engine in my trunk.") The movie *The Love Bug*, which starred a Beetle, was the top-grossing movie in 1969.

THE SYMBOL

The car's symbol was its distinctive shape. The symbol was, without question, an important part of the Beetle phenomenon. First, it represented a car design which was "ugly" in terms of the conventional wisdom of the day. It thus captured the irreverence for convention that was a large part of the image. The point was that no Beetle driver could possibly be concerned with fashionable appearance—economy and reliability had to be the ownership rationale. Second, it was distinctive. For two decades, no competitor was willing to copy the shape. Third, the shape *was* the Beetle: Anyone could identify the beetle (the bug) as the inspiration for the car's shape. In fact, several ads of the era focused *solely* on the shape. One had a line drawing of the silhouette of the car over the caption: "How much longer can we hand you this line?" Another ad (which became a popular poster) showed the rear end of a Beetle penned onto an egg. The caption read: "Some shapes are hard to improve on."

An indicator of the power of the symbol is that it continues to have enough meaning in the 1990s to be used in advertising. For example, Northwest Airlines ran a 1990 ad in which a picture of a Bug is featured under the claim that the Northwest "free travel program" gives you the best mileage you've had in 25 years. And a word-processing program called the Volkswriter is positioned as a low-cost, simple, easy-to-use program.

THE DECLINE

U.S. sales for the Beetle held fairly steady in the early 1970s—from 1971 to 1973 they were around 350,000. (In 1970 they were still over 400,000.) In 1974 the Beetle still sold 244,000 units, despite the fact that the lowest-price Beetle sold for $500 more than the lowest-price Toyota (versus zero premium in 1972). When the Rabbit was introduced the Beetle's sales fell to 92,000. After 1975 the Beetle was no longer a major model in the United States (although it is still made in South America).

There was a host of reasons for the Beetle's decline and the move to the Rabbit. Increased costs from design changes (some mandated by the government) and a sharply weaker dollar caused the price to increase from $1,839 in 1970 to nearly $3,000 in 1973—very damaging to a car positioned as an economical alternative. Datsun and Toyota were aggressively and successfully going after the subcompact market despite similar currency problems. Also, the symbol as a counterestablishment statement had lost much of its magic, since now there were so many Beetles around, and also since the issues that had captured people's imagination (and loyalty to VW) had changed.

However, the symbol still had considerable strength, even in 1975. So you have to wonder if VW was not too hasty in turning away from the Beetle. Perhaps some more persistent publicity and advertising efforts, plus some product refinements, could have slowed the decline. Perhaps, further, the cost disadvantage might have disappeared over time with an effective global manufacturing strategy: Manufacturing operations in Brazil and Mexico were never exploited as a way to deal with the cost problems.

The Rabbit

VW attempted to transfer the equity in the Beetle to the Rabbit, a roomy car with a water-cooled, front-mounted engine which achieved a remarkable second place in U.S. EPA mileage tests. The car, with yet another funky VW name and a cute racing-rabbit symbol, was positioned as a leader in simplicity and practicality—the Bug's legitimate heir. It was supported by Doyle Dane Bernbach ads that were in the Beetle tradition.

The equity transfer did not work as hoped. Rabbit sales in 1976, the first year in which the Beetle was not a factor, were a disappointing 112,000. From 1977 to 1981, sales ranged from a low of 149,000 to a high of 215,000 (in 1979). In 1982, Rabbit sales fell to under 100,000 and VW had, at least for the time, ceased to be a major player in the growing U.S. market for import cars.

The Rabbit had a host of damaging mechanical problems, such as troublesome fuel injectors and rattling air conditioners. These problems of course caused the wrong kind of publicity, especially for a VW car. Loyal owners who had supported the Beetle over the years, not only by buying cars but also by recommending them to others, were disaffected.

There were other problems as well. The boxy Rabbit did not have the counterestablishment élan. Nor was the styling distinctive—in fact it was similar to that of cars from Japan. Further, the brand emphasized its advanced technology in the introduction, which fuzzed up the basic "Bettle" positioning. Moreover, it was introduced one or two years after the Beetle had lost its strong position, was not priced aggressively, and lacked many of the features of the Japanese models.

It is intriguing to speculate on whether the Beetle equity could have been transferred onto the Rabbit if the quality problems could have been avoided. Could VW have done anything else to capture the magic of the Beetle? Or, could the life of the Beetle have been prolonged by managing costs and by continuing product refinements?

Perhaps the Beetle magic of the sixties could not have been maintained or repeated, but only envied and emulated. Whatever the case, it had a great run.

NAMES

The name is the basic core indicator of the brand, the basis for both awareness and communication efforts. Often even more important is the fact that it can generate associations which serve to describe the brand— what it is and does. In other words, the name can actually form the essence of the brand concept. One firm in Germany associated with the consultant Kroeber–Reil developed a line of cookery based upon the name Black Steel. The name had connotations of a clean, strong product which could engage in heavy-duty jobs with style. Would Apple Computer have been able to establish its user-friendly image, in an era in which computers were formidable machines, with another name, or under (say) the Model 700 signature? It is doubtful.

A name can serve as a substantial barrier to entry once it is established. Consider the power of names like Velcro, Formica, and Kodak. In fact, a name can be more useful than a patent, which can be difficult and costly to defend. In contrast, a trademark or service mark can be enforced quickly by the obtaining of a temporary injunction, and need not terminate in some arbitrary time period. If the innovation is closely tied to the name, protection of the name can be enough to protect the innovation.

An established brand can benefit from the establishment of a new subname. A subname can identify a new model which has a particular characteristic, such as the Mercury Sable. It can also identify a group of models which have a common relevant attribute. Consider the Turbo series of computer software products by Borland: Turbo Pascal, Turbo Basic, Turbo C, and Turbo Assembly. The Turbo name has an association with an important attribute, and thus has the potential to create real equity.

Name creation is too important to be relegated to a brainstorming session among a few insiders around a kitchen table or in an executive lunchroom. Excellent managers who would not dream of interjecting their opinions during decision-making sessions involving creating products or ads are for some reason tempted to take over during key name-creation decisions, often in part because a working name is needed quickly, but also in part because name creation seems like the prerogative of the entrepreneur. Yet a name is much more permanent than most other elements of a marketing program. A package, price, or advertising theme usually can be changed much more easily than a name.

The process of both generating alternatives and selecting among them should be systematic, and as objective as possible. The use of a professional firm either to help the process or to take it over should be considered. Whoever does it will need to both generate and evaluate alternatives according to a set of criteria.

GENERATING ALTERNATIVES

Before creating a list of alternatives, it is useful to know which words and phrases will describe the associations that would be useful for the brand name to have. For example, suppose that a name is being sought for a movie video rental service which will deliver to, and pick up from, a box attached to your residence. Referring to a catalogue, you merely call in your selections. Useful associations might be: fast, deliver, wide selection, convenient, easy, friendly, movies, video, rental, competent, in-home selection, express, delivery truck, and order by catalogue. The list can be expanded through word-association research—such as asking members of the target audience to list whatever comes to mind when words from the list are read, or placed on a screen. These associations can be used to generate a set of alternatives by:

• Combining them into phrases—Video Express, Movie Truck
• Generating parts of words and combining them—Rentivideo
• Considering symbols for each—Popcorn Video
• Using rhymes—Groovy Movie
• Using humor—Cecil B. Video
• Adding suffixes or prefixes such as poly, omni, vita, ette, dyne, lite, syn, ad, ix, vita, ada—Moviette

In addition, any set of words that describes objects can be a source of alternatives, such as:

• Animals—Cougar, Greyhound, Linx, Bobcat
• Flower/Tree—Oak Tree, Red Rose
• Person type—Cover Girl, Craftsman
• People—Ford, Regis, Hewlett Packard
• Adjectives—Quick, Clean

A powerful source of a name or slogan is a metaphor. A metaphor is the use of a word or phrase denoting one concept in place of another concept suggesting a likeness between them. A metaphor is a way to communicate very compactly a complex idea. DieHard battery, for example, is a metaphor which suggests that the battery is like a tough person or plant that is hard to kill off. The metaphor desktop publishing really created a whole industry, and stimulated sales of computers and printers in general. Unfortunately for the originators of the metaphor, it was not a trademark which could be protected.

A naming firm, NameLab, uses morphenes as name building-blocks.[2] Morphenes are a set of about 6,000 word fragments capable of stimulating mental images even though they have no meaning by themselves. NameLab came up with Acura (derived from accurate), Sentra (from sentry), and Geo (from geography—a world or global connotation). Another NameLab product was Compaq, the fusion of com (indicating computer and communications) and paq (from compact). The paq was deliberately selected instead of pak, pac, or pach because it stood out as being easy to pronounce yet catchy and unusual. The name also allowed the potential to be linked to other related products, such as wordpaq or datapaq.

In contrast to the approach of using the name to establish desired associations, there is the empty-vase or blank-canvas theory of naming: Use a name with no associations. The name can then be imbued with meaning through product refinement, advertising, and packaging. It may in fact be kept somewhat general or ambiguous, so that it can be attached to a variety of products. Consider names like Kodak, MJB, and Wendy's, all of which started with no meaningful associations.

There should be a set of hundreds of (and perhaps well over a thousand) alternatives. The next step is to evaluate the alternatives, using a set of criteria which should include questioning whether the name is easy to recall, has useful associations, avoids bad associations, will be helpful in generating a logo/symbol, and can be protected legally.

Is It Easy to Learn?

An important aspect of a brand name is thus its memorability: Will it be remembered? Although the memory process clearly is complex, a substantial amount of research into both psychology and consumer behavior has provided at least some insights into which pertinent factors are related to memory.[3] In general, recall will be enhanced:

When a name is different or unusual enough to attract attention, and perhaps to arouse curiosity: "Charlie" was a novel name for a perfume. A bank name like First Federal will not stand out like Red Wagon Bank. Zap Mail is more memorable than Speedy Mail.

When a name has something about it that is interesting—such as rhyme, alliteration, a pun, or humor: Cola-Cola, Toys-R-Us (with a backward R), and The Price of His Toys all provide a spark of interest, as do names with black humor—such as The Texas Chain Saw Manicure Company (a lawn-care service) and The Mad Butcher.

When a name elicits a mental picture or image: Names like Apple, Rabbit, and Cougar should be more memorable than such names as Pledge, Bold, and Tempo. One theory is that a visual image provides a memory trace which is generally easier to retrieve than an abstract concept—in part because it is likely to have more and stronger associations in memory, and in part because it involves a different memory process.

When a name is meaningful: One study demonstrated that recall of names was improved if the name meant something (L'eggs vs. Leget as a name for stockings) and/or if the name fit the product (Letters vs. Economy as a name for a writing pad).[4] The implication is that the use of sets of letters like MCI (vs. Sprint) or words without meaning, like Metrecal (vs. Slender) will be at a disadvantage. Curiously, there is evidence that less-used words have been found to generate higher recognition (as opposed to recall).

When a name has some emotion: Psychological studies have shown that emotionality affects memory. Although negative emotions can rarely be tapped, some product classes lend themselves to positive emotions. Examples are Joy, Caress, Love, My Sin, and Obsession.

When a name is simple: All else being equal, a three-syllable word will be harder to learn than a one- or two-syllable word, particularly if the consumer has little motivation to learn the name. Consider names like Raid, Bold, Bic, Jif, Dash, and Coke. A word which is more difficult to spell or pronounce generally is more difficult to learn and use.

Does It Suggest the Product Class?

Often the brand name can play a key role in achieving an association with the product class, so that the brand will have high recognition/recall within the product class. Some names, such as Go Fly a Kite, Ticketron, Overnight Delivery Services, and Dietayds communicate the involved product class. One obvious problem is that as the name becomes more descriptive of the product class, it will be more difficult to expand the brand to other products. For example, the name Go-Fly-a-Kite provides an unusual, funky, fun name that implies a specialization and expertise in kites that may be very attractive. However, if a store wants to expand into educational toys or adult games, the name may become something of a limitation—perhaps a liability.

Even sets of syllables without meaning can have associations with a product class. A study by two marketing professors of 25 sets of randomly selected letters found that "whumies" and "quax" reminded people of breakfast cereal, and "dehax" and "vig" reminded people of laundry detergent.[5]

WILL THE NAME SUPPORT A SYMBOL OR SLOGAN?

A symbol and slogan can become important assets and need to be solidly linked to the name. When a name can stimulate and support effective symbols and slogans, the task of linking them to the name is made easier. Some names, such as The Swaying Palm, Fat Harry's, and The Red Ribbon, immediately suggest strong symbols and related associations, while others less descriptive do not.

The name Harlem Savings Bank of New York was limiting the bank, which wanted to expand outside of both Harlem and their existing customer base.[6] The cornerstone of their image change was a new name, Apple Bank. The name severed the association with Harlem, and provided access to the associations of apples—something good, wholesome, and simple—and suggested a friendly, fun, somewhat different firm. It was, further, a unique name linked to the city's nickname "the Big Apple." And it provided access to a strong symbol (an apple), a slogan ("We're good for you"), and several promotional lines ("Your money grows and grows at Apple Bank," and "Take your pick from our branches"). The new name was credited with a sharp improvement of several measures of marketing performance.

From fruits to vegetables: A Japanese bank—now termed "the Tomato Bank"—not surprisingly uses a tomato symbol and says "The time is ripe for a new concept in banking," and that they are "bright and cheerful," like the tomato.

DOES IT SUGGEST DESIRED BRAND ASSOCIATIONS?

A brand name like Ultrabrite, The Silent Floor, Airbus, or WordPerfect can also identify brand attributes or other positive associations. Consider the associations of:

- Rent-a-Wreck—with a unique type of [abused] car, a suitably low price range, and an offbeat, humorous management style
- Honda's Civic—with civic-mindedness [a car which minimizes gas consumption and pollution] and with city driving [an easy-to-park car]
- Miller's Magnum Malt Liquor—with strength and masculinity
- Mop 'n Glow—with floor-cleaning and shiny floors
- Head and Shoulders—with dandruff control
- Gee, Your Hair Smells Terrific—shampoo with fresh-smelling hair
- Huggies [introduced as Kimbies]—with comfortable fit close enough to be effective
- Sumitomo—with friendship ["tomo" meaning "friendship" in Japanese]

Again there is the concern that a strong name association with an attribute will be limiting. For example, the name "Compaq" was conceived to represent compact computers. This "compact" association undoubtedly was in part responsible for the product's success. When the firm went into full-size desktop computers the "compact" association needed to be both overcome and sacrificed. The P&G approach, of course, would be simply to generate a new name. Compaq, however, chose to stretch the old name because of its recognition and its association with high quality and successful innovation. At that point in time the "compact" associations were clearly no longer helpful.

Names can also generate positive feelings because they are humorous (Rent-a-Wreck), clever (Go-Fly-a-Kite), associated with something warm (The Teddy Bear Stationers) or likable (The Doughboy Bakery). In fact, one study by two UCLA psychologists measured the feelings that respondents would experience in ideal product-use situations for five product classes: cars, aspirin, toothpaste, candy bars, and wristwatches.[7] Feelings engendered by sets of names attached to these five product classes were also obtained. Brand preference was higher for those names generating the appropriate feelings.

Even word parts or letters can have a strong impact upon associations. An early study showed that the word "mal" consistently was thought to represent a larger object than the word "mil." Similarly, sounds within a word, independent of meaning, can imply movement, shape, luminosity, youth, or gender. For example, masculinity is associated with plosive and guttural sounds (e.g., Cougar), while feminity is associated with the use of "s," soft "c," and weak "f" sounds (e.g., Caress, Silk-Ease).[8]

ARE THERE UNDESIRABLE ASSOCIATIONS?

A name can sound right, and have good associations, to a group of involved people who are considering it from the context of a brand with certain characteristics. But what will a naive person think when exposed to the name for the first time? For example, when United Airlines wanted a new name when they expanded into hotels and rental cars, they picked Allegis, drawn from the words allegiant (meaning loyal) and aegis (meaning shield or protector). Even to those that did pick up the loyalty theme it might have had a negative connotation of royalty demanding subservience—not very suitable for a service firm. Further, to many the new name probably meant allergies. Ultimately, the firm got rid of the Allegis name as well as their hotels and rental cars.

One way to determine the associations elicited by candidate names is

---

Jigglers Works for Jell-O

Jell-O, a strong dessert brand since the turn of the century, was in decline during the 1970s and 1980s. Its top-of-mind awareness fell among younger households, reflecting the fact that young moms didn't use Jell-O the way their moms had.

Jigglers, snack-sized pieces of Jell-O that are solid enough to eat by hand and involving a recipe that requires four packages of Jell-O, provided an answer.[9] The Jigglers effort was supported by a promotion (named the promotion of the year by *Promote* magazine) that offered free Jigglers molds so that children could create Jigglers in varied shapes. Something like a half million molds were distributed in 1990. In addition, over 100,000 special displays holding Jell-O and Jigglers molds were placed in supermarkets. The product was a natural, providing wholesome fun in the Jell-O tradition. And it worked: Sales in 1990 actually increased 7% and image indicators turned as well.

The name Jigglers was a key ingredient in the success of the new use of the product. The name has a good visual image (of Jell-O jiggling in the hand), is associated with jolly, happy people and times, and is a kid's word. In addition, it is linked to Jell-O by the alliteration and by being descriptive of the product.

---

to conduct word-association research: Simply ask members of the target audience to list whatever comes to mind when a word is read or placed on a screen. Among the words, of course, will be the proposed names.

A factor often overlooked is the impact of a name in other languages and cultures. Nova, the name of a GM car, meant "does not work" in Spanish (no va). A telecommunications product called Chat Box became "cat box" in France. Consider the effects of such names as Green Pile (Japanese lawn dressing), Creap (Japanese coffee creamer), Super Piss (Finnish product to unfreeze car locks), and Bum (Spanish potato crisps).

IS THE NAME DISTINCTIVE?

It is important to know in advance whether a name will create an association with a competitive product. In addition to legal considerations there are market reasons why such associations are important. For instance, it can be an advantage for a product to be confused with a prestige brand. Consider for example the private-label grocery products with packages (and sometimes names) similar to those of their higher-priced, national-brand competitors. However, usually the desire is to create a brand and a supporting marketing program that generate an identity separate and distinct from competitors', so that others do not benefit or exploit the equity that is created.

WILL IT BE STRONG LEGALLY?

A prime criteria is that the name be strong legally.[10] The specter of a name which has been used to generate promotional material or, worse, to establish a business, but which then must be discontinued because it has proved not legally defensible, lurks behind every new name. Unilever's [Elizabeth Taylor's] Passion perfume was introduced, only to be prevented from being carried in 55 stores because of a suit by a competitor who had marketed a Passion fragrance. A name which is sound legally must be distinct from the names of competitors, and it must do more than simply be descriptive of the product or service.

A name used commercially by a firm is protected from other competitors whose customers overlap. Thus a proposed name for a movie rental service, such as video express, will not be available in any city or neighborhoods with a store with that name. It is therefore necessary to check in advance the entire potential market area, to see if competitors are using the desired name. Even a *different* name may not be available, if it might be confused with a competitor's name. For this reason a court once concluded that a certain skating rink could not use the name Lollipops because it might be confused by some with an established nearby competitor named Jellibeans.

The name has to do more than just describe the product to be protected. Thus, names such as Air-shuttle, Consumer Electronics, Windsurfer, Dial-A-Ride, and Vision Center would not be protected because they describe a product or service which others could provide. Despite considerable legal effort, Miller would be unable to protect the name Lite that they pioneered for low-calorie beer. The courts held that it is legally equivalent to the word "light," a generic or common descriptive term. For this reason competitors were free to use the term, and Miller lost a golden opportunity to exploit their first mover advantage in the light beer segment. Another example is Coca-Cola, which name itself is protected thanks to vigorous efforts by the firm. However, they were *not* able to prevent the use of the 'cola" term, which describes a drink using the kola nut's extract. Thus we also have Pepsi-Cola and, among many others, RC Cola—and even the Uncola drink, 7-Up.

Early in the evaluation process a checkup using readily available databases should be made as to the availability of candidate names. In some contexts, when the competitive area is broad (both geographically and with respect to competitors), a relatively low percentage of the possible names may be available. However, a potential legal problem should not necessarily exclude a name. Access to protected names can be obtained, and the strength of trademarks can vary widely.

THE SELECTION PROCESS

Usually there are several stages to the selection process. A crude review to eliminate obviously unsuitable candidates, and legal screening for clearly unavailable names, can usually cull the list down to the 20–40 range. Then a more careful subjective evaluation can get it down to 10 or so. These all deserve close examination, including a more thorough legal analysis to determine the legal risks associated with them.

Customer research often is used to gain more accurate information on key characteristics of the names. Among the customer tests that could be conducted are:

• Word associations: Do any undesired associations emerge?
• Recall tasks: Give respondents a list of possible names and ask them

---

Criteria for Name Selection

A proposed name should:

1. Be easy to learn and remember—it is helpful if it is unusual, interesting, meaningful, emotional, pronounceable, spellable, and/ or if it involves a visual image.

2. Suggest the product class so that name recall will be high while still being compatible with potential future uses of the name.

3. Support a symbol or slogan.

4. Suggest desired associations without being boring or trivial.

5. Not suggest undesired associations—it should be authentic, credible, and comfortable and not raise false expectations.

6. Be distinctive—it should not be confused with competitors' names.

7. Be available and protectable legally.

(after a diversion task) to write down all they can recall. This test will determine not only recall but the spellability of the word.

- Scaling the brand: This is done along the important attributes related to the product class and the brand's position.
- Rating brand preferences: Marked differences in preferences often are associated with brand names.

Finally, the strengths and weaknesses of each name, and the bottom-line judgment as to its value to the brand, should be developed. The perspective should include both the critical early stages of the marketing program and the long term as the brand matures.

CHANGING NAMES

When a name has associations that become damaging or limiting, or when new associations incompatible with the old name are needed, a new name may be required. In fact, nearly 2,000 corporate names are changed each year, in large part because the cast-off name no longer reflects the firm's business. As we shall now see, some of these name changes are instructive.

International Harvester found itself in 1985 with the image of a dying (if not dead) farm-equipment manufacturer, despite the fact that it had sold its farm-equipment operation to Tenneco and was at that time the largest U.S. manufacturer of trucks.[11] The key to the image change was changing the name to Navistar (with the tag line "The rebirth of International Harvester"). It was a union of navi (leading or navigation) and star (heavenly body or outstanding performance). The name probably means marine or space-flight equipment rather than the intended associations with trucks and a "customer-driven, aggressive, and risk-taking" firm. However, using a $13 million advertising campaign which included footage of a Navistar truck roaring up a hill, over 85% of the target audience had seen the advertising and could recall the content to the company's satisfaction.

Allegheny Airlines had a geographically restrictive name. They became US Air—a name that had the right nationwide service connotation. Consolidated Foods changed to Sara Lee. Although "Sara Lee" did not reflect what the firm did, it was a well-known, well-liked name that, among other things, would be received well by investors, an important target of the name. Interestingly, the stock market, on average, responds positively to a name change, probably in part because it signals a change in vision or strategy for the firm.

SYMBOLS

The reality is that most firms and products are fairly similar; the differences that do exist, such as service quality, are difficult to communicate in an effective and credible manner. When products and services are difficult to differentiate, a *symbol* can be the central element of brand equity, the key differentiating characteristic of a brand.

The symbol can by itself, as Figure 8–2 suggests, create awareness, associations, and a liking or feelings which in turn can affect loyalty and perceived quality. We know that it is easier to learn visual images (symbols) than words (names). Thus, symbols should help gain brand awareness. However, a symbol rich in associations—such as Mickey Mouse, the Jolly Green Giant, or the Maytag repairman—will contribute much more, and become an important asset for the firm.

Symbols can be nearly anything, including:

- *Geometric shapes*—Prudential's rock
- *Things*—the Wells Fargo stagecoach

FIGURE 8–2 The Role of the Symbol

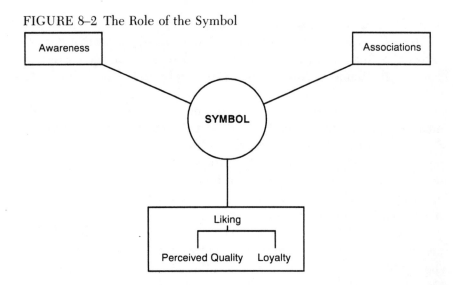

- *Packages*—Morton Salt's blue, cylindrical box
- *Logos*—Apple Computer's apple with a bite out of it
- *People*—the Maytag repairman
- *Scenes*—Marlboro country
- *Cartoon characters*—the Jolly Green Giant

The choice of a symbol and how it is developed will affect the role that it plays in the four dimensions of brand equity. We now consider first its role in developing associations.

ATTRIBUTE ASSOCIATIONS

A symbol can communicate associations—even specific attributes. Consider the Travelers' red umbrella, shown in Figure 8–3, which in a compact way has consistently communicated over time that Travelers protects—it offers protection from the elements by providing a broad shield. Note the slogan: "You're better off under the Umbrella." Similarly, the now stylized Rock of Gibraltar, the symbol of Prudential, means strength, stability, a fortress against adversity. Consider the difficulty of communicating such characteristics without the symbols, and the resulting constraints upon the marketing programs even if such programs were successful. In contrast, the umbrella and rock can be attached to anything the firms distribute, and provide these associations as a bonus.

FIGURE 8–3 The Travelers Umbrella

**INTRODUCING
ONE OF THE MOST DRAMATIC DEVELOPMENTS
IN HEALTH CARE TODAY.**

Something new in affordable health service and protection is unfolding across America.

It's a new level of excellence in meeting the nation's health needs from The Travelers.

It includes growing networks of HMOs, PPOs and other significant innovations in cost management.

For example, The Travelers' Patient Advocate program helps reduce days in the hospital, increases use of out-patient care, and reassures patients by suggesting second opinions.

And our Taking Care health promotion program helps people to adopt healthier lifestyles, become more conscious of good health and to use medical care more efficiently and effectively.

In addition, we've honed the art of fast, accurate claim service to a fine edge and developed one of the most sophisticated information management systems in the industry.

It's all backed by The Travelers' 52 years of health service expertise that now covers over eight million Americans in companies of all sizes.

Today, we are setting the standard of excellence in comprehensive, affordable health service and protection for employers and employees.

As one of America's strongest insurance, financial and health service experts, The Travelers is a force you can count on to develop your health care picture.

The Travelers Insurance Company and its Affiliates, Hartford, CT 06183.

The Travelers
You're better off under the Umbrella.™

Courtesy of The Travelers Corporation.

Consider banking, a service industry in which everyone tends to attempt to develop similar associations to support their services. Those banks that have had the good fortune or foresight to develop symbols have a considerable advantage. For example, Dai-Ichi Kangyo, the largest bank in the world, has a cute, happy little red heart. Customers see the heart everywhere in their interaction with the bank. It symbolizes warmth, a friendly "fun" atmosphere, and an organization that loves its customers. A very large bank needs to fight the impression that, unlike their small local competitors, they are big and impersonal. The value of an active symbol such as the heart is invaluable.

Other symbols that have represented brand attributes include:

• Mr. Clean: The muscular sailor has represented the cleaner's strength.
• Allstate: The "good hands" represent personal care and competent service.
• GM: Mr. Goodwrench means trained, professional, friendly service people.

MULTIPLE ASSOCIATIONS

A study of banks in California confirmed that their associations are very similar with respect to money, savings, checking account deposits, and tellers. Nothing distinctive—with the exception of Wells Fargo, which has had a host of associations going along with their ubiquitous stagecoach. In an industry in which similarity is the norm, the stagecoach is an enormous asset, in part because of the richness of the concept. In addition to providing associations with the Old West, horses, and the gold rush, it also effortlessly is linked to reliability in the face of adversity, adventurousness, independence, and even building a new society out of wilderness.

Other banks, such as Bank of America and Security Pacific, have no such symbol upon which to draw. If they wanted to develop an image of being adventurous and independent, it would be a huge task and would mean the sacrifice of the development of other associations. The richness of the stagecoach symbol does provide such associations as by-products.

POSITIVE FEELINGS: LIKING

Some of the most successful and interesting symbols are cartoon characters that invoke humor and fantasy, symbols such as the Pillsbury

Doughboy (called Poppin' Fresh), the Jolly Green Giant, the Keebler Elves, Charlie the Tuna, Snoopy, and Mickey Mouse. The characters tend to be memorable, likable, and have strong associations. The Pillsbury Doughboy, for example, with its "belly poke and giggle," communicates the plump freshness of bakery products, and also provides a lovable character.

Metropolitan Life, in contrast to competitors such as Prudential, Travelers, and Allstate, had no symbol to aid in recognition and positioning in the mid–1980s. [12] Their solution was to adopt the Charlie Brown characters (by Charles Schultz). The goal was to provide a warm, light, nonthreatening approach to insurance, in direct counterpoint to those of the serious, stolid competitors. There is evidence that the five-year-old program helped awareness (recognition was at 89%) and positively affected feelings toward "Met Life," although the financial performance of the firm had been mixed during this period. Some have argued, however, that the Charlie Brown characters have inhibited the firm from more aggressive factual marketing programs.

The fact that a character is liked or is associated with a positive feeling such as fun or laughter is important. People engage in "affect transfer," which means that they tend to transfer affect (feelings of liking or disliking) from one object to another which is perceived to be connected or related to it in some meaningful way. People are uncomfortable with an inconsistency—such as a neutral feeling toward one object closely associated with another to which a very positive affect is attached. They cope by altering the affect that is not very strong.

Thus, a strong positive affect toward a character like the Pillsbury Doughboy will very likely result in a positive affect toward the Pillsbury baking products to which the Doughboy is associated. Of course, an unsatisfactory baking experience associated with Pillsbury could stimulate a negative-affect link to Pillsbury that might counter or even alter the positive Doughboy influence.

SYMBOLS AS INDICATORS OF
BRANDS AND PRODUCT CLASSES

One role of a symbol, in addition to possibly generating associations, is to be an indicator for a brand. When Wells Fargo Bank wants to associate itself with international capabilities and an international presence, it puts the stagecoach in foreign settings. The result is a useful mnemonic device for the audience. The juxtaposition of a Western symbol linked closely with the bank to a foreign setting like the Ginza or Piccadilly is at once incongruous and meaningful. An exposure to one such scene would be more interesting and memorable than dozens of exposures to the same scene showing a Bank of America sign.

The symbol may also help the brand name to associate with a product class by linking with it. Research in consumer behavior and psychology provides clues as to what sort of symbol characteristics will affect the ability of a symbol to link with brand and product class.

One guideline is to make the symbol unique. There is always the danger that the brand equity of one brand can be co-opted by someone who generates a similar symbol. An important element of the stagecoach to Wells Fargo is its uniqueness in the financial services setting.

Consider a shampoo such as Vidal Sassoon or Head & Shoulders, both of which rely upon their package to act as a symbol. Private-label brands have been produced with nearly identical packages/symbols. One study showed that such products were perceived to have more similar attributes to the national brands (e.g., Vidal Sassoon) than other private labels with dissimilar packaging.[13] The implication is to legally protect symbols from imitators, and to develop symbols which are unique. One way to test a symbol is to use recognition tasks. The symbol could be exposed for a fraction of a second, along with a set of competing symbols. The question is how long the exposure must be before correct recognition occurs. A distinct, differentiated symbol will do well in such a test.

Another guideline is that it is much easier to learn the association between a symbol and a brand if the symbol reflects the brand—for example, if a rocking chair is the symbol for The Rocking-Chair Theater. At its extreme, the symbol and the brand name can be the same—as with Sony, IBM, and GM.

In one study, respondents were exposed to a subset of 48 symbols, each reflecting a brand name.[14] Half of these symbols were interactive, in that they reflected the product class. For example, the Rocket Messenger Service showed a picture of a delivery person wearing a rocket on his back and delivering a package. The other symbols were noninteractive, in that they did not reflect the product class. For example, a sketch of a bear standing near a tree represented the Bear Delivery Service. Respondents, after viewing a set of such stimuli, were asked to name a brand for each product class. When the interactive symbol had been used, a much greater degree of accurate brand recall was evidenced.

There is a trade-off. If the symbol (and brand name) has associations that are extremely strong, the brand's ability to reposition or extend may be reduced. An extension, for example, would not only change the name/

product-class association but also the symbol/product-class association. A symbol which has an inherently weak association with a product class provides strategic flexibility.

UPGRADING THE SYMBOL

With so much invested in a symbol, it is risky to change it because of the relearning that will have to take place. On the other hand, the symbol can become dated and start to develop some undesirable old-fashioned, stodgy connotations. Several firms have successfully updated their symbols over time to keep them in touch with the times while still retaining the heritage and associations.

Aunt Jemima has traded in her kerchief for a stylish, gray-streaked hairdo and has added earrings and a white collar. The change was intended to provide a more contemporary look while preserving the warmth, good taste, and reliability that is associated with the symbol. The Morton Salt girl and Betty Crocker have both kept fashionable over the years with new hairstyles and dresses. The Prudential Rock has become more stylized and contemporary over the decades.

For Coca-Cola, the cans and bottles are key symbols. The core identity elements—the red color, the dynamic curve, the vertical lettering, and the dual brand identities of "Coke" and "Coca-Cola"—were eroded during the mid-1980s with the introduction of new varieties, including caffeine-free drinks (which had a gold package). A review resulted in a more cohesive set design which differentiated the products while still providing more impact on the shelf. There were also some subtle changes in the script that served to help achieve the twin goals of preserving the heritage and distinctiveness of Coca-Cola while legitimatizing the brevity and contemporary impact of "Coke."

GUARDING THE SYMBOL

A symbol, with its associations, will need to be protected over time. It is important to avoid placing the symbol in a context which will jeopardize its associations. For example, Wells Fargo Bank needs to protect and reinforce the stagecoach symbol. When they evaluate any proposed promotions or products, such should be evaluated not only on their own merits but upon their impact on the bank's stagecoach.

Licensing a symbol (such as the Jolly Green Giant) is one way to gain exposure. However, the symbol needs to be restricted to the right settings; any undesirable associations can affect its equity. For example, Mickey Mouse is licensed widely. Several questions may be addressed concerning this fact. What associations are those desired for The Mouse? Are the various licensed products and services consistent with those associations? Will there be overexposure so that boredom or even irritation will emerge?

SLOGANS

A name and a symbol in combination can be an important part of brand equity. However, there is a limit to what a single word and symbol can do. For instance, a name like Ford, with its symbol, is pretty much set in concrete—such a brand usually does not have the luxury of selecting another name and symbol to reinforce a positioning or repositioning strategy. A slogan, however, *can* be tailored to a positioning strategy, and added to a brand name and symbol. It has far fewer legal and other limitations than does either a name or a symbol.

A slogan can provide an additional association for the brand. Ford wanted to add a quality association to its name. The slogan "Quality is Job No. 1" provided the vehicle. Links to the Ford name help provide Ford with a quality association. Similarly, Mazda, a name which by itself has few associations, is aided by the slogan "It just feels right," which summarizes the positioning strategy of a comfortable car and ride. Rice-a-Roni gets mileage out of its "The San Francisco Treat" tag line, what with both "San Francisco" and "treat" having many useful associations.

A slogan can remove *some* ambiguity from the name and symbol. Maybelline has a mixed image, but "Smart, beautiful, Maybelline" is very specific. Cadillac can have different, and not always positive, associations. It can engender visions of ostentatious, gas-guzzling, large cars. However, such associations are much less likely in the context of the slogan "Cadillac style."

Another capacity that a slogan has is its ability to generate equity of its own which can be exploited. Consider AT&T's "Reach out and touch someone" slogan, which has associations with feelings of warmth and friendship, as well as an action component. AT&T drew upon the slogan to help position promotional programs such as the AT&T Reach Out America plan, the AT&T Reach Out World plan, and even a Reach Out Saturday plan.

A slogan also can reinforce the name or the symbol. Thus, the Sharp slogan "From Sharp minds come Sharp products" repeats the brand

FIGURE 8–4 Match the Slogans to the Brands

Slogans	Brands
1. Does she . . . or doesn't she?	1. Ameritech
2. Don't leave home without it.	2. Miller Lite
3. We try harder.	3. Microsoft
4. Everything you always wanted in a beer, and less.	4. American Express
5. When it rains it pours.	5. Toshiba
6. The quality goes in before the name goes on.	6. Zenith
7. In Touch with Tomorrow	7. Mazda
8. The Most Intelligent Cars Ever Built	8. Clairol
9. The Right Choice	9. AT&T
10. You're better off under the Umbrella.	10. Travelers
11. Making It All Make Sense	11. RCA
12. The Heartbeat of America	12. Morton Salt
13. Solutions That Work	13. Avis
14. Giving Shape to Imagination	14. Lockheed
15. It Just Feels Right.	15. Chevrolet
16. His Master's Voice	16. Saab

Note: Answers appear at the end of Chapter 9.

name. The Dai-Ichi Kangyo Bank slogan "We have your interests at heart" builds upon the brand's heart symbol.

As with the name and symbol, a slogan is most effective if it is specific, to the point, and memorable for some reason—interesting, relevant, funny, catchy, or whatever. It also needs to be linked to the brand. Some brands have spent tens of millions, only to find that few shoppers can link the brand with the slogan. Consider the challenge of Figure 8–4. How many names can *you* get correctly?

QUESTIONS TO CONSIDER

1. Consider the names, symbols, and slogans of your competitors. Which are strong, representing competitive advantages? Which are weak?

2. What are the symbols of your brand? What mental image would you like customers to have of your brand in the future? Do your current name, symbol, and slogan deliver that mental image?

3. Develop some alternative symbols and slogans which would reinforce the mental image you would like your brand to have.

9
·

Brand Extensions
The Good, the Bad,
and the Ugly

Brands have become the barrier to entry, but they are also the means to entry.

Edward Tauber

Three things I never lends—my 'oss, my wife, and my name.

Robert Smith Surtees

THE LEVI TAILORED CLASSICS STORY

In the early 1980s Levi Strauss, a $2 billion firm, enjoyed a large market share in its various product categories and felt that it needed to expand its market in order to maintain growth. The expansion decision was guided by a segmentation study of the men's apparel market which revealed five distinct men's apparel segments.

The first, accounting for 26% of men's apparel, was the utilitarian segment. The utilitarian, a Levi loyalist, sought comfortable, durable clothing for both work and play. The second, the mainstream traditionalist, representing 18% of the market, was older and tended to buy polyester suits at department stores. Levi had made good penetration

An early version of this chapter appeared in the *Sloan Management Review*, July 1990.

in this segment with the "Actionwear" line that featured some "give" to accommodate middle-age spread. Levi had also made good inroads into the "price shopper" and "trendy casual" segments. They had, however, *no* presence in the "classic individualist" segment—and thus *any* penetration there would represent a growth opportunity.

A classic individualist was a clothes horse who tended to buy wool-content items and shop in specialty stores. Representing a solid 21% of the market for men's apparel, he was a heavy buyer of suits, with a suit wardrobe much larger than any other segment's. Unlike the mainstream traditionalist shopper, who relied upon his wife's advice, the classic individualist shopped alone and trusted his own judgment on clothes. He was concerned with having the right look and label. Levi had virtually no presence in his apparel purchases.

Targeting this segment, Levi introduced Levi Tailored Classics, a line of men's wool-content suits which were comparable to competitors' offerings in material, workmanship, and fashion. The distribution emphasized department stores rather than specialty stores, in order to exploit the Levi selling presence in department stores. One differentiating feature was the fact that the suits were sold as "separates"—the slacks and coat selected individually. Thus, customers could be fitted better, and the need for tailoring would be reduced. Further, the suits were priced lower than designer suits yet comparable to a competitive (Hager) line.

Despite a costly professional development and introduction effort the product was not successful, and promotional support was withdrawn within a year. An enormous investment in both resources and reputation did not pay off.

In retrospect, there were several "fit" problems that contributed. For one thing, the target segment took both the concept of separates and the department-store outlets as signals of inferior quality and fashion. The most serious fit problem, however (which in fact surfaced in focus-group concept tests) was the Levi name. Levi meant denim, durable, working men, mining, and good value. Extending it via the Actionwear line to the mainstream traditionalists worked: *They* could buy into the concept of Levi making a suit. However, the classic individualists felt (and were not embarrassed to say) that Levi lacked credibility as a maker of suits of top quality and fashion. They also did not feel that a Levi label reflected their self-image, even though they were less likely to verbalize *this* discomfort.

By contrast Dockers, a pants line established in 1986 without a strong link to Levis, has been a smashing success. Cotton pants that are wide at the top and taper toward the bottom, Dockers provide a "looser" fit to the aging baby-boomer. They offer more comfort and fashion than jeans, yet are separated from dress slacks. Dockers, in fact, has become a strong brand name, with associations to both their distinctive pants and (more generally) new casual clothing. Thus the Dockers name illustrates the tactical and strategic advantages of creating a new name.

BRAND EXTENSIONS

Brand extensions, the use of a brand name established in one product class to enter another product class, have been the core of strategic growth for a variety of firms, especially during the past decade. The power of such a strategy is evidenced by the sheer "numbers." One survey of leading consumer product companies found that 89% of new-product introductions were line extensions (such as a new flavor or package size), 6% were brand extensions, and only 5% were new brands. In general, licensed names are a major factor in retail sales. In fact, over one-third of apparel and accessories expenditures involve licensed names.[1]

The attraction of levering the brand name is powerful—often irresistible when the alternatives are considered. The introduction of a new name in some consumer markets can involve an investment of from $50 million to well over $150 million. Yet *no* expenditure level guarantees success. In fact, the batting average of new products, even with substantial support, is not very reassuring. In contrast, the use of an established brand name can substantially reduce the introduction investment and increase the success probability. Of 7,000 new supermarket products introduced in the 1970s, fully two-thirds of the 93 products that resulted in a business whose sales exceeded $15 million annually were brand extensions.[2]

Brand extensions are a natural strategy for the firm looking to grow by exploiting its assets. Indeed, the most real and marketable assets of many firms are the brand names that they have developed. Thus, one strategic growth option is to exploit that asset by using it to penetrate new product categories or to license it to others for use therein. Another option is to acquire a firm with a brand name which can provide a platform for future growth via brand extensions.

However, it is not all peaches and cream. A brand name can fail to help an extension, or (worse) can even create subtle—and sometimes not so subtle—associations that can hurt the extension. Worse still, the extension can succeed, or at least survive, and damage the original brand equity by weakening existing associations or adding new, undesired ones. Because the extension can dramatically affect a key asset (the brand

FIGURE 9–1 Results of Extending a Brand Name

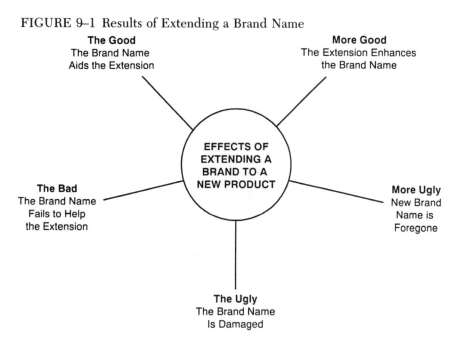

name), both in its original setting and in the new context, a wrong extension decision can be strategically damaging.

The purpose of this chapter is to provide an overview of the brand-extension decision and its possible outcomes as summarized in Figure 9–1—the good, the bad, and the ugly—and to suggest ways to identify the right extensions to pursue. The rationale for an extension (the contributions of both the brand name to the extension, and the extension to the brand name) will be considered first. We will next review the bad (that the brand may harm the extension) and the ugly (that the extension may harm the brand, or prevent a new brand name from being established). Then some suggestions about identifying extension directions will be presented. Finally, several strategy issues involved with the brand-extension decision will be discussed.

THE GOOD: WHAT THE BRAND NAME
BRINGS TO THE EXTENSION

BRAND ASSOCIATIONS

Purchase decisions often are based on a limited number of product attributes. A credible and sustainable point of differentiation with respect

FIGURE 9–2 Leveraging Arm & Hammer's Odor Fighting Association

Arm & Hammer Deodorizer Spray
With Baking Soda
High Recall, Sales-Motivating Commercial

(MUSIC UNDER) ANNCR: (VO) In your refrigerator is the . . .

power to destroy odors.

Arm & Hammer Baking Soda.

(SFX: WHOOSH)

Now the power of baking soda is in New Arm & Hammer Deodorizer Spray.

(SFX: SPRAY) Each spray releases · · ·

deodorizing power crystals. On contact they absorb . . . destroy . . .

even tough household odors. Doesn't just cover them up.

In the air . . . everywhere . . .

safe around food. WOMAN: What a fresh, clean scent.

ANNCR: (VO) Get the power of baking soda in new Arm & Hammer Deodorizer Spray.

Destroys odors in the air . . . everywhere.

The deodorizing power of baking soda in a spray!

Courtesy of Arm & Hammer.

to a key attribute can be difficult to create, especially if one's competitors are established.

If a firm wanted to enter a low-calorie market, for example, it might have to engage in low-calorie shouting matches with competitors as to who has the most low-calorie offering. The result could be an expensive and perhaps impossible positioning task. However, by using the Weight Watchers name, a product line gains a strong set of associations with the Weight Watchers program, and a credible position as an effective component of a weight-control program. The name "Jeep" provided a new line of Jeep shoes with instant associations with upscale casual products for active, adventurous people which would be difficult to achieve without the Jeep name.

A strong association can help the communication task, as well as position a brand. Consider the problem of communicating the idea that a new liquor is rich and creamy. Simply by using the Häagen–Dazs name, Hiram Walker successfully both communicated efficiently a complex message and gained a strong position. Likewise, the Hershey name on a product such as milk immediately communicates not only the chocolate taste but that it will be a "Hershey" taste.

The association needs to get transferred to the new product class. Note the ad for Arm & Hammer Deodorizer Spray shown in Figure 9–2. After the ad reminds the viewer how Arm & Hammer baking soda is used as an odor destroying product in refrigerators, it then helps the view transfer the association to its new product, the Deodorizer Spray. First, it simulates the baking soda being used as a spray in a refrigerator, thus associating baking soda with a spray. Next, it explicitly mentions that the power of baking soda is in the new Deodorizer Spray. An additional link is the use of the words "destroys odors" in both the baking soda and Deodorizer Spray context.

There are a host of brand associations that can provide a point of differentiation for an extension. Edward M. Tauber studied 276 brand extensions and concluded that most fit into seven approaches:[3]

1. *Same product in a different form:* Cranberry juice cocktail and Dole Frozen Fruit Bars
2. *Distinctive taste/ingredient/component:* Philadelphia Cream Cheese Salad Dressing and Arm & Hammer Carpet Deodorizer
3. *Companion product:* Coleman camping equipment, Mr. Coffee coffee, Colgate toothbrushes, and Duracell Durabeam flashlights
4. *Customer franchise:* Visa travelers checks, Sears Savings Bank, and Gerber baby clothes

5. *Expertise:* Honda's experience in small motors helped its lawn mowers, and Bic's razors were aided by a competence in making disposable inexpensive plastic items

6. *Benefit/attribute/feature:* Ivory "mild" Shampoo, Sunkist Vitamin C tablets, and Gillette's Dry Look line

7. *Designer or ethnic image:* Pierre Cardin wallets, Porsche sunglasses, Benihana frozen entrees, and Ragú pasta

QUALITY ASSOCIATIONS

In many situations product-attribute positioning may be futile. A brand can get into a specification battle—the brand with the most fiber, the fastest frequency response, the most effective aspirin, the lowest number of complaints, etc. However, such claims may be short-lived—competitors may alter their product and challenge the claim, or surpass it. Further, customers get confused: They disregard the competing claims and decide on the basis of an intangible perception of quality that is not necessarily based on specific attributes. (Recall the Chapter 5 discussion of "intangibles.")

Competing on the basis of high perceived quality often is an attractive alternative. As noted in Chapter 4, a set of 248 business managers were asked to identify their business's sustainable competitive advantage. By a large margin the most frequent mention was a reputation for quality.[4] The challenge often is to achieve high perceived quality—which sometimes is a more difficult task than actually delivering high quality.

Often the use of established brand names is a good way to achieve a quality perception. Thus, the H-P name provides thousands of products with an umbrella-quality reputation that usually means far more than specifications of individual H-P products. In fact some corporate names (such as H-P, Kraft, GE, and Ford) are on so many products that they lack strong specific associations. Their value, then, is primarily to provide a feeling of perceived quality, and a related feeling that they will be around for some time to come.

The Jaguar name was applied to a line of men's fragrance in part to provide a quality image. The introduction, supported by an ancillary offer of a replica of a Jaguar for $15.00, promised a status scent with drive and passion.

A study of 18 proposed extensions of six brand names—McDonald's, Vuarnet, Crest, Vidal Sassoon, Häagen–Dazs, and Heineken—was conducted by Aaker and Keller.[5] One finding was that the perceived quality of the brand in its original context was a significant predictor of the evaluation of the extension, as long as a fit existed between the two involved product classes. Thus the general perception of quality associated with a name is a key ingredient to the success of its extension. There is little point in extending mediocrity.

AWARENESS/PRESENCE

The first step in gaining acceptance of a new product is developing awareness of the brand name and associating it with the product class. As we saw in Chapter 3, brand-name awareness provides a familiarity which can affect purchases for some low-involvement products (such as gum and detergent) and help determine which brands are considered in other categories (such as cars and computers). For this reason a recognized name can translate directly into a market advantage. Interestingly, the third most mentioned sustainable competitive advantage in the study of 248 business managers was high recognition within the product class—a high visibility or presence.

Creating awareness of a name and associating it with a product class can be expensive. Over $200 million was reportedly spent in changing Esso to Exxon. As noted in Chapter 3, Black & Decker spent over $100 million, mostly on 15-second "spots," to establish its name on the GE line of small appliances it had purchased in 1982. The campaign achieved a 57% awareness level—which was good, but still lower than what GE retained even without making or distributing products in that category.

Many brand names—even some which have not received extensive consumer advertising, such as Winnebago and Arm & Hammer—have recognition levels of over 90%. The use of a recognized brand name on a new product automatically provides name recognition and reduces the communication task to the more manageable one of associating the name to the new product class. We know that it is easier to communicate the fact that the widely known Jell-O now makes Pudding Pops, and later that it makes Gelatin Pops and Fruit Bars, than to communicate the existence of a new name like Swenson's Pudding Pops. One study of 98 consumer brands in 11 markets found that successful brand extensions spent less on advertising than did comparable new-name entrees.[6] Further, the difference increased as the product class matured.

When the brand can support heavy advertising on other categories, the brand-name awareness of the extension will benefit. For example, Helen of Troy, a professional hairstyling tools firm, has built a $100 million retail hair-dryer and curling-wand business by licensing the Vidal Sassoon name. A key ingredient was the massive ongoing advertising support that Vidal Sassoon shampoo and conditioner products received.

TRIAL PURCHASE

A brand name attached to a new product reduces the risk for a prospective buyer. It means that the firm is established, is likely to be

---

A Common Word Part: Inkjet, McMuffin

The use of a common word part can allow the name to accomplish two tasks at once: to indicate an individual product, and to be an indicator of a group of products or a firm.

H-P uses DeskJet, PaintJet, and ThinkJet for three ink-jet printers, and LaserJet IIP and LaserJet III for their laser printers. In sharp contrast, Quame calls their printers Quadlaser, CrystalPrint, LaserTen, ScriptTen, and Sprint. To gain recall and to establish associations for five names is extremely difficult. H-P has the benefit of four advertising efforts to help establish the Jet name. The four other names—Desk, Paint, Think, and Laser—are descriptive variations. When recall of PaintJet, for example, is involved, there are two memory routes, Paint and Jet, that can be accessed. The Jet suffix gives H-P a big advantage.

Consider the value of the Mc word part to represent McDonald's. Again the word part provides an indicator of an individual product, in addition to indicating the firm. Consider the value of the Big Mac as opposed to McDonald's large hamburger, or Chicken McNuggets vs. McDonald's fried chicken morsels, or McKids vs. McDonald's children's clothing.

McDonald's has around 100 names with either Mac or Mc registered, including Big Mac, Chicken McNuggets, Chicken McSwiss, Egg McMuffin, McDonuts, McFortune Cookie, and McRib. They have even developed a McLanguage, including McCleanest, McFavorite, and McGreatest. They protect the Mc word part aggressively, and have objected to a bakery named McBagels, and a McSushi restaurant.

around to support the product, and is unlikely to promote a flawed product. Thus, an IBM or AT&T computer has credibility, while an "Advanced Compute" brand, even with a good product, many have little chance. The established name reduces the risk for the buyer.

In a study of 58 new products introduced into the Philadelphia area, the most important predictor of trial levels was the extent to which a known family brand was involved, and the level of promotion used.[7] Both exceed the impact of distribution, packaging, and brand awareness achieved by advertising. In virtually all new-product concept tests, the addition of an established name such as Pillsbury will greatly enhance initial reaction, interest, and willingness to consider or try the product.

MORE GOOD: EXTENSIONS CAN
ENHANCE THE CORE BRAND

Extensions can (and ideally should) enhance the core brand. Instead of the extension's weakening the brand name and draining its good will, the extension should reenforce its image, providing a building function. Thus, Weight Watchers brand extensions are firmly positioned as weight-control products. They increase the brand's visibility, and support the main association: weight control. Similarly, Sunkist's associations with oranges, health, and vitality are reinforced by the promotion of Sunkist Juice Bars and Sunkist Vitamin C Tablets.

An extension can provide name recognition and associations to new segments. For example, Winnebago Industries sells its expensive campers and motor homes to middle-aged people who can afford the relatively steep price. In 1982, Winnebago licensed a line of camping equipment to build awareness among younger consumers who had not yet heard of Winnebago. At least some buyers of sleeping bags and tents will eventually be prospective buyers of motor homes. Of course, Winnebago runs the risk that, as a result, people will sooner or later feel that the company's campers and motor homes will be made like a flimsy camp stove. However, if the camper and motor-home line is anchored firmly along a quality dimension, and separated from the camping-equipment line in terms of promotion and distribution, this possibility will be reduced.

THE BAD: THE NAME FAILS
TO HELP THE EXTENSION

THE NAME DOES NOT ADD VALUE

When a brand name is added simply to provide recognition, credibility, and a quality association, there often is a substantial risk that even if the brand is initially successful, it will be vulnerable to competition.

Consider Pillsbury Microwave Popcorn, which at first benefited from the Pillsbury name but was vulnerable to the entry of another established name with a parity (or superior) product. The Orville Redenbacher name, for example, entered the category late—and still won with a point of differentiation (expertise in making quality popcorn). The General Mills product, Pop Secret, represented the alternative strategy of developing a new name for the category using one which implies popcorn *and* a product benefit—a secret popping formula. In 1989, Orville Redenbacher held a 36% share of the $420 million microwave popcorn market, while Pop Secret was at 21.7%. Pillsbury, at 4.5%, was one of the also-rans, along with Planters, Jolly Time, Jiffy Pop, and Newman's Own.[8] Pillsbury had a similar experience in microwaveable frozen pizza, where it saw its early gains eroded by those with established pizza names.

It is particularly important for the brand extension to provide a benefit if the product class is well established. For example, a designer name does not always guarantee success, because it does not add value to the product. The Bill Blass name attached to chocolates provided design and prestige associations that were not highly valued by the customer, or at least could not overcome the price premium.

An effort to establish the Beatrice name using the tag line "You've known us all along" did not add any value to the involved brands, such as Wesson and Orville Redenbacher. Further, the effort did not even succeed in making consumers aware that these brands were Beatrice products. There was simply no reason for consumers to make the connection. The result was, at best, wasted awareness-oriented advertising.

A brand attribute and an associated name may only *appear* to offer a benefit. Lilt, a major hair-permanent brand, came out with a shampoo/conditioner designed for hair that had received a perm. For that application, the name Lilt appeared to be a significant asset. However, the focus of the target segment became dry hair rather than permed hair. As a result there was no need or desire for a special perm shampoo: Any shampoo designed for dry hair was acceptable.

It is useful to run a concept test to see if a name actually adds value.

Prospective customers given only the brand name can be asked whether they would be attracted to the product, and why. If they can articulate a reason why the branded new-product concept would be attractive, then the brand is adding value. However, if they are unable to provide a specific reason, it is unlikely that the brand name will add significant value.

NEGATIVE ATTRIBUTE ASSOCIATIONS

There is also the risk that a brand-extension strategy could stimulate negative attribute associations. The Levi Strauss Tailored Classics line of suits failed, in large part because of the negative Levi associations with casual living, rugged material, and the out-of-doors. Examples of brand names which were handicaps to extensions, rather than assets, are not difficult to find:

- The Corn Flakes name reduced the credibility of the honey nut concept of Honey Nut Corn Flakes. The product failed, and was only successful under the Nuts and Honey name without the Corn Flakes association.
- Consumers could not be convinced that Grapefruit Tang would taste like a superior grapefruit drink, because of the strong taste and content associations of the Tang drink.
- Country Time Lemonade had strong taste associations that hurt efforts to extend the name to apple cider.
- Campbell Soup called their line of spaghetti sauces Prego after they found that a Campbell name left a connotation of being orange and watery.
- The Bic name, associated with disposable pens, lighters, and razors, did not work for perfume, in part because cheap/disposable was a handicap in the perfume category.

Log Cabin, the market leader in the griddle-oriented syrup business, was disappointed in its efforts to enter the pancake-mix arena. The association with a sticky, sweet syrup probably did not engender visions of a light and fluffy product. By contrast, Aunt Jemima *was* successful in going the other way—from pancake mix to syrup. Aunt Jemima pancake mix, of course, has links with the Aunt Jemima character—a friendly, warm person who likes to cook pancake breakfasts. These associations were richer and stronger than the Log Cabin associations. Why didn't the Aunt Jemima syrup business come back to damage their core pancake business? The likely reason is that the extensive product experience of Aunt Jemima pancake-mix users, coupled with the strong associations of Aunt Jemima, made it impervious to any impact of the syrup extension.

Sometimes there are some unanticipated subtleties to the transfer. Aaker and Keller found that in testing brand extension concepts, for example, the Crest taste was a problem in Crest gum, but not in Crest mouthwash, although both had positive associations of good tooth care and oral hygiene. Good taste may not be important in mouthwash; indeed, Listerine has associated unpleasant taste with effective freshener action.

Negative associations can sometimes be reduced or suppressed by adding a second brand name with the right connotations, or by elaborating the concept. Thus, there might be a Campbell's Special Torino Spaghetti Sauce: The Campbell's name would be used much like the Kellogg's name on cereals—simply serving to sprinkle some credibility on another brand name. The Special Torino type of subname will cue product-characteristic associations. Alternatively, a concept elaboration could be featured: Campbell's rich, thick, dark spaghetti sauce. The elaboration will reduce the likelihood of Campbell's soup associations emerging.

The Aaker and Keller study showed that product concept elaborations could reduce the incidence of negative associations. An experiment explored whether either of two types of concept elaborations could overcome negative associations engendered by four low-rated brand-extension concepts, such as McDonald's photo processing (e.g., greasy, lack competence). One, elaborating the positive attributes ("The providers of fast, inexpensive, and convenient service") resulted in no improvement in the ratings. The other, elaborating the concept in order to neutralize the negative associations ("Physically separated from the food service and using a well-established camera retailer to process the film") improved the ratings substantially. However, although they went from around 3.5 to 4.0 on a 7-point scale, they were still far short of the successful extension concepts. Success, of course, will depend on the extent to which the negative associations are damaging, and the feasibility and cost of inhibiting their emergence.

An extension that is far removed from the original product (such as Coca-Cola, or McDonald's, and clothing) has the advantage that attributes such as taste cannot be transferred. Thus, where Coca-Cola orange juice would not work, Coca-Cola sweat shirts are acceptable. Of course, in this case the consumer is relying upon the manufacturer of the extension, such as Murjani (Coca-Cola), or the retailer such as Sears (McKid's), rather than on the licensed name to warrant the quality of the clothing.

THE NAME CONFUSES

The name can imply a very different product from what is being delivered. The success of Tuna Helper and Hamburger Helper prompted Betty Crocker to create a chicken version. However, the chicken product required more time, since the chicken content had to be prepared. Further, the name Betty Crocker Cookbook Chicken, which was supposed to suggest a quality homecooked meal, instead was very confusing. Many thought that the product was a cookbook or a recipe. When the name was changed to Chicken Helper, the association with Betty Crocker was reduced and the product was better received.

THE FIT IS POOR

The extension needs to fit the brand. The customer needs to be comfortable with the concept of the brand name's being on the extension. If the fit is poor, desired associations will not transfer but (perhaps worse) will distract, or even precipitate ridicule.

If a premium name such as Rolls–Royce is attached to mundane products such as bicycles or games, customers may feel that the name is being exploited or that it is adding nothing except price. Arm & Hammer was successful, in building on odor-destroying associations, to extend to detergent and oven cleaner, but unsuccessful in extending to an underarm spray deodorant. The thought of an ingredient used in oven cleaners being applied to a sensitive part of the body was unpalatable. In a similar vein, even though Dole has associations with Hawaii, the introduction of Dole Hawaiian resorts or travel services might not be acceptable because it is too far a stretch.

A basis of fit can be provided in a variety of ways, as Figure 9–3 illustrates. One basis of fit can be links between the two product categories. Aaker and Keller found that two types of relationships between product classes were related to the acceptance of extension concepts:

1. *Transferability of skills and assets:* The "brand" is perceived to have the necessary skills and assets needed to make the extension. Crest mouthwash worked, in part because a toothpaste firm is assumed to have the capability to make a mouthwash.

2. *Complementarity:* The extension is used with the product class associated with the brand. Thus, Vuarnet skis worked, even though

FIGURE 9–3 Bases of Fit

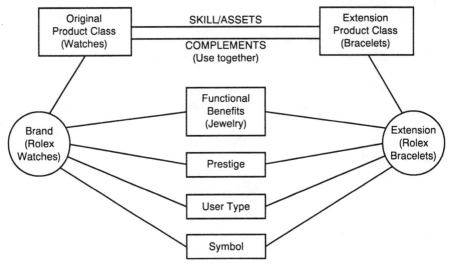

skis are technologically far removed from sunglasses, because Vaurnet sunglasses had developed a close association with skiing.

Fit can also be based on functional attributes relating to brand performance, or on intangible attributes such as prestige or status. Park, Milberg, and Lawson compared extensions for Timex, a watch with strong functional associations, with those for Rolex, a prestige name in watches.[9] The extensions were for products which were either oriented toward prestige (bracelet, necktie, cufflinks) or function (flashlight, calculator, or batteries). The Rolex name was significantly more helpful for the prestige products than was the Timex name, but the reverse was true for the functionally oriented products.

Park, Milberg, and Lawson in a related study asked people to identify four extension possibilities for both Rolex and Timex, and to identify the basis of fit for each suggested extension. The Rolex name generated significantly more names than the Timex name, leading the authors to conclude that when prestige is the basis of fit, a brand can stretch further than when a functional attribute is the basis.

Clearly there can be many sources of a common association, including user types (for babies), sources (Beverly Hills), ingredients (contains oats), and symbols (stagecoach). For example, Wells Fargo generates associations of stagecoach, Old West, safes, and pioneers, as well as banking associations. Thus, the stagecoach and Western associations might suggest a line of Western clothing or a Western theme park. The safe association might suggest burglar-alarm systems or cash-transfer services. McDonald's is associated with Ronald McDonald and his friends, and fun times for kids, making the concept of a McDonald's theme park acceptable.

POOR QUALITY PERCEPTIONS

Tab flavors, such as ginger ale and root beer, were an idea that made sense when Tab was Coca-Cola's diet-drink entry and they wanted to compete in other flavor categories. The concept failed, in part because substantial segments felt that Tab had a disagreeable taste; it was basically perceived as low-quality by large parts of the market.

Even when a brand is generally well regarded there will be some who will have had bad experiences with it, or for some other reason have the impression that it is of low quality. Thus, the use of an extension will limit the market to those who are *not* unfavorably disposed to the brand.

THE EXTENSION IS NOT SUPPORTED

There always is a temptation to establish a new entry "on the cheap," relying on the power of the brand name. Diet Cherry Coke established a substantial business without *any* advertising support, in part because of the strength of the brand name. However, other extensions, such as Cuisinart's spice chopper, which attempted to rely too heavily on a brand name and thus skimped on advertising and promotion support, have not fared so well. Their failure may be mistakenly attributed to the concept rather than to inadequate support.

THE UGLY: THE BRAND NAME IS DAMAGED

The brand name often is the key asset of the firm. It can be more important than the bricks and mortar—or even the people—in terms of replacement investment. It is tempting to evaluate the extension as a business decision on its own merits. However, a key consideration should be the possible damage it could cause to the brand franchise. Having the extension fail is usually not nearly as bad as having it "succeed," or at least survive, and damage the brand name by creating undesirable attribute associations, damaging the brand's perceived quality, or altering existing brand associations.

UNDESIRABLE ATTRIBUTE
ASSOCIATIONS ARE CREATED

An extension will usually create new brand associations, some of which can be potentially damaging to the brand in its original context. Miller High Life declined substantially during the 1980s. One frequently proposed theory is that Miller Lite, by creating lite beer associations, is partially to blame for the decline. A lite beer, to some, means fewer calories achieved by its watery taste. The theory is that the "low-calorie taste" could become associated by some High Life drinkers with the Miller name, which has a lingering "Champagne of Bottled Beer" association. As sales of Miller Lite went from 9.5% share of the U.S. beer market in 1978 to 19% in 1986, the Miller High Life brand declined from 21% to 12% in the same period.

There is certainly the possibility that Sunkist Fruit Rolls hurt the Sunkist health image, that Black & Decker small appliances hurt their power-tool image, and that the Sears Financial Network hurt the retailer's image of value—and, conversely, that the Sears associations hurt Dean Witter, that Carnation Pet Food hurt their other food items, and that Lipton Soup at one time hurt the image of a purveyor of fine teas. One study showed that a brand with products high on a "gentleness" scale had this position adversely affected by a proposed extension that was perceived to be inferior on this dimension.[10]

Such a predicted transfer of negative associations does not always occur. General Mills was very reluctant to disturb the Cheerios brand associations of being a nonsugar cereal. They tested Honey Nut Cheerios for a long time, and even tested an adult cereal position, in order to avoid the Cheerios core market. However, the extension did not damage the sales of Cheerios at all, even though it was used by the same customers. It instead cut into the presweetened portion of their diet. Further, Apple Cinnamon Cheerios was introduced in 1989, gaining a 1.5% share of the cold-cereal market without affecting the share held by either Cheerios (4.8%) or Honey Nut Cheerios (3.1%).[11] The Diet Coke story is similar.

Under what conditions will an extension's potentially negative association be transferred to the original brand context? The transfer should be less likely if (1) the original brand associations are very strong, (2) there is a distinct difference between the original brand and the extensions, and (3) the difference between the original brand and the extensions is not so extreme as to make the extension appear incongruous. Thus, Cheerios has strong associations with oats, the doughnut shape, and "nonsugar." Honey Nut Cheerios, being a presweetened cereal, has a distinct difference which allows the product to be categorized in memory separately. The two categories, while distinct, are *not* incongruous. A Cheerios candy bar, however, might well create a problem for Cheerios.

EXISTING BRAND ASSOCIATIONS ARE WEAKENED

The brand associations created by the extension can fuzz a sharp image which had been a key asset. The danger is particularly acute when a brand's key association is a product class—Kleenex, Perrier, and Tampax, for example, all are synonymous with a product category. Cadbury's association with fine chocolates and candy certainly weakened when it got into such mainstream food products as mashed potatoes, dried milk, soups, and beverages.

Trout and Ries suggested that the meaning of the Scott name became confused when extensions such as ScotTowels, ScotTissue, Scotties, Scottkins, and Baby Scot were added.[12] The names tended to confuse a shopping list and were in sharp contrast to the strong product-class identity of Bounty, Northern, Pampers, and Kleenex. Interestingly, Scott in the mid-eighties sharply reduced its consumer advertising expenditures, backing away from efforts to create strong brands. Instead, their revised strategy was to be a maker of cheap, high-volume products.

It is important to make a distinction between adding associations and diluting them. Jell-O used its association with pudding and creamy taste, plus its wholesome/family-setting associations, to introduce Jell-O Pudding Pops. The Jell-O name helped communicate the product concept and assisted recognition and credibility as well. They then extended Jell-O Pudding Pops to Jell-O Gelatin Pops and Jell-O Fruit Bars.

The question is whether the frozen-novelty association dilutes the original pudding associations or simply adds an association without changing the original. Does the Jell-O name still mean pudding, but also frozen novelties, or is the pudding association weakened? The answer largely involves the strength of the original associations. Some names and symbols (such as the Pillsbury Doughboy and Hewlett-Packard) are so strong that it is very difficult to damage or change existing associations. New associations are simply added—e.g., H-P makes computers as well as test equipment.

As a brand is extended its product-class associations may be weakened, but it may also develop a useful association with a type of product. Thus, Armour (meats), Pillsbury (flour/baking products), Green Giant (vegetables), and Pepperidge Farm (upscale frozen bakery products) retain useful associations with groups of products. One consideration in making extension decisions, then, is whether an extension set can form a coherent whole so it includes useful specific product-oriented associations. In contrast, other brands (such as General Electric and Kraft), and many Japanese and Korean firms (such as Goldstar and Samsung) are associated with so many diverse product classes that their value is mainly on providing name recognition and perceived quality.

When the brand association is not product-related, there is more latitude. Thus, when the dominant association is the personality of Aunt Jemima, the life-style of the Sharper Image customer, the technological superiority of H-P, or the fashion/style of Vuarnet, the extension can go farther afield without affecting the existing associations.

QUALITY IMAGE IS AFFECTED

A reputation for perceived quality is the basis of sustainable competitive advantage for many businesses. There should be a concern that an extension widely exposed but of inferior quality might damage this reservoir of good will.

General Mills attempted to capitalize on the Lacoste alligator, an authentic status symbol during the 1970s, by extending the name into a wide variety of clothing items and by reaching out into new target markets. Observers have attributed the resulting sharp sales fall-off (starting in 1982) to a weakening of the upscale sportsman association.[13] All of a sudden the alligator no longer was a status symbol. Similarly, the failure of the IBM Junior product undoubtedly tarnished the IBM quality reputation, particularly for the low-end "home" market. And the undisciplined use of the Gucci name—at one point there were 14,000 Gucci products—was one of the contributing factors in the fall of Gucci.[14]

Even if an extension is successful, there will be those who dislike some aspect of it or its positioning, and others who have had a bad use experience with the extension. This group may become a problem for the original brand, as their loyalty may be reduced. In the long run, the more exposure that the brand receives via extensions, the larger will the group of people be who will have had a bad experience, or hold a negative attitude toward the brand in some setting.

Attaching the brand to a lower price point enhances the risk that the quality image of the brand itself will be affected. If Hilton were to introduce a set of low-price hotels under some variant of the Hilton name, the core Hilton chain could well suffer. Rolls–Royce once supplied car engines to a limousine selling at one-third of the Rolls–Royce price, and allowed their brand name to be used in the promotion of the cut-price limos—at some cost to their image.

Cadillac introduced the Cimarron in the early 1980s as a version of both GM's Pontiac 2000 and the Chevrolet Cavalier with a bit more gold trim and leather. The Cimarron wasn't aimed at the traditional Cadillac buyer but rather at a less affluent one who would like to move up to a Cadillac name without a Cadillac price tag and who might otherwise buy a BMW. The analysis that there would be little cannibalization was correct. However, the associations with the Cimarron and its target buyers undoubtedly hurt the Cadillac name. In the Landor Associates' 1988 study of brand names, the Cadillac had the 16th spot in awareness but only the 84th place in "esteem." The ill-fated Cimarron effort could well have been a contributing factor.

There is evidence that a very strong brand can withstand a weak extension without being damaged. For example, the Green Giant received no detectable damage from a six-year effort to establish a line of frozen dinners. In another laboratory study, Keller and Aaker found that a brand with a strong perceived quality rating can be surprisingly unaffected by failed extensions (although the failed extensions can affect the ability of the firm to extend *further*).[15]

A DISASTER OCCURS

A disaster out of control of a firm, such as the discovery that an Ivory model was a porno star, that Tylenol boxes had been tampered with, or that Rely products presented a serious health hazard, can happen to almost any brand name. To the extent that the name is used on many other products, the damage will be more extensive.

In Chapter 7, the alleged sudden-acceleration problem with Audi 5000 cars, Audi's response—to blame American drivers—and the Audi sales slump were discussed. A study of the incident's impact on the depreciation rates of other Volkswagen products is illuminating.[16] The Audi 4000, which had no such problem, was impacted nearly as much as the Audi 5000 (7.3% vs. 9.6% respectively), whereas the Audi Quattro suffered a smaller effect (4.6%). Because the Quattro was less closely tied to Audi, its name was separated from the Audi identity on the car, and Quattro ads often did not mention Audi at all. Further, other Volkswagen names (such as Porsche and Volkswagen) were not affected.

The threat of a disaster to the Fisher–Price name has inhibited them from going into the child-care business. They have had very positive associations of quality playthings for children that could very likely be transferred to child care. However, just one child-molestation incident, or even accusation, might cause serious damage to the whole Fisher–Price equity.

THE BRAND FRANCHISE IS CANNIBALIZED

An important part of brand equity is a brand's customer loyalty. If sales of a brand extension come at the expense of the original brand (the original brand's sales are cannibalized), the extension's sales may not compensate for the damage to the original brand's equity.

Gillette had a strong brand name in the shaving-cream market—Right Guard—and wanted to attack Barbasol with a low-end entry. The vehicle was their Good News! line of razors that was positioned as a low-end line and carried a low price. Gillette thus tested a Good News! Shaving Cream by Gillette. The test showed that it took sales instead from Right Guard. In part, the problem was that consumers felt that they could save money by buying Good News! and still get a Gillette product.

Campbell's, after trying a series of extensions such as Campbell's Cup, Campbell's Chunky, Campbell's "Home Cookin'," Campbell's Golden Classics, and Campbell's Creamy Natural, introduced a soup line under the Prego name. The Prego brand provides an Italian soup position that is likely to sharply attack the Progresso line of Italian-style soups, which had been taking share from Campbell's, without cannibalizing the basic Campbell's line.

A key question in this whole area is the degree of overlap between segments. If the crossover between canned and dry cat food, or powdered and liquid detergent, for example, is low, then cannibalization may be low.

MORE UGLY: A NEW BRAND
NAME IS FOREGONE

Perhaps the worst potential result of an extension is a foregone opportunity to create a new brand equity. Consider where P&G would be without Ivory, Camay, Dreft, Tide, Cheer, Joy, Pampers, Crest, Secret,

Sure, Folger's, Pringles, and their 70 or so other brands. Consider how much more value is represented by the P&G brands than a set of brands such as P&G bar soap, P&G laundry detergent, P&G dishwashing detergent, P&G diapers, P&G toothpaste, P&G deodorant, P&G coffee, and P&G potato snacks.

Establishing a new brand name provides a vehicle with which to generate a set of distinct associations without being burdened with an existing set. If the Macintosh computer had been named the Apple 360, it would not have developed the associations, loyalty, and equity of the Macintosh name. Contrast the Apple branding strategy with that of H-P: It can be argued that H-P has been handicapped by its decision not to establish distinct names, first for its calculators and subsequently for its computers. A different name in each case might have helped to differentiate the H-P lines.

Consider the value of the name Dustbuster as opposed to Black & Decker's Portable Vacuum. The Dustbuster name provides a dramatic message of cleaning effectiveness. It also provides a unique (and possibly superior) indicator for the product that could well serve to differentiate it in the future. There is also the possibility that the name may allow Black & Decker to capitalize on being the first to enter the market with such a product by having the name *mean* the product (the Xerox phenomenon).

A new brand also provides a platform for growth. For example, after introducing Campbell's Prego name for a line of spaghetti sauces to compete with Ragú, the Prego name was then available for use in other lines, such as frozen Italian entries. Too, as noted above, it has even been used for a soup line to compete with the Italian-style Progresso.

The establishment of a unique new brand name, then, involves the consideration of:

—the strength of the name associations and their usefulness in telling the brand story. Does the name help the communication task? Does it make learning the brand message easier?

—the strength and usefulness of the name in creating long-term loyalty and advantage. Is it unique, and likely to be superior to competitors in stimulating associations?

—the cost of establishing the name, of gaining awareness and associations. Can the brand justify marketing support adequate to establish the name? (While Honda could develop the Acura line in the U.S., it chose to retain the Honda name in the smaller European countries.)

HOW TO GO ABOUT IT

Developing a brand extension systematically involves three steps: identifying brand associations, identifying products linked to those associations, and selecting the best candidates from that product list for concept testing and new-product development.

WHAT ARE THE ASSOCIATIONS?

The first step is to determine the associations with the brand name. As discussed in Chapter 6, a variety of techniques can be employed, such as:

• Name associations: What comes to mind when the following brands are mentioned?
• Projective techniques: Jan had just finished eating Campbell's tomato soup and felt . . .
• Exploring perceptual differences: What other brands is it different from, and why?

For example, Vuarnet generates associations with expensive, skiing, quality, style, fashion, trendy, and UV protection. Vidal Sassoon generates associations with expensive, good scent, brown bottle, French, hair designer, fashionable, hair salons, and hair care.

Typically, a large set of associations emerges, from say 10 or 20 all the way up to over 100. Judgment will be needed to reduce this list to the most promising set of 5 to 15 on which to focus. One criterion is the strength of association with the brand. Is it extremely strong? (Nearly everyone associates McDonald's with kids, for example.) Or is it weak? A list of associations could be scaled by a set of customers asked to indicate how much the word reminds them of McDonald's.

Associations will be more useful if they can provide a link (a basis of fit) with other categories, and provide competitive leverage for extensions. In that respect, associations with a product class usually are limiting. The association of Chanel with perfume (or even with a female personal-grooming product) is more limiting than a French association or a style association.

DETERMINING CANDIDATE PRODUCT CLASSES

For each of the major associations, or sets of associations, the next step is to identify related product categories. Again, customers could be asked directly to generate names of products related to the associations. Thus, McDonald's could build on the "kids" association to have a line of toys, clothing, or games directed at children. The "efficient, low-cost" association might allow them to enter any service in which those qualities might be valued. A McDonald's clothing store would therefore be expected to sell clothes at a relatively low price and in an efficient manner.

Table 9–1 shows the results of a search for extension products for Vaseline Intensive Care Lotion that used this approach.[17] Eight primary

TABLE 9–1 Vaseline Intensive Care Associations and Related Products

Associations	Related Products
Moisturizer	Soap
	Face cream
	Skin cream
Lotion	Sunburn
	After-shave
	Baby lotion
Medicinal	Antiseptic
	First-aid cream
	Hemorrhoid cream
Purity	Cotton
	Gauze
	Sterile pads
Body care	Emery boards
	Muscle toner
	Cotton swabs
Pump bottle	Liquid hair-net
	Mustard
	Glass cleaner
Baby care	Diapers
	Powder
	Oil
Fragrance	Perfume
	Room deodorizer
	Deodorant

SOURCE: Adapted from Figure 3 in Edward M. Tauber, "Brand Franchise Extension: New Product Benefits from Existing Brand Names," *Business Horizons*, Vol. 47, March–April 1981, pp. 36–41.

associations were obtained. For each, three related categories are shown. The sharp differences in brand vision that emerge are shown graphically. If the brand should build on a moisturizer association it could go into soap, face cream, and skin cream, all with a moisturizer position. In contrast, if it were to build on the medicinal association, antiseptic, first-aid cream, and hemorrhoid cream would be logical. Clearly, the choice of the first extension would tend to solidify an association and influence the choice of subsequent extensions.

In fact, Vaseline did build on the lotion and moisturizer associations, but positioned them as medicinal/therapeutic, thereby drawing on the third association.[18] Their first extension, Vaseline Lip Therapy (introduced in 1976), was followed by Vaseline Intensive Care Foam Bath and Vaseline Intensive Care Skin Lotion. The use of "Therapy" and "Intensive Care" signaled the medicinal/therapeutic position. Note the ad shown in Figure 9–4. All have done well in the market, as has Vaseline Baby Oil, a close competitor with Johnson & Johnson. Not so successful, however, is Vaseline Hair Tonic. Perhaps a moisturizer association is not helpful in that category—or, more likely, the product is perceived as being greasy.

Another approach is to focus on such bases of fit as complementarity, transferability of skills and assets, user types, attributes, benefits, components, and symbols. Consider complementarity—which other products would be used in the same application (perfume with lipstick, for example). Transferability of skills and assets reflects the fact that makers of a product (such as potato chips) will be perceived to have a capability of making some other products (such as pretzels) better than others (such as pickles). A common attribute such as aroma could lead to products that have aroma as a key attribute.

SELECTING CANDIDATE PRODUCTS

From the resulting list of products, the next task is to select a limited number to explore through a concept-testing stage. Two primary criteria should be used. First, the brand should be perceived to fit the extension. Second, it should provide some point of advantage.

The extension needs to fit the brand—the customer should be comfortable with the concept of the brand being on the extension. If the brand is to help the extension by transferring a perceived quality or an association, a basis of fit will make that transfer more feasible. If the

FIGURE 9–4 A Vaseline Extension

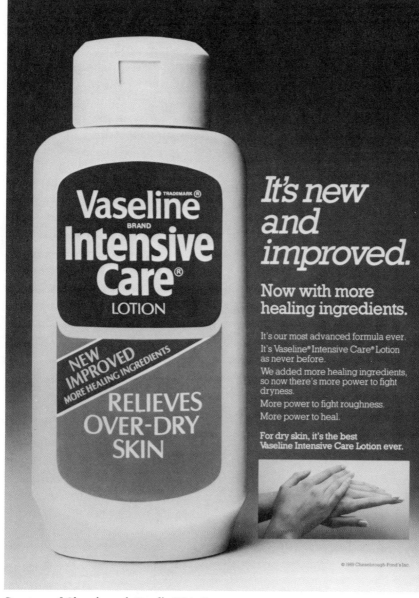

Courtesy of Chesebrough-Pond's USA Co.

customer perceives a lack of fit, he or she may become distracted, focus upon the fit issue, and not allow the desired transfer to occur. At the extreme, a perceived incongruity could stimulate ridicule and laughter.

One approach to the evaluation of fit is simply to ask respondents whether a brand name fits a series of alternative product classes. A low fit rating, however, is not necessarily fatal. Some products that don't appear to fit may actually do so if positioned in such a way as to accentuate a link between the brand and the product class. Thus, an attractive extension (it involves an attractive market, for example) may merit a more extensive concept test, even if there appears to be a fit problem.

A particularly common fit problem occurs when a brand is used on a trivial (for the brand) product class, a product class in which there is little perceived differentiation. The brand will then be perceived to be exploiting its name because it has little to offer. Further, it will probably be perceived as being overpriced. Aaker and Keller found such a situation with the concept of Heineken popcorn.

A second criterion to be used in selecting candidate extensions is that the extension should provide a point of advantage. If a customer cannot say why he or she would like a proposed extension, there is cause for concern. The name should provide a reason to buy. It should suggest a benefit such as higher quality, more chocolate, more reliable performance, or a feeling of status.

Again, market research can provide guidance. Prospective customers can be asked to identify competitors of the proposed extension, and to list ways in which the extension may be superior to the offerings of each competitor (or sets of competitors), and ways in which it will be inferior. To gain insight as to whether the benefits of the extension are sufficient, customers can be asked to provide an overall evaluation on the basis of just the name. Asking next for the reasons for the evaluations can provide insights into the importance of the potential benefits and liabilities of the extension. Of course, such an approach will not, however, reflect the impact of any new association which could be created as part of the brand-extension positioning strategy.

STRATEGY CONSIDERATIONS

Since the brand-extension decision is in fact a strategic one, in making such a move several strategic issues should be considered.

WHEN DOES AN EXTENSION MAKE SENSE?

A brand extension will tend to be the optimal route when:

1. Strong brand associations provide a point of differentiation and advantage for the extension.
2. The extension helps the core brand by reinforcing the key associations, avoiding negative associations, and providing name recognition. When the brand name provides only name recognition and a perceived quality umbrella, often the extension will be vulnerable to competition.
3. The category will not support the resources needed to establish a new name, or a new name will not provide a useful set of associations or a platform for future growth.

THINK STRATEGICALLY

Since an extension builds upon the associations of a brand name it is important to think beyond the first extension to future growth areas, as was seen in the Vaseline case. A brand name such as Rossignal will have a set of associations like French, skiing, technology, quality, and style. The first extension will probably build up some of those associations and weaken others. The resulting set will then provide the basis for future extensions, and inhibit others. Thus, it is important to think through which umbrella associations should ultimately provide the brand group with a fit logic and a source of differentiation and advantage. Unless this thought process occurs before the first extension, significant opportunities might be lost.

USE NESTED BRAND NAMES

It is possible to develop brand names within brand names and use them to develop associations and platforms for new growth. For example, Black & Decker had a line of appliances designed to be mounted off the kitchen counter. The phrase "Spacesaver," developed as an umbrella name for the line, provided a link to the key customer benefit of saving shelf space. Jell-O introduced Deluxe Bars, an extension of Jell-O Pudding Pops providing peanut- and chocolate-covered flavors not offered in the standard Pudding Pop line.

A nested brand name provides the reassurances of an established name and the product-attribute associations as well. The only problem is that it still represents a new name which needs to be established. Unless there is the sales base, and the will and ability to establish the name, the name may provide confusion instead of value.

Campbell's, which has Manhandler, Homestyle, and Special Request in addition to distinct lines of Chunky, Home Cookin', Golden Classics, Gold Label, Creamy Natural, Soup du Jour (a frozen microwave soup), Cookbook Classics (a microwaveable, shelf-stable soup), and Fresh Chef (refrigerated soups), may have too many. Each of these was costly to establish, and added to the potential for confusion. Eventually the cost in dollars and confusion to establish such a variety of names may surpass their value in terms of offering associations.

HEDGE YOUR BETS

The risk of a brand extension can be reduced if the brand name is not linked too closely with the new product. A problem with, say, Kellogg's Product 19 (e.g., if it contained an ingredient involved in a cancer scare) might then be isolated to the Product 19 line. Cup-a-Soup from Lipton represents less risk to its core-brand name than if the core brand were a part of the labeled name, as it is in Campbell's Cup. Distancing the brand name from the extension is particularly helpful in vertical brand extensions, whereby a brand is extended down to a lower-quality product, and it is important that the original price/quality positioning remain unaffected by the extension.

Marriott was very concerned about how to use the Marriott name in their new hotel lines. Figure 9–5 shows their decision. The top-line Suites Hotel carries the Marriott name, and should reinforce its progenitor's awareness and perceived quality. The others represent problems, since they are a cut below the flagship Marriott name. The solution: Have a "by Marriott" connotation. For example, "Courtyard by Marriott," in which Courtyard is the featured name, provides the essence of the reassurances of the Marriott association, but with less risk to the parent organization than would a name that more prominently featured the magical word "Marriott."

The use of the Marriott name, especially by the economy-positioned Fairfield Inn line, is a Marriott risk. Travelers may well think they are getting Marriott quality when staying at Courtyard, or even Fairfield. But at least some of the core Marriott clientele are sure to turn (or return) to less-"contaminated" prestige hotels.

FIGURE 9–5 The Marriott Line

The use of a corporate name to endorse a weak brand, such as putting the name Nabisco on Royal Pudding, will usually be of limited help. It may help reassure first-time purchasers, but it also may have little ability to add credibility and perceived quality—because of a perceived fit problem with the product class, or because its perceived quality is not exceptional.

THE STAGE IN THE PRODUCT LIFE CYCLE

A brand extension has a larger comparative advantage in an established product class when the brand name helps generate awareness, associations, and distribution in a cluttered marketplace. By contrast, the risk to a brand name is greatest when a product class is young. Consistent with these judgments, the aforementioned study of 98 consumer nondurable brands in 11 markets (page 213) found that all but two of the 11 pioneer brands (the first brands into the market) were new-name brands (both the extensions actually failed), that the use of brand extensions by the new entrants increased as the product class matured, and that the survival rate of the nonpioneering new entrants using extensions was greater than that of those using new-name brands.

PROTECTING AND NURTURING THE BRAND NAME

Clearly, the viability of growing by using extensions is based on the equity of the original brand name. Consequently, it is crucial that the name be protected and nurtured. Since its associations can be influenced by any market activity, the marketplace needs to be actively managed. In particular, sales promotions, product composition decisions, distribution decisions, and pricing policies can affect the brand. When those decisions are made, the concept of brand equity should be at the forefront.

QUESTIONS TO CONSIDER

1. Develop a list of candidate brand extensions that have logical links to your brand.
2. For several candidate brand extensions analyze them in terms of their implications—the good, the bad, and the ugly (see Figure 9–1).
3. Think strategically. Jumping ahead of a logical brand extension,

what should be the set of brands and subbrands in the future? How should they interrelate?

4. What is the role of the corporate name? How should it be used in supporting other brands?

Answers to the slogan test from Figure 8–4 in Chapter 8.

1. Clairol	9. AT&T
2. American Express	10. Travelers
3. Avis	11. Microsoft
4. Miller Lite	12. Chevrolet
5. Morton Salt	13. Ameritech
6. Zenith	14. Lockheed
7. Toshiba	15. Mazda
8. Saab	16. RCA

10

Revitalizing the Brand

A rough sea makes a great captain.

Marketing should focus on market creation, not market sharing.

Regis McKenna

THE YAMAHA STORY

Yamaha Pianos offers an example of how a declining market can be revitalized.[1] After decades of investment and effort, Yamaha had succeeded in capturing 40% of the global piano market. Unfortunately, this market was declining by 10% every year and low-cost Korean firms were entering. It was a classic time to milk the brand equity and try to recover as much return as possible. Clearly, to even maintain share was going to be difficult and unrewarding.

Yamaha responded by developing the Yamaha Disklavier (shown in Figure 10–1). Introduced into the U.S. in January of 1988, the Disklavier functions and plays just like comparable Yamaha pianos, except that it also includes an electronic control system. This system is based on a combination of digital and optical technology which can distinguish among 127 different degrees of strength and speed of key touch. Because of the digital base, each keystroke can be recorded with great accuracy and stored on a 3.5″ disk. The disk can be used to replay a piece exactly

FIGURE 10–1 The Yamaha Disklavier

The concert season at 930 Morningstar Lane
will feature Steve Allen, George Shearing, Peter Nero
and the Yamaha Disklavier piano.

Of course, the artists won't appear at the Henderson residence in person, but the
performances will be extraordinarily live just the same... with PianoSoft™

pre-recorded disks and the Disklavier™
piano. ■ *Listening Series* disks
reproduce every nuance
of the artist's
original performance when played back on the
Disklavier.™ ■ So, if you're not invited to the
Henderson's concert series,
audition the PianoSoft™
library and the Disklavier™
piano at your authorized
Yamaha piano dealer and
begin planning your own
star-studded concert season.

YAMAHA **disklavier** PIANO

© 1990 Yamaha Corporation of America, Keyboard Division, P.O. Box 6600, Buena Park, CA 90622

KPARMS

Courtesy of Yamaha Corporation of America.

as it was played; every nuance of phrasing is meticulously reproduced.

In addition to reproducing the original performance the Disklavier can also modify it. The tempo can be adjusted up to 20% faster or 50% slower in order to capture a different sound. The composition can also be transposed into a different key, again allowing a different sound. Or a portion of the sound (such as the upper half of the keyboard) can be deleted so that a student can practice using only the right hand while the left-hand part plays, or vice versa. Although the Disklavier *is* a piano (termed an "acoustic" piano to distinguish it from electronic synthesizers that only produce a piano sound), it can be connected to digital instrumentation which will provide the professional musician additional flexibility in producing music.

The Disklavier offers considerable benefits, especially for the professional. We have already seen that a composer or arranger, using the instrument to alter the key and/or the tempo of the piece, can explore variations of an execution. Additionally, a vocalist or instrumentalist can have the piano accompanist's part recorded on a disk so that it will be available for other practice sessions. No longer will practice depend upon a live accompanist: A lounge or store with a Disklavier piano can replace that artist with the recorded version.

A teacher can use the record/replay, especially with the slow-down option, to demonstrate technique or to help display errors or deficiencies in play. Linking the piano with a source of background music can serve to make scale drills more useful and enjoyable for the student. Practice with one hand can be more meaningful if the music from the other hand is being played by the Disklavier. A disk of a student's early efforts can provide a baseline record against which to demonstrate later improvement, and perhaps a record to place beside a periodic photo album as a journal of formative experiences.

Most intriguing, however, is the value of the Disklavier to those who do not play the piano well enough to provide entertainment to others. These unfortunates now have the potential to have Vladimir Horowitz, George Shearing, or Liberace play in their home. A library of disks, the Yamaha PianoSoft Library, allows a user to obtain and present specially prepared recorded versions of selected live performances of the best artists. The piano therefore does not have to stand idle when a family member is not practicing, or (more importantly) when the last family member gives up on learning and practicing the piano.

In essence Yamaha reinvented the player piano, which in its heyday of the 1920s provided music to the home, and *still* enjoys associations with family, fun, and "live" music. The Disklavier, of course, provides a level of reproduction quality that is a far cry from the limited quality of the old player piano with its key-activating, punched-paper rolls.

In part, the piano industry was being undercut by the clever gimmickry of electronic keyboards and organs, which had special appeal for the gimmick-loving younger crowd. The high-end piano was being replaced in the market by keyboards costing a small fraction of the price—but the Disklavier provided a response. Those who were proud of their furnishings, and/or wanted the look, sounds, and feelings associated with a *real* piano, now had another option.

The Disklavier and (as one might expect) its competitors appear to have revitalized a declining industry. Three years after its introduction the Disklavier, which sold for $9,000 to $25,000, was the industry leader, and represented 20% of Yamaha's piano sales. The instrument got a big boost when it was used early in 1990 to recreate a performance of George Gershwin playing "Swanee." Interestingly, over half of its buyers do not play the piano, suggesting that the player-piano legacy is an important driver of purchase decisions. Also, over half (50% of grand buyers and 63% of upright buyers) of the buyers have already had a piano. Thus, for some at least, the Disklavier is undoubtedly making the traditional piano obsolete.

Another intriguing music-oriented business, this pioneered by firms such as PianoDisc and QRS Music Rolls, provides a "retrofit kit" (for around $2,500 to $4,000) which turns existing pianos into a version of the Disklavier. There is a base of something like 40 million pianos in the U.S., many of which have become pieces of furniture producing memories rather than music. The kids either have left home or become involved in competing activities. Meaningful sales of the retrofit kit would provide a substantial side market for digital disks (not to be confused with CDs), and even for piano tuners. People would now have an incentive to have their piano tuned regularly.

Faced with a declining market, the conventional approach in the piano world as elsewhere is simply to compete harder by cutting costs, adding differentiating features to improve margins and market share, or milking the business by drawing down the equity. Instead of trying to beat competition in a rather sick business area, Yamaha developed a product breakthrough which created a new niche, one with high growth potential in which they could develop substantial competitive advantages. The result appears to be the dramatic transference of a declining, unattractive business area into an exciting growth context.

REVITALIZATION OPTIONS

What if brand equity has stagnated? Must a firm be satisfied with
maintaining a brand which is old and tired or just a plodder? In this
chapter we consider the possibility of revitalizing a brand which may be
old in spirit but, redirected, may have planty of life left. In revitalizing
the brand, the goal is not only to generate added sales levels but to have
them based upon enhanced equity, a move which often involves improved
recognition, enhanced perceived quality, changed associations, an expanded customer base, and/or increased loyalty.

In fact, the revitalization of a brand usually is substantially less costly
and risky than introducing a new brand, which can cost tens of millions
and will more likely fail than succeed. Firms look at brands something
like the way homeowners view homes: It is cheaper, and often better,
to fix one up or add onto it than to buy a new one.

Not all brands are candidates for revitalization, however. Often there
is a temptation to try to revive an old friend that simply cannot overcome

FIGURE 10–2 Revitalizing the Brand

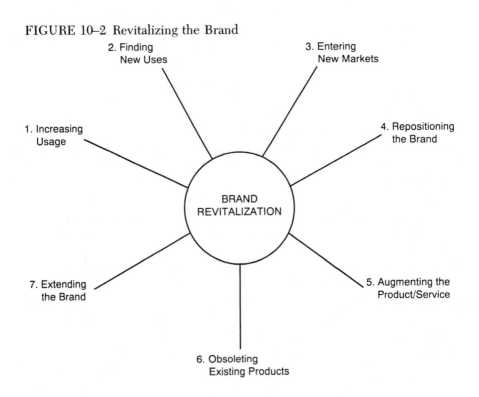

either its liabilities or a sinking market. There has to be a workable concept to breathe new life into the brand. The final section of this chapter considers problems of product "old age," when maintenance is required and even when product "death" must be looked in the face.

There are seven avenues for brand revitalization. One (number 7 in Figure 10–2), by exploiting brand equity through brand extensions, was discussed in detail in Chapter 9. The six other approaches are shown in Figure 10–2, and discussed in the following pages of this chapter. Although each provides a useful perspective, providing a different route to revitalization, none is mutually exclusive. For example, the Yamaha Piano case involved virtually all of them: (1) product usage was increased, (2) new uses were found, (3) a new market was attacked (those who didn't play), (4) the brand was repositioned, (5) the product was augmented, (6) the current product was obsoleted, and (7) the brand name was extended.

It is useful to have seven different ways of looking at the revitalization objective even though several of them may come up with the same solution. Each has a different perspective, and the use of several maximizes the possibility that a good approach will be found. This all follows a prime tenet of creative thinking: Looking at a familiar problem from a different perspective can be the key to finding a novel, creative solution.

1. INCREASING USAGE

Attempts to revitalize a brand by improving its market share through improving the brand or using more aggressive marketing will often stimulate a vigorous competitive response. The alternative of attempting to increase usage among current customers is usually less threatening to competitors, and thus can be a more effective way to increase the size of the brand's sales base, and thus its equity. Instead of trying to get a bigger slice of the pie, it's usually easier and more rewarding to attempt to make the pie bigger.[2]

When developing programs to increase usage, it is useful to begin by asking some fundamental questions about both the user and the consumption system in which the product is embedded: Why isn't the product or service used more? What inhibits the usage decision? How does the light user differ from the heavy user in terms of attitudes and habits?

Increased product usage can be precipitated in two ways, as detailed

TABLE 10–1 Increasing Usage in Existing Product-Markets

Approach	Strategy	Examples
Frequency of Use/ Consumption	Reminder communication	Jello Pudding
	Position for frequent use	Shampoo, car care
	Position for regular use	Flossing teeth after meals
	Make the use easier or more convenient	Dixie Cup dispenser, microwaveable
	Provide incentives	Frequent-flyer plan
	Reduce undesirable consequences of frequent use	Gentle shampoo
	Use on different occasions	Cereal as snack vs. breakfast
	Use at different locations	Radio in shower
Level of Use/ Consumption	Reminder communication	Increase insurance coverage
	Provide incentives	Special price for accessories
	Influence norms	Use of larger containers
	Reduce undesirable consequences of increased use level	Low-calorie candy
	Develop positive associations with use occasions	Frito–Lay—"Can't Just Eat One"

in Table 10–1: by increasing the frequency of use, and by increasing the quantity used in each application.

INCREASING THE FREQUENCY OF USE

Reminder Communication. In some contexts, awareness as reflected in top-of-mind recall of either the brand or the use occasion (or both) is the driving force. A problem here is that whereas some people know about the brand and/or their use of it, they simply do not think of using it without being prodded. In these cases, reminder advertising may be what is needed. Steak sauce and other condiment brands conduct reminder advertising campaigns to obtain more-frequent usage. A manufacturer of canned spiced ham found that most customers kept the product in their pantry "just in case." The problem was to get it used in recipes. The strategy employed was a reminder-advertising and promotion campaign. General Foods conducted a reminder campaign for Jell-O Pudding, with Bill Cosby asking, "When was the last time you served pudding, Mom?"

Routine maintenance functions like dental checkups or car lubrication are easily forgotten, and reminders can make a difference. An Arm & Hammer consumer survey revealed that people who use baking soda as a deodorizer in refrigerators thought that they changed the box every four months when actually they do so every 14 months.[3] An advertising campaign, geared to seasonal reminders to replace the box, attempted to change these habits.

Position for Frequent or Regular Use. Products can change an image of occasional usage to one of frequent usage by a repositioning campaign. For example, the advertising campaigns for Clinique's "Twice-a-Day" moisturizer and "Three glasses of milk per day" both represent efforts to change the perception of the products involved. A related approach is to position for regular use, because a usage habit is the best guarantee that the usage will be maintained. An advertising campaign, for example, might emphasize the need for a brush-after-every-meal habit, or the desirability of phoning a relative once a week.

Make the Use Easier. Asking why customers do not use the product or service more often can lead to approaches for making product use easier. For example, a Dixie Cup or paper-towel dispenser encourages use by reducing the usage effort. Packages that can be placed directly in a microwave make usage more convenient. A reservation service can help those who must select a hotel or similar service. Frozen waffles and Stove-Top Stuffing are examples of product modifications that increased consumption by making usage more convenient.

Provide Incentives. Incentives can be provided to increase consumption frequency. Programs such as the airlines' frequent flyer plans can affect usage. A problem is to structure it so that usage is affected and so that it does not simply become a vehicle for debilitating price competition. Price incentives (such as two for the price of one) can also be effective—but also risk stimulating a focus upon price.

Reduce Undesirable Consequences of Frequent Use. Sometimes there are good reasons why a customer is inhibited from using the product more frequently. If such reasons can be addressed, usage may increase.

For example, some people might believe that frequent hair-washing may not be healthy. A product designed to be gentle enough for daily use might alleviate the worry and stimulate increased usage. A low-calorie, low-sodium, or low-fat version of a food product may sharply increase the market. The brand that becomes best associated with the product change will be in the best position to capitalize on the increased market.

Use at Different Occasions or Locations. Increased usage can be obtained by asking customers when and where the usage is occurring. Can new times and/or places be introduced? Makers of fruit juices have attempted to move their products from the highly competitive breakfast-only beverage business to snack uses. A fertilizer product can be used on shrubs and trees as well as on lawns. A radio called "Wet Tunes— The Shower Radio" was designed for use in the shower.

INCREASING THE QUANTITY USED

Similar techniques can be employed to increase the quantity used on each occasion:

1. An insurance customer can be reminded to consider increasing the coverage on a house whose replacement value increased. A shirt buyer might be reminded to consider a tie or other accessory.

2. Incentives can be used. A fast-food restaurant, for example, might attempt by pricing or promotion to increase the number of items purchased at a meal. A special price would be available if say a drink and fries were ordered with a hamburger.

3. Efforts can be made to affect the usage-level norms. The size of a "normal" serving might be influenced by creating a larger container and getting it accepted.

4. The perceived undesirable consequences of heavy consumption might be addressed. Thus, a light beer or a low-calorie salad dressing could remove a reason to restrict the usage level. Life-Saver candies have advertised that one piece has fewer calories than most people think.

5. Positive associations with use occasion might be developed through advertising. Thus, a sense of fun and refreshment associated with Pepsi-Cola might encourage heavier usage. Frito–Lay has used the "Can't just eat one" tag line to emphasize the taste pleasure. A computer equipment firm could associate increased business efficiency with buying a more powerful system with more terminals.

2. FINDING NEW USES

The detection and exploitation of a new functional use for a brand can rejuvenate a business which has been considered a has-been for years. A classic example is Jell-O, which began strictly as a dessert product but found major sources of new sales in applications such as Jell-O salads.

Arm & Hammer Baking Soda's annual sales were around $15 million and stagnant in the early 1970s, when the suggestion of using the well-known product to deodorize refrigerators was advanced.[4] The results, stimulated by a 1972 advertising campaign, were spectacular. The number of households that reported using the product in this application rose from 1% to 57% in just 14 months. Later campaigns suggested its use as a sink deodorizer, a freezer deodorizer, a cat-litter deodorant, a dog deodorant, and a treatment for swimming pools. By 1981, Arm & Hammer was a $150 million business. Extending the brand into deodorizer products (recall Figure 9–2 in Chapter 9), dentifrices, and laundry detergent, by 1990 the brand had sales exceeding $400 million.

Other brands successfully finding growth by means of new applications are:

- Grape Nuts, used as a garnish, is served over yogurt or ice cream; and microwaved with milk makes a fast, hot breakfast or snack.
- A chemical process developed for use in oil fields to separate water from oil is now used by water plants to get rid of unwanted oil
- Lipton Soup includes recipes for new uses on boxes and in ads that suggest "Great meals start with Lipton—recipe soup mix—soup." The recipe concept is even in the slogan.

The identification of new uses can best be obtained by market research determining exactly how customers use the brand. From the set of uses that emerge, several can be selected to pursue. For example, users of external analgesics were asked to keep a diary of their uses.[5] A surprising finding was that about one-third of Ben-Gay's usage, and over 50% of its volume, went for arthritis relief instead of muscle aches. A separate marketing strategy was developed for this use, featuring dancers (e.g., Ann Miller) and football players (e.g., John Unitas) who now have arthritis, and the brand caught a wave of growth.

Another tack is to look at application areas of competing product forms. The widespread use of raisins prompted Ocean Spray to create dried cranberries. They are used in cookies, and in cereals such as Muesli, with a "Made with real Ocean Spray cranberries" seal on the package.

They also are being tried as a snack food, tentatively called Ocean Spray Craisins.

Sometimes a larger payoff is to the firm that can provide applications not currently in general use. Thus, surveys of only current applications may be inadequate. Firms such as General Mills have sponsored recipe contests, one objective of which has been to create new uses for the product by discovering a new "recipe classic." For a product (like stick-on labels) which can be used in many ways, it might be worthwhile to conduct formal brainstorming sessions or other creativity exercises.

If some application area has been uncovered that could create substantial sales, it needs to be evaluated. *First*, a market survey or other forecasting device might be used to estimate the potential level: How many customers could use the product in that way? What level of product purchase would that application support for each customer? Arm & Hammer conducted over 150 market research studies to support its development of new-use applications and new products.

Second, the feasibility and costs of exploiting the application area need to be assessed. Some new applications can require substantial marketing programs. Angostura Bitters, a 160-year-old brand used primarily in Manhattans, decided to promote nonalcoholic drinks, starting with the Charger.[6] The Charger, a drink which was around bars for decades, consisted of sparkling water, bitters, and lime. Canada Dry was enticed to promote it by putting a packet of bitters with a recipe on the necks of bottles of Canada Dry Seltzer. Tastings were organized at museums and street fairs. Radio ads with a "Charger" theme were run. Other drinks, such as the Caribbean (made with cranberry juice, pineapple juice, and bitters) followed.

Third, the possibility that a competitor will take over the application area by product improvement, heavy advertising, or other means, or will engage in price warfare, needs to be analyzed. The issue is whether the brand can achieve a sustainable advantage in the new application. Ocean Spray has an association with cranberries that might protect an entry into a cranberry snack, but their name will be of less help in a processed application such as cookies and cereals.

3. ENTERING NEW MARKETS

An obvious way to generate growth is to move into a new market area with the potential for new growth. Heretofore that market may not have been ready for the product, or the price may have been excessive for that market, or perhaps no firm had even thought of that market. In any case, it nevertheless represents untapped sales potential for the industry.

In some cases the new markets may require product modifications. Texas Instruments looked at the previously neglected women's market for calculators as a way to revitalize this mature, competitive business.[7] Around 60% of all calculators were (and are) purchased by women, but few were designed specifically for them. The approach was to turn calculators into fashion accessories under the name Nuance. Nuance—shown in Figure 10–3—looks like a compact and has a latch-key cover which protects the keyboard in a purse or briefcase. Available in a sophisticated purple and a soft beige, its rubber keys are contoured for comfort, and staggered so that women with longer nails can avoid double strokes. The solar-powered unit never needs batteries, and will work in low light levels. Too, the "four-function" keyboard includes a percent key for discounts and sales tax.

A proposed caffeine-laden Diet Pepsi, named Pepsi A.M., represents an entry into the breakfast market.[8] It provides an alternative to coffee. The advertising calls the product "The great-tasting cola that beats coffee cold!"

There are many examples of firms that have found growth in mature, competitive industries by looking toward new markets:

• Vans, long used for delivery by businesses, represented a rather mature market until they were adapted for consumer use and sales exploded.

• The small refrigerator allowed the product to move from the home to the office or student dormitory. The same can be said for microwave ovens.

• Johnson & Johnson's baby shampoo was languishing until they looked toward adults who wash their hair frequently, and their need for a mild shampoo: "If it's gentle enough for baby. . . ." The result was a market share gain from 3% to 14%.

How to Find New Markets

There are several guidelines that can help to find and select new markets. First, consider a wide variety of segmentation variables such as age, geographic location, benefits sought, and gender. Sometimes a different way to look at the market will uncover a useful segment. Second, consider growth segments within declining or mature industries—for example, light beer and nonalcoholic beer are growth segments in the

FIGURE 10–3 Pretty Enough to Show—Practical to Use

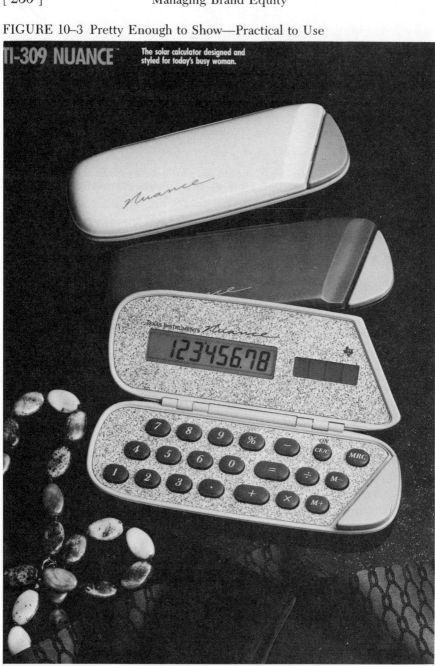

Courtesy of Texas Instruments.

mature beer industry. Third, identify segments that are not served well such as the women's calculator market or the fashion needs of older people. Those segments represent opportunities if their needs can be served better. Fourth, segments should be sought for which the brand can be adaptable and for which the brand can provide value.

4. REPOSITIONING THE BRAND

CHANGING ASSOCIATIONS

A positioning strategy can become inappropriate because it becomes obsolete over time, the target market ages, or the association becomes less appealing (or even a source of ridicule) as tastes and fashions change.

Cheez Whiz was introduced by Kraft in 1956 as a sandwich spread, for snacks, and for casual eating—primarily by kids.[9] By the 1980s, however, the business was sinking at the rate of 2% a year, in part because of the associations. The product has been described as the culinary equivalent of a velvet painting of Elvis Presley. The film *The Revenge of the Nerds II* was said by one critic to be so dumb that it makes you feel as if your head has been hollowed out and pumped full of Cheez Whiz. Kraft, however, repositioned the brand as a cheese sauce for the microwave oven which can be used on a variety of dishes—including casseroles, vegetable side-dishes, and baked potatoes. Figure 10–4 illustrates. Supported by an increased advertising effort of $6 million (up from $2 million), the brand received a 35% jump in sales.

A positioning strategy can also simply wear out. The target segment becomes saturated; new associations and associated segments are needed to generate growth. V-8 Cocktail Vegetable Juice had been positioned as a better-tasting drink than tomato juice.[10] But in the early 1970s, sales became stagnant. Tests revealed that changes in advertising expenditures and/or prices did not help. What *did* work was a repositioning as a healthy drink which would help in weight control. Using the "I coulda had a V-8" slogan, the new positioning created a 20% sales increase.

Among the brands that have achieved a boost by repositioning have been:

• Campbell's Soup, once positioned as a lunch supplement: Mothers received a guilt trip if they did not provide the "M'm, good!" soup. As kids eating lunch at home became history, repositioning the soup as a main-meal substitute for adults ("Soup is good food") made sense.

FIGURE 10–4 Changing Cheez Whiz Associations

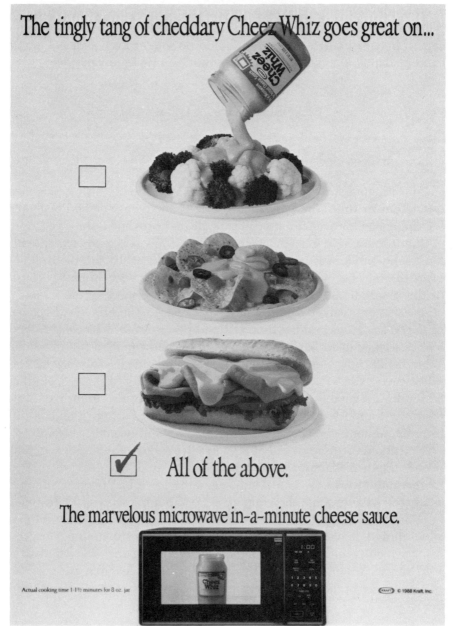

CHEEZ WHIZ is a registered trademark of Kraft General Foods, Inc. Reproduced with permission.

- Geritol, the iron and vitamin supplement: Once a favorite potion of the Lawrence Welk generation, now it is the brand for amorous middle-aged people.
- A dormant headache powder which repositioned by returning to its roots—the original package, a bitter taste, graphic events such as bass-fishing tournaments, and the blue-collar Southwestern user.[11] It had unsuccessfully attempted to stimulate sales by modernizing its package and changing the product's taste.

ADD VALUE BY DIFFERENTIATING: NEW ASSOCIATIONS

Sometimes as it matures a product becomes a commodity, and price pressures make the business unprofitable. One therapeutic approach is to attempt to reposition the commodity as an upscale branded product.

In the 1960s, chickens were a pure commodity, sold pretty much like a homogeneous grain or raw material. Frank Perdue, tired of being in a commodity business, changed all that by creating Perdue chickens. He completely repositioned his product as a high-quality branded product, largely on the basis of an advertising campaign that featured himself—a colorful, crusty character—and the line "It takes a tough man to make a tender chicken." The campaign was a convincing story about the superiority of the brand on the basis of better feed, careful processing, ice-packed storage, the upscale retailers who handled it, and (mainly) the will of Frank Perdue. And it employed humor: Perdue bragged about his tender chickens having a soft life in $60,000 homes, getting eight hours' sleep, avoiding junk food, and drinking pure well-water ("Your kids never had it so good"). Sales margins and profits were dramatically affected.

5. AUGMENTING THE PRODUCT/SERVICE

The following scenario is all too common: Product-class sales are stagnating or declining. The product is looking more and more like a commodity. The brand assets (used to differentiate) that once seemed so strong have finally been matched by several competitors, and customers seem more and more concerned with price. It is more difficult to find customers willing to pay a premium price for a brand which has performed historically a bit more reliably and competently. The temptation is to become resigned to a very competitive environment.

In this context it can be useful to buy into Theodore Levitt's position that *any* product or service, even a commodity, can be differentiated.[12] When the product is close to becoming a commodity, says Levitt, consider augmenting it, providing services or features not expected by the customer as they go beyond anything being offered. There really are two ways to win: Do something better, or do something extra or different. With a mature product, it often is more feasible to do something extra or different than better.

Improving the package is one way to offer a differentiating extra which can stimulate a new look to a tired product class. McCormick created a pepper container whose cap allowed the container to double as a pepper mill. Nestlé packaged its chocolate in tiny tubs similar to the packets of preserves found in restaurants, so that children could make a hot chocolate or sundaes with the help of a microwave. Sometimes too the new package can solve a customer problem. P&G's Citrus Hill offers a screw-cap juice carton which allows customers to shake the contents without having spillage. And Campbell's Chunky Soups added ring-pull tops to provide easy access for those who can use a microwave.

The L'eggs market effort in the early 1970s provides a classic example of an augmented product. The firm increased sales from $9 million in 1970 to $290 million in 1974, in the face of a declining hosiery industry. The cornerstone of the L'eggs effort, the concept of selling high-quality hosiery in supermarkets, was supported by a total marketing program. The unique egg-shaped package was difficult to shoplift, and enhanced the use of the catchy, memorable name. A vertical display managed by a staff of route salespeople eliminated the disorder usually associated with prior efforts to put hosiery in supermarkets. Selling on consignment reduced the investment involved and helped the line to be very profitable for supermarkets.

Another example is Foremost–McKesson, in drug wholesaling, who used a computer-based information system to provide a myriad of services to the druggist, including virtually taking over inventory management, reorder decisions, and pricing decisions. The system also processed medical insurance claims, and provided information on drug interactions and Medicaid numbers for store customers. McKesson also set up labeling systems and computerized accounts-receivable programs, and developed a "rack jobber" service which took over the management of the shelves for at least some products.

As a result, the large McKesson sales force engaged in store-level selling was replaced by a very small force which serviced the systems.[13] The large order-processing department no longer was needed. Customers, very sensitive to item pricing, became committed to McKesson's systems. Despite shedding some business areas, McKesson grew from $1 billion in 1978 to $5 billion 10 years later, while making a 20% return on assets—all in a business area which looked unattractive in 1975.

The need is to find augmentations that the customer will really value, and that are linked enough to the product so that it will in fact benefit. The process starts by understanding the customer: What are the problems that are really irritating to the customer—that make a difference? Is there any way that added services can deal with them? In what way is the customer dissatisfied? What can be done? Consider the system in which the product is embedded, including the decision to buy, the ordering process, and logistics. Can anything be done to improve efficiencies, perhaps by getting more involved in the ordering system as McKesson did?

CUSTOMER INVOLVEMENT

When providing a product or service to an organization, a key is to get the customer involved in the process of finding ways to augment the product or service. Customer involvement not only helps to identify the most appropriate areas on which to work but also makes the effort visible to the customer, and helps the implementation of any proposed solution.

The textile firm Millikin formalizes the process, using Customer Action Teams (CATs).[14] A CAT is a self-contained effort to seek a creative solution to both better serving current customers and developing new ones. To launch a team, the customer is required to supply team members to join with Millikin representatives—usually including manufacturing, sales, finance, and marketing. Millikin launches hundreds of CATs each year, and their success stories provide incentives for customers to join.

A series of CATs turned Millikin's shop towel (industrial rag) business from a commodity to a value-added service business. Millikin now virtually runs the business of their customers, industrial laundries. Millikin now provides computerized ordering and logistics systems, market research assistance, leads from trade shows, audiovisual sales aids, operations seminars, sales-force training, and so on.

6. OBSOLETING EXISTING PRODUCTS WITH NEW-GENERATION TECHNOLOGIES

Sometimes a sleepy industry can be revitalized by a product which obsoletes the existing installed base and accelerates the replacement cycle. Certainly the Yamaha Disklavier is such an example. Others include the large-head tennis racket, color television, and the transistor radio.

Such a rebirth happened in the home audio market in the early 1980s, after it had been stagnant for a decade. Compact discs were perhaps the major factor. By providing the ability to upgrade the sound of an audio system, they not only generated sales but stimulated users to upgrade their speakers and receivers as well. The advent of stereo television sets was also a factor. U.S. stereo sales moved to a growth rate of around 10% in the mid-eighties.

The decision to pursue new technologies is particularly tricky for a market leader who has a vested interest in the old technology but faces competitive risks due to a strategy of delay and disinterest. The Gillette experience of the early 1960s illustrates. Gillette resisted the stainless-steel blade technology because the product's durability meant that people would need far fewer blades, and because the cost to change its manufacturing and marketing efforts would be high.[15] (The company was making in excess of 40% return on investment.) As a result, the small British "stainless" innovator, Wilkinson, and their American rivals, Eversharp and Schick, made major and permanent inroads into Gillette's share and profits. Gillette's share fell from 70% to 55%, and their return fell to below 30%. It is remarkable how rarely new-generation technology comes from the market leader, even when it is investing large amounts in R&D.

ALTERNATIVES TO REVITALIZATION:
THE END GAME

The prospects for any brand will depend upon the strength of the brand, its equity, the intensity and commitment of the competition, and the market demand for the product class. When one or more of these factors become(s) unfavorable, then the options of milking the brand or exiting the market should be considered.[16]

There are substantial risks in investing in a declining industry, especially with a brand which shows signs of weakness. First, the investment may not pay off. Sailing against a current is difficult, especially with a craft not designed for that. Although success is not impossible, it is hardly guaranteed. Further, a strategy of investing, for a multibrand organization, may draw resources away from other brands or business areas that are more attractive. All brands should not be given equal access to resources; some will by their very nature have more attractive prospects than others.

If every brand receives a commitment to survive, or even to reinvest its profits, there will be some brands (especially newer ones) that will be starved for resources. An optimal strategy is to withhold resources from some brands, and upon occasion even allow a brand to die. Relegating a brand to die (or even to a milking strategy) can be difficult, of course, particularly if the brand is an old friend and if the brand management team is still enthusiastic. The bottom line here is that *every* brand's management, in addition to pondering generating revitalization alternatives, should also consider the "milk" and "exit" options.

THE MILKING OPTION

A milk (or "harvest") strategy involves avoiding investment in the brand, attempting instead to generate additional cash flow from it. In general, a milking strategy will accept a decline in sales and profits, and the risk that the brand will eventually go under. A common way to exploit brand equity, its underlying assumptions are: (1) that either a faltering brand, strong competition, or eroding market demand make the present business area unattractive; (2) that the firm has better uses for the funds; (3) that the involved brand is not crucial to the firm, either financially or synergistically; and (4) that milking is feasible (as well as desirable) because sales will decline in an orderly way.

There are variants to a milking strategy. A "hold" or "maintain" variant will allow enough investment in the brand to hold or maintain its position, but to avoid growth-motivated investment. A "fast milking" strategy involves sharp reductions in operating expenditures, and perhaps price increases, to maximize short-term cash flow and minimize the possibility that any additional money will be invested in the business. A fast milking strategy will accept the risk of a sharp sales decline's precipitating a market exit. The common denominator is a restriction in the resources that are put behind the brand.

A good example of a milking strategy is that of Chase & Sanborn discussed in the accompanying insert. Another is Unilever's Lux Beauty Bars once "Used by nine out of ten Hollywood stars."[17] It now has less than 3% of the market, and hasn't advertised in more than 15 years. It just rides the truck with the stronger Lever products, generating $25 million in sales—about half of which is gross profit.

The Chase & Sanborn Story

Chase & Sanborn illustrates the potential of a milking strategy.[18] The brand, introduced in 1879, became the first American company to pack roasted coffee in sealed cans. In 1929, Chase & Sanborn, then a major player in the coffee market, combined with Royal Baking Powder and Fleischmann to form a company called Standard Brands. During the 1920s and 1930s, Chase & Sanborn advertised heavily and dominated the coffee industry. "The Chase & Sanborn hour," starring Edgar Bergen and Charlie McCarthy, was one of the most popular radio shows of its time.

After World War II, instant coffee and General Foods' Maxwell House both appeared. Instead of fighting the heavy advertising of Maxwell House, Chase & Sanborn chose a milking strategy. Over the years, advertising support for the brand was reduced until, finally, advertising was stopped entirely. In 1981, Standard Brands merged with Nabisco, which then sold off the coffee business for about $15 million to a small Miami firm, General Coffee.

Three years later, General Coffee was bought by Hills Bros., who found that brand awareness for Chase & Sanborn was exceptionally high despite the fact that the brand had not been advertised for over 15 years. About 88% of consumers in the Northeast and Southeast recognized the name. Just by putting the brand on shelves in that region, a market share of 0.41% was obtained, a share much higher than P&G's High Point and a more recent entry, Mr. Coffee.

Standard Brands also followed the slow milking strategy with Royal Pudding when that product was faced with another General Foods brand, Jell-O.

Several situational characteristics can lead to a milking strategy rather than an exit strategy:

1. The industry decline rate is not exceedingly steep. There are pockets of enduring demand in the industry that will ensure that the decline rate will not suddenly become precipitous.
2. The price structure will be stable at a level which allow profits to be made among the efficient firms.
3. The brand has enough customer loyalty, perhaps in a limited part

of the market, to generate sales and profits in a milking mode. The risk of losing relative position with a milking strategy is low.

4. The brand creates some value to the firm by providing economies of scale, or by otherwise supporting other brands.
5. A milking strategy can be successfully managed.

Implementation of a milking strategy can be difficult. One of the most serious problems is that a suspicion that a milking strategy is being employed can create a momentum of its own, which may upset the whole strategy. In fact, the line between a milking strategy and abandonment is sometimes very thin. Customers may lose confidence in the firm's product, and employee morale may suffer. Competitors may attack more vigorously. All these possibilities can create a sharper-than-anticipated decline. To minimize such effects, it is helpful to keep a milking strategy as inconspicuous as possible.

Another serious problem is the difficulty of placing and motivating a manager in a milking situation. Most brand managers have neither the orientation, the background, nor the skills to engage in a successful milking strategy. Adjusting the performance measures and rewards appropriately can be difficult for both the organization and the involved managers. One reasonable solution—use a milking specialist—often is not feasible, simply because such manager types are rare.

The most serious concern, however, is that the premises upon which the milking strategy is based will turn out to be wrong. Information regarding market prospects, a competitor move, a cost projection, or some other relevant factor, could prove erroneous. Another possibility is that the circumstances may change. For example, products such as oatmeal have seen a resurgence in sales because of its low cost and high associations with naturalness and health.

In a milking strategy a firm may be slow to detect changes, or may be reluctant to make appropriate investments, and thus may miss opportunities. For example, two large can manufacturers, American and Continental, were engaging in a milking strategy and lost share when they missed the industry move to produce two-piece cans.

DIVESTMENT OR LIQUIDATION

When prospects for the brand are bad and a milking strategy does not seem feasible, the final alternative—divestment or liquidation—is precipitated. Among the conditions that would suggest an exit decision rather than a milking decision are:

1. The decline rate is rapid and accelerating, and there are no pockets of enduring demand that are accessible to the business.
2. The price pressures are anticipated to be extreme, caused by determined competitors with high exit barriers and by the lack of brand loyalty and product differentiation. A milking strategy is unlikely to be profitable for anyone.
3. The brand position is weak, and there exist(s) one or more dominant competitors who have achieved irreversible advantage. The business is now losing money, and future prospects are dim.
4. The firm's mission changes as the role of the business becomes superfluous or even unwanted.
5. Exit barriers, such as specialized assets or long-term contracts with suppliers, can be overcome.

Managerial pride often inhibits the exit alternative. Professional managers tend to view themselves as problem-solvers and are reluctant to accept the judgment that a turnaround is not worthwhile. Further, there is the emotional attachment to a brand that has perhaps been in the "family" for many years, and indeed may even have been the original brand upon which the rest of the firm was created.

A serious concern is that a business area might be killed off while potentially profitable business activity remains. IBM, for example, felt that its 286 series machine was going to be replaced by the 386 series, and effectively eliminated it from its line. In fact, the 286 machines provided the basis for dozens of companies to erode IBM's position. IBM belatedly put a version of the 286 back into its line—but damage had been done.

SELECTING THE RIGHT END GAME: MILK VS. EXIT

The selection of a milk or exit strategy involves an analysis of the three determinants of brand profitability: brand strength, market demand, and competitive intensity. Figure 10–5 shows a set of questions under each category which can be a guide to the investment decision in a declining industry.

Market Prospects. A basic consideration is the rate, pattern, and predictability of decline. A precipitous decline should be distinguished from a slow, steady decline. One determining factor is the existence of pockets of enduring demand, segments that are capable of supporting a core demand level. The overall cigar industry has experienced a slow, steady

FIGURE 10–5 The Investment Decision in a Declining Industry: Some
Strategic Questions

Market Prospects

1. Is the rate of decline orderly and predictable?
2. Are there pockets of enduring demand?
3. What are the reasons for the decline—is it temporary? Might it be reversed?

Competitive Intensity

4. Are there dominant competitors with unique skills or assets?
5. Are there many competitors unwilling to exit or contract gracefully?
6. Are customers brand-loyal? Is there product differentiation?
7. Are there price pressures?

Brand Strength and Organizational Capabilities

8. Is the brand strong? Does it enjoy high recognition and positive, meaningful associations?
9. What is the market share position and trend?
10. Does the business have some key competitive SCAs with respect to key segments?
11. Can the business manage a milking strategy?
12. Is there synergy with other businesses?
13. Does the brand fit with the current firm's strategic thrust?
14. What are the exit barriers?

decline, in part because the premium segment is stable and loyal. Contrariwise, the vacuum-tube industry has continued to have strong replacement demand, even after vacuum tubes have all but disappeared from new products. And, in the leather industry, leather upholstery is still healthy—imitations notwithstanding.

Competitive Intensity. A second consideration is the level of competitive intensity. Is there one or more dominant competitor(s) with substantial shares, and a set of unique assets and skills which form formidable and sustainable competitive advantages? Is there a relatively large set of competitors not disposed either to exit or to contract gracefully? If the answer to either of these questions is yes, the profit prospects for others may be dismal.

Another perspective comes from the customers. A key to making profit in a declining industry is price stability. Are customers relatively price-insensitive, such as buyers of premium cigars or replacement vacuum tubes? Is there a relatively high level of product differentiation and brand loyalty? Or has the product become a commodity? Are there costs involved in switching from one brand to another?

Brand Strength and Organizational Capabilities. Sources of brand strength in a declining environment often are quite different from those in other contexts. What is helpful in a declining industry are:

- Established strong relationships with the profitable customers, especially those in the pockets of enduring demand
- Strong associations (at this stage it will be difficult for competitors to alter their image significantly)
- The ability to operate profitably with underutilized assets
- The ability to reduce costs as business contracts
- A large market share if economies of scale are present

QUESTIONS TO CONSIDER

1. Why aren't customers using the product more often? Why don't they use it in greater quantity? Would reminders help? What about incentives? Is the use inconvenient? Are there undesirable consequences of usage that could be overcome? Could users be encouraged to use the product in different contexts? Could users expand the usage level? The potential for increased usage is usually greater with the heavy-user segment—look there first.

2. How do your customers use your brand? Analyze the potential of each application area: What *is* the potential? What marketing effort would be required?

3. What are the brand's primary markets? How is the brand positioned in each market? Is the current market saturated? What are some alternative positioning strategies? Would any open up new growth prospects? What are alternative markets? Evaluate the potential of each.

4. What are the unmet needs of the customer? Customer problems and annoyances? Consider not only the customer's interaction with the product but also the system in which the product is embedded. Could an extra service, product feature, or product modification be helpful to the customer? Are any competitors offering extras that are valued? Consider firms in similar industries: What "extras" serve to differentiate? Would any work in your context?

5. Should milking or exiting be considered? Consider the questions in Figure 10–5.

11
·
Global Branding
and a Recap

The game's not over 'til it's over.

THE KAL KAN STORY

Early in 1989, Mars changed the name of its Kal Kan cat food to Whiskas in the U.S., to complete the creation of a worldwide name.[1] There were several motivating reasons. With more communication among global marketing professionals at Mars, the use of the same name made it more likely that ideas—and perhaps advertising campaigns— could be shared. Further, pet owners travel and might switch if their familiar brand was not available somewhere. Just two years earlier, Mars had created two other global brands by changing the name of its Kal Kan dog food in the U.S. to Pedigree, and its Mealtime dry dog food to Pedigree Mealtime. Judging by U.S. market-share data, those changes also were successful.

The risk associated with the Kal Kan name changes was mitigated by the fact that although the Kal Kan name had substantial equity, it did not have a great name. "Whiskas," by contrast, was more likable and was perceived as being much more feline-sounding. Similarly, "Pedi- gree" was associated with a quality, expensive pet that would be served only the best food. Kal Kan had lacked such positive attributes—it seemed

[263]

to serve only as a reminder that the container was a can. Hardly an association that contributed much to the brand.

THE PARKER PEN STORY

Parker Pen in 1985 launched a global business strategy in order to combat Cross from above and the Japanese from below.[2] The centerpiece of the effort was a new pen, called the Victor, and a common advertising campaign (built around the theme "It's wrought from pure silver and writes like pure silk"), a common slogan ("Make your mark with a Parker"), and a common pricing strategy. The effort was a disaster—so bad in many of its 150 markets that local units resisted pressures to adopt it.

The common pricing was a problem, as market conditions in some countries made the standardized price and resulting quality positioning untenable. The selected name did not have the greatest associations in all countries, either. And the advertising and its resulting associations were judged by many to be ordinary.

Among the casualties of the global branding strategy were some effective local branding efforts. For example, the offbeat agency of the highly profitable Parker unit in England, one of 40 agencies used by Parker prior to globalization, had developed a particularly successful campaign. It associated the brand with people with the élan to deliver a well-crafted insult written with a Parker. One such insult was a note to an airline, reading "You had delusions of adequacy?" Unfortunately the campaign's humor was very British and would not have worked well outside the Empire.

A GLOBAL BRAND?

Should there be a global brand—a single name, symbol, and slogan together with common associations? Should the same one familiar brand name (such as Kodak, McDonald's, Sony, IBM, or Coca-Cola) be used throughout the world? Or should a variant, a related but different brand name, be adapted for each country, or even for different regions within a country? If different brands are now used, should they be replaced by a global brand name?

The case for global products and marketing efforts have been argued by several leading management thinkers including Harvard's Theodore

Levitt, and Kenichi Ohmae of McKinsey in Japan. They note that tastes and styles throughout the world are becoming more homogeneous, in part due to television and travel and also because of the spread of affluence. As a result, a product and appeal that are effective in one area are likely to be effective in another. Further, all areas want—indeed demand—the best quality and most advanced features. Thus, it is necessary to provide the finest product design and accompanying associations all over the world.

A key to the argument for a global product is the economies of scale that result from the world-wide volume—regarded as crucial to being competitive in many industries. Of course, some manufacturing and product design economies of scale do not depend upon the use of a global brand. However, there will exist sometimes substantial economies of scale in the design of advertising, promotions, packaging, and other aspects of the brand that will be affected by a global branding policy. The development costs can be spread over a larger market. Another perspective is that the smaller markets will have access to the resulting efforts involving larger budgets.

A global brand can have substantial advantages in gaining brand awareness when customers travel between countries. The presence of advertising and distribution can impact upon country visitors. In Europe and elsewhere where between-country travel is extensive, such exposure can be important to a brand. Another efficiency issue involves situations where media coverage overlaps countries. In that case, a global brand can buy exposures much more efficiently. In particular, as the European Common Market matures there is likely to be more and more media overlap and customer crossover and thus more payoff to a global brand strategy.

A global brand can have some useful associations. Just the concept of being global can symbolize the ability to generate competitive products in addition to strength and staying power. Such an image can be particularly important in pricey industrial products or consumer durables like cars or computers where there are customer risks that a product may be unreliable or be technologically surpassed by a competitor. Such Japanese firms as Yamaha, SONY, Cannon, and Honda that operate in markets where technology and product quality are important have benefited from a global brand association.

A global brand often provides a country association for a brand which is very established in one country and for which the country association is part of the essence of the brand. For example, Levi is U.S. jeans, Chanel is a French perfume, Dewar's is a Scotch whiskey, Kikorian is a Japanese soy sauce, and Bertolli is an Italian olive oil. In each case, the brand is established in the home country and the country itself is part of the essence of the brand. In such a context, a global brand will tend to be worthwhile.

TARGETING A COUNTRY

Even if the name is not established, the constraint that the name, symbols, and associations work in all countries is very confining. Most names, especially names with useful associations, will have a damaging meaning (or will be preempted) in some countries. For example, P&G's Pert Plus, the very successful combination shampoo and conditioner, is sold as Rejoy in Japan, Rejoice in much of the Far East, and Vidal Sassoon in the U.K. because the Pert Plus name or something similar was preempted. It is no coincidence that many of the global brands and symbols like IBM and SONY are, by themselves, not association rich.

A similar problem exists for symbols and associations. Those that are "universal," that work in all settings, are not necessarily the most effective. Consider, for example, Heinz baby food and Levi jeans which both have a strong value position in the U.S. and a premium position in other markets. Clearly, two such very different tacks will need to involve very different symbols and associations.

A local brand can benefit from distinct associations that can be useful— even pivotal: Is there any tendency to "buy home-grown," or any positive feeling toward local traditions or characteristics, that can be integrated into the brand's positioning strategy? Or, does the global brand have negative associations locally because it has an undesirable meaning in some countries, or is it tied to a country's politics and thus subject to the ups and downs of international events?

A worldwide association may simply not be appropriate in some countries because of the *competitive* context. A British Airways globalization effort involved the centralization of advertising, which resulted in a "The world's favorite airline" theme. It featured a 90-second commercial which showed the Manhattan skyline rotating slowly through the sky. Even in the U.S., where the campaign originated, managers wondered if the replaced campaign (which had emphasized traditional British values with the theme "We'll take good care of you") was not more effective. In countries where British Air was an also-ran, the claim did not make much sense. Further, there were operational problems. For example, 90-second ads could not be used in South Africa.

In primary market areas, local marketing units may generate better ideas than big-budget global efforts. Further, ten different ideas from ten countries may be more likely to emerge, with something really good among them, than one "global" idea, even if the "global" one was created by a large budget and the best talent. When Polaroid was repositioning from a "party camera" platform to a more serious, utilitarian platform, a campaign which was developed in Switzerland was the most effective.[3] It promoted the functional use of instant photography as a way to communicate with family and friends—the "Learn to speak Polaroid" campaign. If local units had not been free to generate their own campaigns, this superior campaign would not have surfaced.

The rush to global branding is somewhat ironic as, in the U.S., there is a strong move to regional marketing. Firms such as P&G and Campbell's are giving local marketing units responsibility for sales promotions and advertising which had previously been centralized.

ANALYZING THE CONTEXT

A proposal for globalization of the brand—the symbol, the slogan, or associations—should be accompanied by a country-by-country (or region-by-region) analysis. As Figure 11–1 summarizes, there are a set of advantages and disadvantages to a global brand that can guide the analysis. Assume that there is a global brand option that will be driven by the largest markets or by the most established markets. For each country or region several questions need to be addressed. As compared to using a global brand:

What is the cost of creating and maintaining awareness and associations for a local brand? How significant is the customer cross-boundary

FIGURE 11–1 Global vs. Local Branding

Global Brands Provide:	Local Brands Provide:
Scale Economies in the Development of Advertising, Packaging, Promotion etc.	Names, Symbols, and Associations That Can Be • Developed Locally • Tailored to Local Market • Selected without the Constraints of a Global Brand
Exploitation of • Media Overlap • Exposure to Customers Who Travel	
Associations • Of a Global Presence • Of the "Home" Country	Reduced Risk from "Buy Local" Sentiments

travel and the resulting brand exposure? Is there significant media overlap that makes local advertising and promotion inefficient?

Are there economies of scale in the creation and implementation of advertising and other components of the brand's marketing program?

Is there value to associations of a global brand or of a brand associated with a "home" country?

What local associations will be engendered by the global name/symbol/slogan/associations? What are their positive or negative marginal value(s)?

Is it feasible culturally and legally to use a brand name, symbol, and associations across countries? What does the name and symbol mean in different countries? Is it pronounceable? Consider Meiieselex cereals and Freixenet champagne.

What is the value of the awareness and associations that a regional brand might develop? Is the product relatively culture bound? An in-home product like frozen food will tend to be more linked to the local language, symbols, and culture than will an industrial product like computers.

One common misconception is that globalization is an all or nothing proposition. In fact, globalization can involve some elements of the brands—the name, the symbol, the slogan, the perceived quality, or the associations—it need not involve all of them. It may be optimal to globalize some but not all elements of the brand.

Even Coca-Cola found that it could not use Diet Coke in much of Europe because of local restrictions regarding the use of the word "diet" and because it had medicinal connotations in some markets. Instead, the drink is called Coca-Cola Light in Europe. Thus Coca-Cola, perhaps the classic example of global branding, is not using a global brand name on a key product!

The trick will be to globalize those elements for which there is a resulting payoff in cost or impact, and allow the other elements of brand equity to be customized to local markets.

A RECAP

After spending 10 chapters discussing brand equity and its management, it is time to sit back and reflect—to take as it were a stroll down memory lane. First, a summary model of brand equity will be presented, a more complete structure than the one presented in Chapter 1. Second, a set of observations will be drawn from each chapter, representing points about brand equity and its management that deserve highlighting: They serve to provide a reminder of some issues and findings. Clearly, this brief review indicates that considerable progress has been made toward the management of brand equity. However, it also reminds that there is much to be done.

A BRAND EQUITY MODEL

In Chapter 1 a Figure was presented which provided an overview structure for the brand-equity concept. The five asset dimensions that underlie brand equity (brand loyalty, brand awareness, perceived quality, brand associations, and other proprietary brand assets) were shown as creating brand equity. Further, the value that brand equity generates to the customer and to the firm was detailed as an "output" of brand equity.

In each of the following four chapters, ways in which each of the dimensions of brand equity might create value were suggested and discussed. In Figure 11–2, a *revised* brand-equity model integrates these contributions into Figure 1–3 (Chapter 1). Brand equity is shown to consist of the five asset dimensions. Ways in which each dimension might create value for the customer and/or the firm are now in the model. These paths to value creation are then distilled into a compact, summary set of ways (shown at the right of the figure) in which brand equity can provide value to the customer and to the firm.

In any given context some of these potential sources of value may not apply, but others will. However, the model does provide a starting point for analysis for any decision that will impact upon brand equity.

CHAPTER OBSERVATIONS

Chapter 1: What Is Brand Equity? Brand equity is here defined as the set of brand assets and liabilities linked to the brand—its name and symbols—that add value to, or subtract value from, a product or service. These assets include brand loyalty, name awareness, perceived quality, and associations.

There are considerable pressures for short-term performance, in part driven by the dictum that shareholder wealth is a primary goal of business,

FIGURE 11–2 Brand Equity

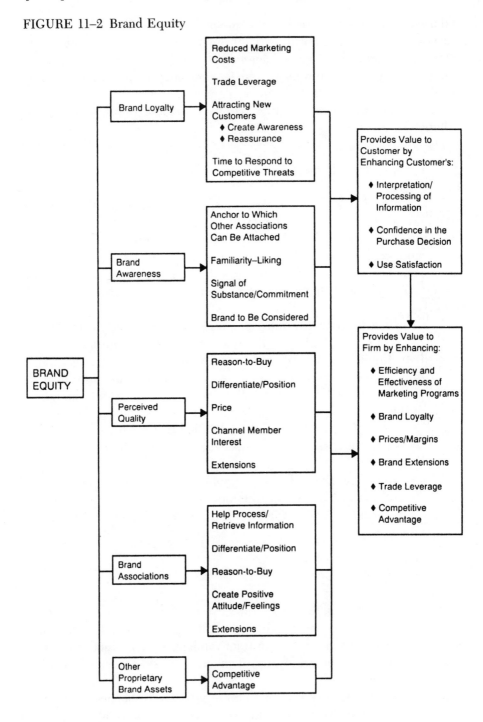

and the reality that stock prices are responsive to short-term performance measures. Short-term activities (such as price promotions) can show dramatic results, while brand-building activities (such as image advertising) may have little immediate impact. The challenge is to understand better the links between brand assets and future performance, so that brand-building activities can be justified.

Estimating the value of a brand can help show that the underlying assets do have worth. The assessment of the value of brand equity can be based on the price premium that the name supports, the impact of the name on customer preference, the replacement cost of the brand, and the stock value minus the value of other assets. The most persuasive measure, however, may be a multiplier of the earning power of the brand. The multiplier would be based upon an analysis of the relative strength of the brand assets.

Chapter 2: Brand Loyalty. The core of brand equity is the loyalty of its customer base—the degree to which customers are satisfied, have switching costs, like the brand, and are committed. A loyal set of customers can have substantial value which is often underestimated. They can reduce marketing costs, since a customer is much less costly to keep than to gain or regain, and provides leverage over others in the distribution channel. Customers can create brand awareness and generate reassurance to new customers. Loyal customers will also give a firm time to respond to competitive advances.

Retaining old customers and building loyalty involve active management; they do not happen automatically. What will help is treating the customers right: Do the little things, stay close to the customer, measure satisfaction, create switching costs, provide extras, and, in general, over-invest in your customer. Organizations of all kinds have found the implementation of a customer orientation difficult, even though it sounds simple and obvious.

Chapter 3: Brand Awareness. Don't underestimate the power of brand awareness—recognition, recall (your brand is recalled as being in a product class), and top-of-mind (the first recalled). People like the recognizable. Further, recognition is a cue for presence, substance, and permanence. Recall can be a necessary condition to being considered, and can have a subtle influence on purchase decisions as well. It also provides the anchor to which other associations are linked.

Building awareness is much easier over a longer time-period because learning works better with repetition and reinforcement. In fact, brands with the highest recall are generally older brands. Event sponsorship, publicity, symbol exposure, and the use of brand extensions all can improve awareness. However, developing recall requires a link between the brand and the product class, and just name exposure will not necessarily create that link.

Chapter 4: Perceived Quality. Perceived quality pays off. According to studies using data from thousands of businesses in the PIMS database, it improves prices, market share, and ROI. In addition, it was the top-named competitive advantage in a survey of managers of business units. It provides a reason-to-buy, a point of differentiation, a price premium option, channel interest, and a basis for brand extensions.

The key to obtaining high perceived quality is to deliver high quality, to identify those quality dimensions that are important, to understand what signals quality to the buyer, and to communicate the quality message in a credible manner. Price becomes a quality cue, especially when a product is difficult to evaluate objectively or when status is involved. Other quality cues include the appearance of service people, stereo speaker size, and the scent of a cleaner.

Chapter 5: Brand Associations. A brand association is anything mentally linked to the brand. The brand position is based upon associations and how they differ from competition. An association can affect the processing and recall of information, provide a point of differentiation, provide a reason to buy, create positive attitudes and feelings, and serve as the basis of extensions.

Positioning on the basis of an association with a key tangible product attribute is effective when the attribute can drive purchase decisions, but often it can also result in a specification-shouting match. The use of an intangible attribute such as overall quality, technological leadership, or health and vitality can sometimes be more enduring. The association with a customer benefit is another option. One study showed that the combination of a rational benefit and an emotional benefit was superior to a rational benefit alone.

The relative price position often is central: Is the brand to be premium, regular, or economy—and, further, is it to be at the top or bottom of the selected category? Among the other association types to consider are use applications, product users, celebrities, life-styles and personalties, product class, competitors, and country or geographic area.

Chapter 6: The Measurement of Brand Associations. Insights about what a brand means to people and what motivations it taps often can be obtained by using indirect methods of eliciting associations. A customer, for example, can be asked to describe a brand user or use experience, to generate free associations with the brand, or to indicate how brands differ from each other. Another way to gain a rich profile of a brand is to ask people to consider the brand as a person (or animal, activity, magazine, etc.), and probe as to what type the brand would be.

A companion method would usually involve a representative sample of a customer segment which would scale the brand and its competitors with respect to such positioning dimensions as product attributes, customer benefits, user characteristics, use situations, or competitors. The result is a perceptual map which graphically identifies the important perceptual dimensions and shows the position of the brand for the customer sample.

Chapter 7: Selecting, Creating, and Maintaining Associations. A successful brand position will usually follow three tenets: (1) Don't try to be something you are not. (2) Differentiate your brand from competitors'. (3) Provide associations that add value and/or provide a reason-to-buy.

A key to creating associations is to identify and manage signals. The label "35-mm single-lens reflex" signals that a camera has certain characteristics. A promotion can signal that non-price attributes are not important unless it is structured so that it reinforces the desired image. To deliver an attribute and communicate that it exists may not be enough if the appropriate signals are not managed properly.

Being consistent over time and over elements of the marketing program is crucial in maintaining associations. When a disaster hits, the best strategy is usually to avoid arguing over who is to blame, and to attempt to resolve it quickly.

Some organizations have attempted to protect brand equities by adjusting the organizational reward structure, and even by creating equity managers.

Chapter 8: The Name, Symbol, and Slogan. The name, symbol, and slogan are critical to brand equity, and can be enormous assets, because they serve as indicators of the brand and thus are central to brand recognition and brand associations.

A name should be selected by a systematic process involving the creation of a host of alternatives based upon desired associations and metaphors. The name should be easy to recall, suggest the product class, support a symbol or logo, suggest desired brand associations, not suggest undesirable associations, and be legally protectable. There usually are trade-offs to be made. For example, a name which suggests a product class might be strategically limiting when brand extensions are considered.

A symbol such as the Wells Fargo stagecoach or Travelers (red) umbrella can create associations and feelings. A symbol such as IBM or SONY that is based upon the name will have an edge in creating brand recognition. However, a symbol such as the Morton Salt label (showing salt raining upon a girl holding an umbrella) that includes the product class (e.g., salt) should help in brand recall where the link to the product class needs to be strong.

A slogan can be tailored to a positioning strategy, and is far less limited than a name and symbol in the role it can play. A slogan can provide additional associations, or focus existing ones.

Chapter 9: Brand Extensions. One way to exploit brand equity is to extend the name to different products. An extension will have the best chance when the brand's associations and/or perceived quality can provide a point of differentiation and advantage for the extension. Extensions rarely work when the brand name has nothing to offer beyond brand awareness.

An extension should "fit" the brand—there should be some link between the brand and the extension. The fit could be based upon a variety of linking elements, such as common-use contexts, functional benefits, links to prestige, user types, or symbols. Any incongruity could damage, and result in the failure of, desired associations to transfer. In addition, there should not be any meaningful negative association created by the brand name.

There is a risk that an extension will damage the core brand by weakening either its associations or its perceived quality. As illustrated by such extensions as Diet Coke, Honey Nut Cheerios, and Green Giant frozen entrees, that will not necessarily happen, especially if the original brand name and its associations are strong and there is a distinct difference between the original brand and the extensions. In fact, an extension will usually help brand awareness and, in the best situation, will reenforce the brand associations.

Probably the biggest risk of an extension is that the potential of a new brand name with unique associations may be lost.

Chapter 10: Revitalizing the Brand. One option for a brand which is old and tired is to pursue one of the seven routes to brand revitalization. One (increasing usage by existing customers, perhaps through reminder advertising or making the use easier), often is both relatively easy and unlikely to precipitate competitive reaction. A second is to find a new product use which can be feasibly stimulated by the brand (using Arm & Hammer baking soda as a refrigerator odor-fighter, for example). A third is to find new markets (such as moving into Europe) or attacking a neglected market (such as calculators for women).

A fourth revitalization route is to reposition by changing associations (i.e., Cheez Whiz as a sauce) or adding new associations. A fifth is to augment the product or service by providing features or services that are not expected. A sixth is to obsolete existing products with new-generation technologies, as the Yamaha Disklavier did. The seventh is the extension option covered in Chapter 9.

Revitalization is not always possible or economically justifiable, especially in the face of a brand which lacks a strong position, is facing a declining market and dominant competitors, is not central to the long-range thrust of the firm, and lacks a revitalization strategy. One option is to divest or liquidate. Another, to milk the brand, would be preferred when there is an enduring niche that remains loyal to the brand, the decline is orderly (with relatively stable prices), and the milking option seems feasible.

A PARTING WORD

In a growing number of contexts, the brand name and what it means combine to become the pivotal sustainable competitive advantage that firms have. The name is pivotal because other bases of competition (such as product attributes) usually are relatively easy to match or exceed. Further, customers often lack the ability or motivation to analyze the brand-choice decision at a sufficient depth to allow specifications to win the day.

Brand equity does not just happen. Its creation, maintenance, and protection need to be actively managed. Further, it involves strategic as well as tactical programs and policies. This book has attempted to provide some hows and whys of that management task.

Notes

CHAPTER 1
What Is Brand Equity?

1. The P&G story is in part drawn from a special issue of *Advertising Age* titled "The House That Ivory Built," August 20, 1987, from the book by Oscar Schisgall, *Eyes on Tomorrow: The Evolution of Procter & Gamble* (Chicago: J. G. Ferguson Publ. Co., 1981); from the 1984 P&G booklet "Celebrating 100 years of Ivory Soap"; and from selected P&G annual reports. The note on detergent is drawn from Philip Kotler and Gary Armstrong, *Marketing*, 2d ed. (Englewood Cliffs, NJ: Prentice–Hall), pp. 200–202.

2. The history on branding draws from Peter H. Farquhar, "Managing Brand Equity," *Marketing Research*, September 1989, pp. 24–34.

3. Henry Schacht, "Ripe Business in Trademark Licensing," *The San Francisco Chronicle*, April 26, 1989, p. C1.

4. Paul M. Schmitt, "Research Tools for the Nineties" (Chicago: Nielsen Marketing Research, 1989), and Tod Johnson, "The Myth of Declining Brand Loyalty," *Journal of Advertising Research*, February/March, 1984, pp. 10–17. Although given the measures used, a 9% change over eight years seems substantial; Johnson described it as modest.

5. "Focus: A World of Brand Parity," Report published by BBDO Worldwide, 1988.

6. Kevin Kerr, "Consumers Are Confused by Sears' New Policy," *Adweek's Marketing Week*, June 12, 1989, pp. 30–31.

7. George Garrick, "Properly Evaluating the Role of TV Advertising," Proceedings of the ARF Conference, 1989.

8. Schmitt, op. cit.

9. Garrick, op. cit.

10. Garrick, op. cit.

11. David A. Aaker, "Managing Assets and Skills: The Key to a Sustainable Competitive Advantage," *California Management Review*, Winter 1989, pp. 91–106.

12. Gregg Cebrzynski, "Researchers Get Advice on Brands, International Market," *Marketing News*, September 3, 1990, p. 38.

13. Anthony Ramirez, "Fake Fat: Sweet Deal for Monsanto," *The New York Times*, May 28, 1990, pp. 21–22.

14. B. G. Yovovich, "What Is Your Brand Really Worth?" *Adweek's Marketing Week*, August 8, 1988, pp. 18–24.

15. Bill Saporito, "Has-Been Brands Go Back to Work," *Fortune*, April 28, 1986, pp. 123–124.

16. Carol J. Simon and Mary W. Sullivan, "The Measurement and Determinants of Brand Equity: A Financial Approach," Working Paper, The University of Chicago, 1990.

17. David Fredericks, "The Lights Are On but Nobody's Home—Again," Presented at the MSI Branding Conference, December 1990.

CHAPTER 2
Brand Loyalty

1. The MicroPro story was drawn in part from a variety of published sources including Cheryl Spencer, "The Rebirth of a Classic," *Personal Computing*, February 1987, pp. 63–73; Kate Bertrand, "Can MicroPro Catch Its Fallen 'Star'?" *Business Marketing*, May 1989, pp. 55–66; Christine Strehlo, "What's So Special About WordPerfect?" *Personal Computing*, March 1989, pp. 100–116; Paul Freiberger, "MicroPro Future Unsure," *San Franciso Examiner*, April 4, 1989, p. C-1; Steven Burke, "WordStar Names New Chief," *PC Week/Business*, October 15, 1990, p. 161; *Computer Reseller News*, February 26, 1990, p. 15.

2. Jim Seymour, "Leave a Wake-Up Call for December 1990," *PC Magazine*, January 16, 1990, p. 15.

3. Alix M. Freedman, "Perrier Finds Mystique Hard to Restore," *The Wall Street Journal*, December 12, 1990, pp. B1-B4.

4. Ronald Alsop, "Brand Loyalty Is Rarely Blind Loyalty," *The Wall Street Journal*, October, 19, 1989, p. B1, and Thomas Exter, "Looking for Brand Loyalty," *American Demographics*, April 1986, pp. 33.

5. Frederick F. Reichheld, "Making Sure Customers Come Back for More," *The Wall Street Journal*, March 12, 1990. Mr. Reichheld is an executive at Bain & Co.

6. Frederick F. Reichheld and W. Earl Sasser, "Zero Defections: Quality Comes to Services," *Harvard Business Review*, September–October, 1990, pp. 105–111.

CHAPTER 3
Brand Awareness

1. The Nissan material is in part drawn from Anastasia C. Jackson, "The Value of a Japanese Brand: The Demise of Datsun by Nissan," Unpublished Paper, 1990. Also, Cleveland Horton, "Nissan: Is It Losing Its Edge?" *Advertising Age*, October 27, 1986, p. 4. John Revett, "Nissan Change May Work, but Price Is High," *Advertising Age*, July 27, 1981, p. 24.

2. Mim Ryan, "Assessment: The First Step in Image Management," *Tokyo Business Today*, September 1988, pp. 36–38.

3. "Shoppers Like Wide Variety of Housewares Brands," *Discount Store News*, October 24, 1988, p. 40.

4. The distinction between recognition and recall and their role in advertising planning is described in John R. Rossiter, Larry Percy, and Robert J. Donovan, "A Better Advertising Planning Grid," Working Paper 890–039, The University of New South Wales, 1989.

5. The concept of a dominant brand is discussed in Peter H. Farquhar, "Managing Brand Equity," *Marketing Research*, September 1898, pp. 24–33.

6. R. B. Zajonc, "Feeling and Thinking," *American Psychologist*, February 1980, pp. 151–175.

7. Prakash Nedungadi, "Recall and Consumer Consideration Sets: Influencing Choice without Altering Brand Evaluations," *Journal of Consumer Research*, December 1990, pp. 263–276.

8. Arch G. Woodside and Elizabeth J. Wilson, "Effects of Consumer Awareness of Brand Advertising on Preference," *Journal of Advertising Research*, Vol. 25, August/September 1985, pp. 41–48.

9. David A. Aaker and George S. Day, "A Dynamic Model of Relationships Among Advertising, Consumer Awareness, Attitudes, and Behavior," *Journal of Applied Psychology*, Vol. 59, June 1974, pp. 281–286.

10. Mim Ryan, op. cit.

11. Michael Lev, "Assessing Nissan's Zen Effort," *The New York Times*, May 14, 1990, p. 24.

12. Bill Saporito, "Has-Been Brands Go Back to Work," *Fortune*, April 28, 1986, pp. 123.

13. Leo Bogart and Charles Lehman, "What Makes a Brand Name Familiar?" *Journal of Marketing Research*, February 1973, pp. 17–22.

14. Thomas S. Wurster, "The Leading Brands: 1925–1985," *Perspectives*, The Boston Consulting Group, 1987.

15. Henry J. Claycamp and Lucien E. Liddy, "Prediction of New Product Performance: An Analytical Approach," *Journal of Marketing Research*, November 1969, pp. 414–420.

16. Kevin Lane Keller, "Memory Factors in Advertising: The Effect of Advertising Retrieval Cues on Brand Evaluations," *Journal of Consumer Research*, Vol. 14, December 1987, pp. 316–333.

17. Joseph W. Alba and Amitava Chattopadhyay, "Salience Effects in Brand Recall," *Journal of Marketing Research*, November 1986, pp. 363–369.

CHAPTER 4
Perceived Quality

1. The Schlitz story comes in part from Susan Anderson, "Evaluation of Brand Equity" MBA Thesis, University of California at Berkeley, June 1989; Jacques Neher, "What Went Wrong?" *Advertising Age*, April 13, 1981, pp. 46–64, and April 20, 1981, pp. 49–52; and "Anheuser Finds Quality Pays Off. . . But Schlitz Encounters Problems," *Financial World*, June 4, 1975, pp. 16–17. The Busch quote is from the *Financial World* article. The Schlitz ad manager quote is from the April 20 *Advertising Age* article (p. 52).

2. For a literature overview see Valarie A. Zeithaml, "Consumer Perceptions of Price, Quality, and Value: A Means–End Model and Synthesis of Evidence," *Journal of Marketing*, July 1988, pp. 2–22.

3. David A. Aaker and Kevin Lane Keller, "Consumer Evaluations of Brand Extensions," *Journal of Marketing*, Vol. 54, January 1990, pp. 27–41.

4. Robert D. Buzzell and Bradley T. Gale, *The PIMS Principles* (New York: The Free Press, 1987), Chapter 6.

5. Robert Jacobson and David A. Aaker, "The Strategic Role of Product Quality," *Journal of Marketing*, October 1987, pp. 31–44.

6. David A. Aaker, "Creating a Sustainable Competitive Advantage," *California Management Review*, Winter 1989, pp. 91–105.

7. David A. Garvin, "Product Quality: An Important Strategic Weapon," *Business Horizons*, Vol. 27, May–June 1984, pp. 40–43

8. David Woodruff, "A New Era for Auto Quality," *Business Week*, October 22, 1990, pp. 84–96; Alex Taylor III, "Why Toyota Keeps Getting Better and Better and Better," *Fortune*, November 19, 1990, pp. 66–79.

9. A. Parasuraman, Valarie A. Zeithaml, and Leonard L. Berry, "A Conceptual Model of Service Quality and Its Implications for Future Research," *Journal of Marketing*, Fall 1985, pp. 41–50.

10. David Walker, "At Sheraton, the Guest Is Always Right," *Adweek's Marketing Week*, October 23, 1989, pp. 20–21.

11. Valarie A. Zeithaml, Leonard L. Berry, and A. Parasuraman, "Communication and Control Processes in the Delivery of Service Quality," *Journal of Marketing*, April 1988, pp. 35–48.

12. Amna Kirmani and Peter Wright, "Money Talks: Perceived Advertising Expense and Expected Product Quality," *Journal of Consumer Research*, Vol. 16, December 1989, pp. 344–353.

13. Akshay R. Rao and Kent B. Monroe, "The Effect of Price, Brand Name, and Store Name on Buyers' Perceptions of Product Quality: An Integrative Review," *Journal of Marketing Research*, Vol. 26, August, 1989, pp. 351–357.

14. Harold J. Leavitt, "A Note on Some Experimental Findings About the Meaning of Price," *Journal of Business*, Vol. 27, July 1957, pp. 205–210.

15. Jacobson and Aaker, op. cit.

CHAPTER 5

Brand Associations: The Positioning Decision

1. The Weight Watchers story is drawn in part from Rebecca Fannin, "Shape Up," *Marketing & Media Decisions*, February 1986, pp. 54–60; Brian O'Reilly, "Diet Centers Are Really in Fat City, *Fortune*, June 5, 1989, pp. 137–140; Warren Berger, "The Big Freeze at Heinz," *Adweek's Marketing Week*, August 21, 1989, pp. 20–25; Gregory L. Jiles, "Heinz Ain't Broke, But It's Doing a Lot of Fixing," *Business Week*, December 11, 1989, pp. 84–88; "Anthony O'Reilly—What's on His Plate?" *Advertising Age*, February 26, 1990, pp. 1 and 16; and annual reports of H. J. Heinz Company.

2. "Anthony O'Reilly—What's on His Plate?" *Advertising Age*, February 26, 1990, p. 16.

3. Warren Berger, "The Big Freeze at Heinz," *Adweek's Marketing Week*, August 21, 1989, pp. 20–25.

4. Regis McKenna, *The Regis Touch* (New York Addison–Wesley, 1986), p. 41.

5. Joseph W. Alba and J. Wesley Hutchinson, "Dimensions of Consumer Expertise," *Journal of Consumer Research*, Vol. 13, March 1987, pp. 411–454.

6. Jerry Flint, "A Brand Is Like A Friend," *Forbes*, November 14, 1988, pp. 267–270; and "Shirley Young: Pushing GM's Humble-Pie Strategy," *Business Week*, June 11, 1990, pp. 52–53.

7. Stuart Agres, *Emotion in Advertising: An Agency's View*, The Marschalk Company, 1986. Also see a selection by the same title which appears in Stuart J. Agres, Julie A. Edell, and Tony M. Dubitshy, *Emotion in Advertising: The Critical or Practical Explorations* (New York: Quorum), pp. 3–18.

8. Glen L. Urban, Philip L. Johnson, and John R. Hauser, "Testing Competitive Market Structures," *Marketing Science*, Vol. 3, Spring 1984, pp. 83–112.

9. Aimee L. Stern, "Maybelline Ascendant," *Adweek's Marketing Week*, April 3, 1989, pp. 22–28.

10. Stan Luxenberg, "Cadbury Trusts Anyone Over 30," *Adweek's Marketing Week*, August, 22, 1988, pp. 18–21.

11. "Perfect 10s Give Way to Families of Four," *Adweek's Marketing Week*, March 27, 1989, p. 34.

12. Tom Murray, "The Wind at Nike's Back," *Adweek's Marketing Week*, November 14, 1986, pp. 28–31.

13. Keith Reinhard, "How We Make Advertising," presented to the Federal Trade Commission, May 11, 1979, pp. 22–25.

14. Roger Enrico, *The Other Guy Blinked* (New York: Bantam Books, 1986).

15. C. Min Han and Vern Terpstra, "Country-of-Origin Effects for Uni-National and Binational Products," *Journal of International Business Studies*, Summer 1988, p. 242.

16. N. G. Papadopoulos, L. A. Heslop, F. Graby, and G. Avlonitis, "Does 'Country-of-Origin' Matter?" Working Paper, Marketing Science Institute, 1989.

CHAPTER 6

The Measurement of Brand Associations

1. Drawn from Douglas Scott and Flaurel Englis, "Tracking Automotive Intentions and Imagery: A Case Study," *Journal of Advertising Research*, February/March 1989, RC-13 to RC-20.

2. Joseph S. Newman, *Motivation Research and Marketing Management* (Boston: Harvard University Press, 1957), p. 143.

3. David A. Aaker and Douglas M. Stayman, "Implementing the Concept of Transformational Advertising," *Psychology & Marketing*, 1991.

4. Joseph T. Plummer, "How Personality Makes a Difference," *Journal of Advertising Research*, Vol. 24, December 1984/January 1985, pp. 27–31.

5. Rena Bartos, "Ernest Dichter: Motive Interpreter," *Journal of Advertising Research*, February–March 1986, pp. 15–20.

6. Annetta Miller and Dody Tsiantar, "Psyching Out Consumers," *Newsweek*, February 27, 1989, pp. 46–47.

7. Plummer, op. cit.

8. Bartos, op. cit.

9. Joel N. Axelrod and Hans Wybenga, "Perceptions That Motivate Purchase," *Journal of Advertising Research*, June/July 1985, pp. 19–22.

10. Mason Haire, "Projective Techniques in Marketing Research," *Journal of Marketing*, April 1950, pp. 649–656.

11. Sidney J. Levy, "Dreams, Fairy Tales, Animals, and Cars," *Psychology & Marketing*, Vol. 2, Summer 1985, pp. 67–81.

12. Axelrod and Wybenga, op. cit.

13. Thomas J. Reynolds and Jonathan Gutman, "Advertising Is Image Management," *Journal of Advertising Research*, Vol. 25, February–March 1984, pp. 29–37; and Jonathan Gutman, "A Means–End Chain Model Based on Consumer Categorization Processes," *Journal of Marketing*, Vol. 46, Spring 1982, pp. 60–73. See also S. Young and B. Feigin, "Using the Benefit Chain for Improved Strategy Formulation," *Journal of Marketing*, Vol. 39, July 1975, pp. 72–74.

14. For more detail on scaling, see David A. Aaker and George S. Day, *Marketing Research*, 4th ed. (New York: John Wiley, 1990), Chapters 9, 17, 18, and 19.

15. George S. Day, Allan D. Shocker, and Rajendra K. Srivastava, "Customer-Oriented Approaches to Identifying Product Markets," *Journal of Marketing*, Vol. 43, Fall 1979, pp. 8–19.

CHAPTER 7
Selecting, Creating, and Maintaining Associations

1. Iegor Siniavski, "Communication at Honeywell France," Unpublished Master's Thesis, University of California at Berkeley, 1990.

2. "Dutch Boy's Image Gets a Fresh Coat of Paint," *Adweek's Marketing Week*, May 22, 1989, pp. 65–67.

3. Joseph M. Winski, "No Caffeine—Choice: 7-Up," *Advertising Age*, May 30, 1983, p. 3.

4. Keith Reinhard, "How We Make Advertising," presented to the Federal Trade commission, May 11, 1979, pp. 22–25.

5. Regis McKenna, *The Regis Touch* (Boston: Addison–Wesley, 1986), Ch. 3.

6. Mita Sujan, "Consumer Knowledge: Effects on Evaluation Strategies Mediating Consumer Judgments," *Journal of Consumer Research*, June 1985, pp. 31–46.

7. Nicholas Glenn, "Auto Rebates Don't Cut the Mustard," *Promote*, April 9, 1990, p. 21.

8. Gary J. Gaeth, Irwin P. Levin, Goutam Chakraborty, and Aron M. Levin, "Consumer Evaluation of Multi-Product Bundles: An Information Integration Analysis," Working Paper, The University of Iowa, 1990.

9. R. T. J. Tuck and W. G. B. Harvey, "Do Promotions Undermine the Brand?" *ADMAP*, January 1972, pp. 29–33.

10. David Kiley, "Can J. C. Penney Change Its Image Without Losing Customers?" *Adweek's Marketing Week*, February 26, 1990, pp. 20–24.

11. Robert F. Hartley, *Marketing Mistakes*, 4th ed. (New York: John Wiley, 1989), pp. 117–153.

12. David Kiley, "How Suzuki Swerved to Avoid a Marketing Disaster," *Adweek's Marketing Week*, October 24, 1988, pp. 27–28.

13. Hartley, op.cit., pp. 30–45.

CHAPTER 8
The Name, Symbol, and Slogan

1. Material is drawn from Andy Keane, *The Volkswagen Story*, MBA Thesis, University of California, Berkeley, 1990; "A Battered VW Begins the Long Road Back," *Business Week*, February 5, 1972, pp. 52–56; and David Kiley, "Can VW Survive?" *Adweek's Marketing Week*, May 1, 1989, pp. 18–24. (The sales figures were provided by Volkswagen of America.)

2. Robert A. Mamis, "Name-Calling," *INC.*, July 1984, pp. 67–70.

3. Kim Robertson, "Strategically Desirable Brand Name Characteristics," *The Journal of Consumer Marketing*, Vol. 6, Fall 1989, pp. 61–71.

4. R. N. Kanungo, "Brand Awareness: Effects of Fittingness, Meaningfulness, and Product Utility," *Journal of Applied Psychology*, Vol. 52, 1968, pp. 290–295.

5. Robert A. Peterson and Ivan Ross, "How to Name New Brands," *Journal of Advertising Research*, Vol. 12, December 1972, pp. 34–39.

6. Jerome R. McDougal, "Apple Name Change Polishes Image of Thrift," *Bank Marketing*, February 1987, pp. 18–20.

7. Albert Mehradian and Robert DeWetter, "Experimental Test of an Emotion-Based Approach to Fitting Brand Names to Products," *Journal of Applied Psychology*, Vol. 72, 1987, pp. 125–130.

8. Robertson, op. cit.

9. Lorraine C. Scarpa, "Brand Equity at Kraft General Foods," Paper written for the Marketing Science Institute Brand Equity Conference, 1990; and Laurie Petersen, "Promotion of the Year," *Promote*, December 10, 1990, p. 36.

10. An excellent short book on naming products which provides good insight into the legal aspects is Henri Charmasson, *The Name Is the Game* (Homewood, Ill.: Dow Jones–Irwin, 1988), Ch. 5.

11. Rich Zahradnik, "More than Pretty Pictures," *Marketing & Media Decisions*. Business-to-Business Guide 1986, pp. B34–B41.

12. Dan Keoppel, "What Have Snoopy and Gang Done for Met Life Lately?" *Adweek's Marketing Week*, November 13, 1989, pp. 2–3.

13. James Ward, Barbara Loken, Ivan Ross, and Tedo Hasapopoulos, "The Influence of Physical Similarity on Generalization of Affect and Attribute Perceptions from National Brands to Private Label Brands," 1986 AMA Conference Educator's Proccedings, Chicago: American Marketing Association, 1986, pp. 25–20.

14. Kathy A. Lutz and Richard J. Lutz, "Effects of Interactive Imagery on

Learning: Application to Advertising," *Journal of Applied Psychology*, Vol. 62, November 1977, pp. 493–498.

CHAPTER 9

Brand Extensions: The Good, the Bad, and the Ugly

1. See Edward F. Ogiba, "The Dangers of Leveraging," *Adweek*, January 4, 1988, p. 42; and Lori Kesler, "Extensions Leave Brands in New Area," *Advertising Age*, June 1, 1987, S1.

2. Edward M. Tauber, "Brand Leverage: Strategy for Growth in a Cost-Controlled World," *Journal of Advertising Research*, August–September 1988, pp. 26–30.

3. Tauber, op. cit.

4. David A. Aaker, "Managing Assets and Skills: The Key to a Sustainable Competitive Advantage," *California Management Review*, Winter 1989, pp. 91–106.

5. David A. Aaker and Kevin Lane Keller, "Consumer Evaluations of Brand Extensions," *Journal of Marketing*, Vol. 54, January 1990, pp. 27–41.

6. Mary W. Sullivan, "Brand Extension and Order of Entry," Working Paper, University of Chicago, February 1989.

7. Henry J. Claycamp and Lucien E. Liddy, "Prediction of New Product Performance: An Analytical Approach," *Journal of Marketing Research*, November 1969, pp. 414–420.

8. Bradley Johnson and Julie Liesse Erickson, "Popcorn Leaders Make Light Moves," *Advertising Age*, July 24, 1989, p. 2.

9. C. Whan Park, Sandra Milberg, and Robert Lawson, "Evaluation of Brand Extensions: The Role of Product Level Similarity and Brand Concept Consistency," Working Paper, University of Pittsburgh, 1990.

10. Deborah Roedder John and Barbara Loken, "Diluting Brand Equity: The Negative Impact of Brand Extensions," Working Paper, University of Minnesota, 1991.

11. John C. Maxwell Jr., "New Cereal Brands Put Snap in Market," *Advertising Age*, July 23, 1990, p. 43.

12. Al Ries and Jack Trout, *Positioning: The Battle for Your Mind* (New York: McGraw–Hill Book Company, 1985).

13. Walter Kennedy, "Marketing Solutions," *Adweek's Marketing Week*," January 2, 1989, pp. 44–45.

14. John Rossant, "Can Maurizio Gucci Bring the Glamor Back?" *Business Week*, February 5, 1990, pp. 83–84.

15. Kevin Lane Keller and David A. Aaker, "Managing Brand Equity: The Impact of Multiple Extensions," Working Paper, University of California at Berkeley, February 1990.

16. Mary Sullivan, "Measuring Image Spillovers in Umbrella Branded Products," Working Paper, University of Chicago, 1988.

17. Edward M. Tauber, "Brand Franchise Extension: New Product Benefits from Existing Brand Names," *Business Horizons*, Vol. 47, March–April, 1981, pp. 36–41.

18. David Kiley, "Chesebrough–Pond's Squeezes Another Brand Out of Vaseline," *Adweek's Marketing Week*, July 18, 1988, p. 21.

CHAPTER 10
Revitalizing the Brand

1. This section was stimulated by Kenichi Ohmae, "Getting Back to Strategy," *Harvard Business Review*, November–December 1988, pp. 149–156. (Carter Schuld of Yamaha provided helpful information.)

2. This section draws upon the excellent paper by Philip E. Hendrix, "Product/Service Consumption: Implications and Opportunities for Marketing Strategy," Working Paper, Emory University, 1986.

3. Barnaby J. Feder, "Baking Soda Maker Strikes Again," *The New York Times*, June 16, 1990, p. 17.

4. Jack J. Honomichl, "The Ongoing Saga of 'Mother Baking Soda'," *Advertising Age*, September 20, 1982, pp. M2–M3.

5. Linden A. Davis, Jr., "Market Positioning Considerations," in E. L. Bailey (Ed.), *Product-Line Strategies* (New York: The Conference Board, 1982), pp. 37–39.

6. Robert Hanson, "Angostura's Past Helps Revive Bitters," *Adweek's Marketing Week*, May 23, 1988, pp. 53–55.

7. Aimee Stern, "TI Liberates the Calculator," *Adweek's Marketing Week*, August 22, 1988, p. 3.

8. Matthew Grimm, "Waterloo, Iowa Wakes Up and Smells the Pepsi," *Adweek's Marketing Week*, November 27, 1989, pp. 2–4.

9. Ronald Alsop, "Giving Fading Brands a Second Chance," *The Wall Street Journal*, January 24, 1989, p. B1.

10. Joseph O. Eastlack, Jr. and Ambar G. Rao, "Modeling Response to Advertising and Pricing Changes from 'V-8' Cocktail Vegetable Juice," *Marketing Science*, Vol. 5, Summer 1986, pp. 245–259.

11. Ronald Alsop, "Folksy Ads Help in Reviving Old-Time Headache Powder," *The Wall Street Journal*, January 20, 1987, p. 18.

12. Theodore Levitt, "Marketing Success Through Differentiation—of Anything," *Harvard Business Review*, January–February 1989, pp. 83–91.

13. Foremost–McKesson: "The Computer Moves Distribution to Center Stage," *Business Week*, December 7, 1981, pp. 115–119; and Tom Peters, *Thriving on Chaos* (New York: Knopf, 1987), p. 110.

14. Tom Peters, *Thriving on Chaos* (New York: Knopf, 1987), pp. 56, 57, and 112.

15. Robert F. Hartley, *Marketing Mistakes*, 3d ed. (New York: Wiley, 1986), pp. 91–105.

16. For an excellent treatment of strategies in declining industries see Kathryn Rudie Harrigan, *Strategies for Declining Businesses* (Lexington, Mass.: Lexington Books, 1980); and Kathryn Rudie Harrigan and Michael E. Porter, "End-Game Strategies for Declining Industries," *Harvard Business Review*, July–August 1983, pp. 111–120.

17. Bill Saporito, "Has-Been Brands Go Back to Work," *Fortune*, April 28, 1986, pp. 123–124.

18. Milton Moskowitz, "Last Days of Chase & Sanborn," *The San Francisco Chronicle*, February 22, 1982, p. 56; and Ruth Stroud, "Chase & Sanborn Gets Back in the Chase," *Advertising Age*, Februry 25, 1985, p. 12.

CHAPTER 11
Global Branding and a Recap

1. David Kalish, "Cat Fight," *Marketing & Media Decisions*, April 1989, pp. 42–48.

2. Joseph M. Winski and Laurel Wentz, "Parker Pen: What Went Wrong?" *Advertising Age*, June 23, 1986, pp. 1, 60, 61, and 71.

3. Kamran Kashani, "Beware the Pitfalls of Global Marketing," *Harvard Business Review*, September–October 1989, pp. 91–98.

Index